The Communist Movement
since 1945

HISTORY OF THE CONTEMPORARY WORLD

Consultant Editors: Dr Peter Catterall &
Professor Lawrence Freedman

This series aims to provide students of contemporary history, politics and international relations with concise, critical overviews of the major themes and the development of key geographical regions that have dominated discussion of world events in the twentieth century. The emphasis in the regional histories will be on the period since the Second World War, but coverage will extend to the earlier twentieth century wherever necessary. The books will assume little or no prior knowledge of the subject, and are intended to be used by students as their first point of entry into a wide range of topics in contemporary international history.

Published

The Causes of the Second World War
Andrew J. Crozier

The Communist Movement since 1945
Willie Thompson

Forthcoming

South Africa in the Twentieth Century:
From Empire to Nation
James Barber

The West and the Third World
D.K. Fieldhouse

Decolonization and its Impact
Martin Shipway

The Communist Movement since 1945

Willie Thompson

BLACKWELL
Publishers

First published 1998

Blackwell Publishers Ltd
108 Cowley Road
Oxford OX4 1JF
UK

Blackwell Publishers Inc.
350 Main Street
Malden, Massachusetts 02148
USA

British Library Cataloguing in Publication Data

A CIP catalogue record for this book is available from the British Library.

Library of Congress Cataloging in Publication Data

Thompson, Willie.
    The Communist movement since 1945 / Willie Thompson.
       p. cm.—(History of the contemporary world)
    Includes bibliographical references and index.
    ISBN 0–631–19969–1.—ISBN 0–631–19971–3
    1. Communism. 2. Communist parties. 3. World politics—1945–
I. Title. II. Series.
HX44.T5365 1998
320.53′2′09—dc21   97–8617
                                                                       CIP

Typeset in 10½ on 12½ pt Bembo
by Graphicraft Typesetters Ltd, Hong Kong
Printed in Great Britain by MPG Books Ltd, Bodmin, Cornwall

This book is printed on acid-free paper.

Contents

Figures

Acknowledgements

My thanks are due to my colleagues, students and other writers and teachers in this field who have stimulated my thinking through interchange and dialogue. Especial thanks are owed to Dr Peter Catterall, who proposed the idea of this volume, my editor, Tessa Harvey, and Professor Walter Connor of Boston University, whose scrutiny saved me from many unforgivable errors. All shortcomings of fact or interpretation are of course my own.

W.T.

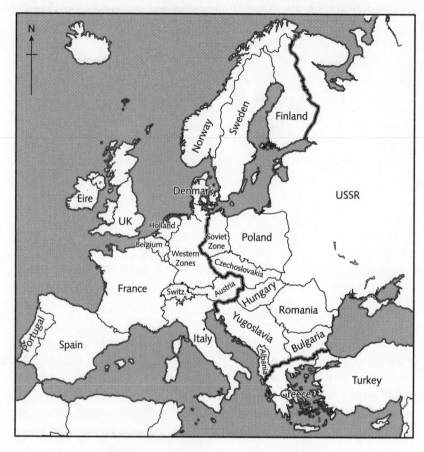

Figure 1 The Iron Curtain, late 1947

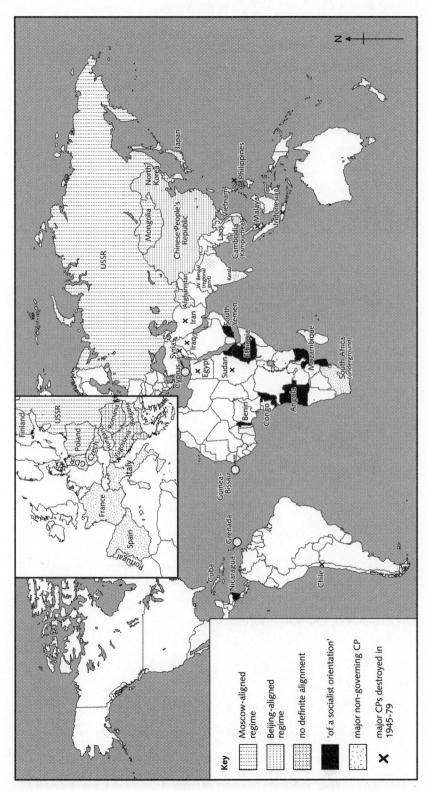

Figure 2 The communist world, late 1979

Introduction

Anyone who tries to write a history of communism as a movement is faced with particular organisational difficulties. This movement was not a single or a simple political entity but, quite apart from the fact that it was made up in the later half of the century of nearly a hundred separate national parties, was divided into two broad and very different sectors, namely the parties which held state power and those which did not. The complexity does not stop there, for one of these parties, the Communist Party of the Soviet Union, initially stood in a central relation to all the others and to a greater or lesser degree determined their ideological outlook. It was also capable, when its leaders thought the circumstances justified, of exercising or trying to exercise detailed organisational control over the others' affairs.

Matters become yet further complicated from the sixties when major rupture between the ruling communist parties of the USSR and China (following the less significant one with Yugoslavia in the forties) established two rival and antagonistic centres of communist leadership, each claiming to be the true proponent of the ideology, while in the seventies further alternative streams emerged which did and yet did not mark themselves off from the Leninist tradition and the states which claimed to embody it.

We are therefore faced with an amazingly complicated and differentiated reality which still at some level continued purporting to be a unity and to constitute a world political movement. Any attempt to trace or interpret its development – for it had a determinate beginning and effectively a determinate end even in the states like China which maintained continuity of regime – is therefore liable to grow diffuse and over-extended. The only answer to this problem is unavoidable and drastic simplification. Any account, including this one, which tries to make sense of the phenomenon is obliged to leave out a great deal[1] and to concentrate on what appear to be the key relationships and processes necessary to understand the career of a political force which in long perspective came from virtually nowhere to rule a third of the world's population and profoundly influence the remainder, which appeared on the face of things to be set for centuries of development and whose catastrophe was as sudden an unexpected as any in recorded history. One area of omission ought to be particularly noted. The question of the role of women within the communist movement, both the ruling and non-ruling parties, deserves a study of its own. The movement prided itself on its commitment to gender equality, but this was understood in purely formal terms, and indeed had the effect of making it all the easier for communist men to accept unthink-ingly that women should continue to fulfil traditional roles, especially domestic ones. Such was the case wherever communist power was established.[2] Though there were a lot of female members in com-munist parties, they were disproportionately underrepresented in com-parison to the population, and this circumstance became steadily more marked as the hierarchies were ascended. There were very few women at the top of any CP. This survey, as an overall sketch, is regrettably but inevitably very male-orientated, for such was the nature of the movement.

No history of this sort can avoid comparison with the late Adam Westoby's magisterial *Communism since World War II* (1981), and this one has no pretensions to match Westoby's comprehensiveness or depth of analysis. His date of publication, however, precludes any consideration of the final decade and the eventual denouement which closed the movement's history.[3] Moreover, the focus is very much upon communist parties in power, while this volume attempts to give greater attention to the significance of the non-ruling commun-ist parties.

A further consideration, with wide implications for the histori-ography as well as the history of the movement, is the question of the social character of the communist regimes, one that very much exercised the entire left while the Soviet bloc existed and which runs all the way through Westoby's analyses. No dispassionate observer could possibly accept the self-definition of the regimes, namely that they represented the ruling power of their national working classes in fraternal association with other non-antagonistic social elements such as the peasantry and intelligentsia. It was clear that in all of them a ruling elite, through a varying mix of exhortation, manipulation and terror, exercised unaccountable power over a politically dispossessed mass of citizens. Traditional Trotskyist interpretations have viewed this as a representing a parasitic bureaucratic excrescence on a basically healthy social body, brought about initially by political usurpation in the early Soviet Union and later imposed in all the regimes controlled or influenced by Moscow. This perspective denies that the governing elites could be termed genuine ruling classes, on the grounds that their power derived only from political and not proprietorial relationships. Within this paradigm disagreement existed on the degree of degeneracy afflicting the elites. Rival analyses rejected the orthodox Trotskyist interpretation and defined the communist rulers as authentic ruling classes and their regimes as ones of 'bureaucratic collectivism' or else 'state capitalism'.

These conflicting theories were politically as well as intellectually contentious, for they related to whether or not the regimes, while preserving the institutions of socialised property, could be expected to reform in the long term towards genuine democracy and 'socialism with a human face'. My own view during those years, being a Communist Party member, was that the prospects, though paved with repeated disappointments, were basically favourable and that reform impulses could emerge within ruling CPs themselves, as they had done in Czechoslovakia in 1968 and might one day do so in the USSR. In retrospect, however, the argument advanced by Hillel Ticktin that the Soviet regime – and by implication the others – was intrinsically unreformable and doomed to crash, appears to have greater weight.

On this thesis the collapse of the Soviet bloc (and, one may surmise, reversion to capitalism by the Chinese regime) was not a product of accidental or avoidable circumstances but the natural unfolding of its essential nature. In Ticktin's analysis the Soviet state was indeed ruled by a parasitic elite, but one which was incapable of controlling its long-term development. The Soviet economy was administered, but *not* planned, for because both workforce and elite were alienated from overall social purposes, concerned only with fiddling short-term targets to their own immediate advantage and in the latter case in preserving its privileges, the system was essentially out of control, generated enormous waste and could achieve growth only by raising inputs disproportionately. If the contradiction was severe enough in Stalin's day when economic mobilisation could be inspired by terror, it became even more pressing after the dictator's death, when terror was abandoned as a routine instrument of control.

> The result is massive overproduction of producer goods in spite of the desires of the administrators. *This is not a historically viable system and is inherently unstable* . . . . In a situation where people subjectively wish to change the system but cannot do so we must conclude that there is some social law lying beyond their will to change.[emphasis added][4]

Written in 1973, this must be acknowledged to show unusually perceptive foresight. So far as the regimes are concerned, the interpretation being put forward here has therefore overtones of a chronicle of death foretold – and the same applies, though in a different fashion, to the Asian regimes as well as the Soviet bloc. The implications of the demise of communist regimes for the non-governing CPs is also striking and suggestive. In spite of the constantly reiterated claims to ideological and organisational independence made by most of the latter and their increasingly national postures, hardly any proved viable in the aftermath and most changed their character fundamentally or else closed down. This examination attempts to interpret the historical logic behind that development.

A further issue affecting the historiography of the movement is not so much the question of what its leaders – and pre-eminently the regime leaders – actually *were* doing but rather what they *thought* they were doing. It relates to the manner in which a historian reads the literature and the pronouncements emanating from the movement, again principally its ruling regimes. Quite clearly this cannot be taken at face value. Its discourse is ideological in the most derogatory sense of the term, representing a false consciousness, but the problem goes even further. Westoby observes that the function of the ruling system of ideas in all sorts of traditional class societies is to make the prevailing class arrangements appear natural and inevitable – if not divinely inspired – but in the communist regimes it was to assert as unquestionable truth what everybody knew to be false.

It is understandable therefore that both Westoby and Ticktin treat the communist elites as motivated by conscious cynicism, concerned only to justify their usurpation of the power rightfully belonging to the working class. In this light the vast output of propaganda which they produced and which presented their movement as a universal emancipatory project, is to be seen as nothing more than deceitful persiflage. In this respect I believe the two writers to be mistaken. For reasons which are explained in the text I regard it as making better sense to assume that the spokespeople of the regimes even at their most mendacious (and mind-bendingly boring) really did in a certain fashion mean what they said; in other words, that the official Marxist–Leninist ideology has to be taken seriously – though requiring of course to be read between the lines. It served the function not simply of cover-up but of reconciling the contradiction between the realities of which the leaders of both ruling and non-ruling parties were well aware and the emancipatory claims of their cultural tradition – Marxism and the Bolshevik Revolution.

In other words, the ideas embodied in the official texts provide an insight into the perceptions and intentions of the communist leaderships – it is not *simply* a question of raw power relationships being tricked out in cynically manufactured propagandist garb. The arguments and interpretations in what follows therefore do treat them seriously as reflections of the movement's consciousness. Only published material is employed in this volume, not archival research. The reasons for this are organisational and pragmatic, though it is worth noting that the very limited opening of Soviet archives that has occurred since the regime fell has not produced any dramatic new interpretations of its history but, except in details, mostly confirmation of what was already known or suspected.

A Note on Terminology

Communist discourse used certain terms in a manner different from that in which they are normally employed. Some understanding of this (beyond the simple expedient of attaching terms of approval such as 'democracy' to realities of the opposite kind) is necessary for our purpose. The most important is the word 'socialism'. It is essential to appreciate that none of the regimes governed by a communist party defined itself as 'communist'. In their own perception they were at the stage between the anti-capitalist revolution and the achievement of 'communism' – in other words, they were 'socialist', so that for example a 'state with socialist orientation' was one which was not formally a member of the bloc but leaned towards it; and reference would be made to 'the socialist community' or 'socialist world' rather than the 'communist' one. The word 'communist' in the title of ruling parties indicated an aspiration, not what was considered to be an achieved reality. Confusion of course is liable to arise for an outsider when reference is simultaneously being made to Socialist parties in the West – communists would normally refer to them as 'social

democratic'. In the text that follows the usage is that of the movement itself – the context will make it clear in what sense 'socialism'
is being employed.

'Marxism–Leninism' was the movement's official ideology, adhered
to up to the end by most (though not all) of the parties. The term
was concocted by Lenin's heirs and there is certainly argument as to
how far Leninism can be regarded as a genuine extrapolation of Marx's
doctrines. However, I am using it simply as a shorthand designation
for the framework of doctrine which was actually common to the
movement, while leaving on one side the issue of its philosophical
validity. The term 'soviet' is printed thus when reference is being made
to the councils for whose name the Russian word is a translation; when
capitalised it refers to the title of the state. The word 'West' when
capitalised refers to the regimes opposing communism; uncapitalised,
it means the geographical direction.

1

The Movement's Turning-point

When in May 1945 the guns fell silent on the European battlefields the official communist movement, as represented by the parties of that name and their subsidiary organisations, stood throughout the Continent in higher public esteem than it had ever done before or was ever to reach again.

The regime which was up to that point the sole[1] embodiment of communist state power, the USSR, though physically shattered by four years of total conflict, incalculable human losses and comprehensive material devastation of its most productive regions, had not only achieved unqualified victory but risen to the rank of a superpower, a member of the Big Three, with its armies positioned deep in central Europe. The lustre of its military performance, moreover, had made its domestic principles, its ideology and its ruling party the object of widespread foreign acclaim. Elsewhere throughout Europe communist parties shared in a greater or lesser degree the credit accorded to the USSR for its role in the war. In addition many of them enjoyed far-reaching domestic approval for the energy and commitment with which they had participated in resistance movements against German occupation. Surveying a wider horizon, the movement at that point engaged the sympathies of millions more in Asia and Latin America. The question was, how far it could be regarded as the same movement which had come into being twenty-five years earlier?

The internationalism of the political movement which brought about the October Revolution[2] in Russia cannot be emphasised too

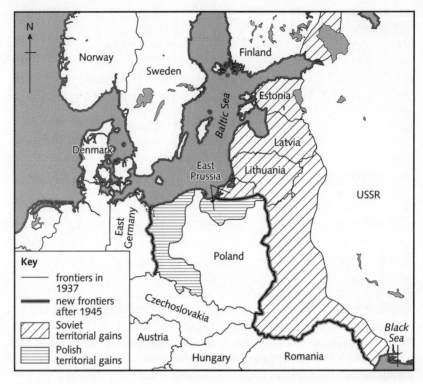

Figure 3 Soviet territorial gains in Europe after the Second World War

strongly. The Europe-wide organisation of socialist parties which had existed since the late nineteenth century termed itself the Socialist International,[3] although this was more a statement of aspiration than of actuality, for in reality it comprised more a collection of nationally jealous and mutually suspicious parties than an international organisation in any true sense. Nonetheless, its components (including the rival factions, Bolsheviks and Mensheviks, of its Russian member) aspired to the replacement, whether rapid or gradual, peaceful or violent, of the existing order of – as they saw it – capitalist productive anarchy, poverty, oppression and war, with an international regime of classless mutual co-operation, peace and production for use instead of profit – the socialist commonwealth. '[s]ocialism shared much of the self-confidence of propertied society in Western Europe, its sense that it stood at the forefront of human achievement and that it pointed the way forward for less advanced societies'.[4]

The onset of European war in 1914 shattered the illusion of internationalism. All the major socialist parties and their leaders threw their support behind their national governments in prosecuting the war effort, although in previous years congresses of the International had resolved to act to put an end to any general war if it broke out. Lenin, the implacable revolutionary, then an exile in Switzerland, was initially shattered at the news of such backsliding. He defined the conflict as a fight between imperialist robbers for redivision of the spoils, the final bankruptcy of the global capitalist order and an opportunity that should be grasped for revolutionaries to settle accounts with the bourgeoisie in the main centres of its power. He did his utmost over the following three years to publicise the slogans 'The enemy is at home!' and 'Turn the imperialist war into civil war!'

These efforts initially evoked only a minimal response, although sufficient to establish a rudimentary network of anti-war socialists across the battlefields. When in February (March) 1917 defeat, war-weariness and mismanagement resulted in the collapse of the Tsar's regime, Lenin described this not primarily in Russian terms but as 'the imperialist chain snapping at its weakest link'. Thereafter all his endeavours were directed towards the establishment in Petrograd of what he regarded as the regime of workers' power, whose installation would provide the signal and the encouragement for the working class in the factories and the trenches throughout Europe to turn their guns against their rulers and validate Marx's historical perspective of a world won by the proletariat.

It was to further this same vision that in 1919, while the Bolshevik regime precariously held on to power in a Russia ravaged by civil war of incomparable savagery, the Communist (or Third) International was established in Moscow, the new capital. The rallying cry for a new revolutionary International had been sounded from the moment of the 1914 debacle, but in addition, since the Bolshevik takeover Lenin and his colleagues had come to view with concern the fitness of the revolutionary groups outside Russia for replicating the Bolshevik achievement:[5] they were thought to lack the experience, political understanding and revolutionary 'will to power' which the Bolsheviks, now retitling themselves communists, imagined that they possessed. Consequently the Comintern, as it was commonly referred to, was not a federation of separate revolutionary-minded parties, but in principle a single global party with its directing centre in Moscow,[6] to which all its national sections were rigorously subordinated, and with membership conditions purposely designed to exclude waverers. Lenin defined it as 'the general staff of the world revolution'.

> In short, the power of the International had all the majesty of the Revolution. It penetrated into the far corners of the huge phenomenon that the world knew as the global communist movement. Moscow's wishes carried the weight belonging to a country where socialism had been constructed. Impressive, far away, perplexing, experimental, excessive, informed and complicated, the Komintern's authority was somewhat akin to 'the law and the prophets,' absolute but hermetic.[7]

The early communist movement was thus distinguished from all other political forces by its revolutionary internationalism (though it fostered nationalist movements directed against the European empires) and thus, not surprisingly, attracted the hatred and fear of the world economic and political order against which it was aimed. Even more than the defeated Germany of the early twenties, Soviet Russia, the embodiment of anti-capitalist revolution, was treated as a pariah state. Until 1923 its leaders continued to expect the imminent overturn of the world capitalist order, the source of the Comintern's appeal to the adherents of the early communist parties. Fantastical though this must appear in historical retrospect, the course of events between 1914 and 1917 had provided some convincing grounds for such a prospect, and instilled in the Bolsheviks and their would-be imitators a super-confidence in the historical destiny of the industrial working class under Bolshevik-style leadership. The Bolshevik success having been born out of war, extreme violence and relentless discipline, it is again not surprising that those conditions and qualities were taken as universal requirements for the advancement of the world revolutionary project.

Revolution Isolated

By 1923 Lenin was incapacitated and his successors struggling among themselves for predominance. At the same time, following the failure of yet another attempted insurrection in Germany, it dawned upon them that the surge of revolutionary advance beginning in 1917 had – they believed temporarily – exhausted itself. Even two years earlier its ebb had compelled adjustments to be made both in the postures of the Comintern and the internal Soviet regime. The former adapted its tactics away from frontal assaults and to first winning the majority within the European working classes. The latter, under the New Economic Policy of 1921, instituted a version of 'market socialism' which left the numerically predominant peasantry, in effective possession of the land, to exchange their produce in the market through the mediation of petty traders while industrial production, such as it was, underwent drastic deregulation. The events of 1923 underlined and reinforced these trends.

Such was the form of developments: their inner content marked the beginning of the communist movement's transformation into the shape it was to retain throughout its subsequent existence. Although nothing was further from the intentions of the leaders who initiated these redirections, they implied, in both instances, an edging towards national in the place of international agendas. The tactic of the 'united front' required the opening of lines of communication with the members of social democrat parties, the political heirs of those which had taken a nationalist stand in 1914 and whose outlook was informed by a primary loyalty to their own state. It also meant that the individual CPs, however passionately they might repudiate nationalism and assert their primary international loyalty, had to give greater attention perforce to their individual national identities. An example of the relationship can be noted in the British case, in which the CPGB participated in the General Strike under the leadership of a TUC whose strike newspaper was the significantly titled *British Worker.*

By the the time of that incident the subordination of the international parties to their Soviet mentor was complete, a state of affairs which contradicted the original purposes and conception of the Comintern. Although that had been a Soviet creation, brought into being by the energies of Lenin's emissaries and sustained with Soviet funds,[8] it was in principle a collective of equal members, to which all were equally subject; conceding no formal pre-eminence to the party of the state in which the organisation was located, but at most a priority of esteem to the party which had led a successful revolution and represented the principal embodiment of Bolshevik understanding and experience. In reality matters were very different. The Soviet leaders, principally in the person of Grigory Zinoviev, who was both the President of the International and a member of the triumvirate (he regarded himself as the senior triumvir) which was running the Soviet state, had by the mid-twenties turned the leaders of the other communist parties into their satraps. Those too independent-minded to conform had been removed from their leadership positions or excluded altogether from the communist movement.[9]

These kinds of relations were established partly by a combination of intrigue, money and Zinoviev's overbearing personality, but it would be an error to imagine that disreputable explanations are the most important ones. More significant was the relationship of *ideological* dependency which overtook the non-Soviet CPs in the absence of any other successful revolution. On an immediate or pragmatic level, the success of the CPSU(B) was emphasised and highlighted against the failure of all of its counterparts and constituted an unanswerable argument in any disagreement. More fundamentally, the passionate longing for a new order of things and commitment to revolutionary internationalism which animated the communist militants, finding no realisation in terms of their original concept, became increasingly focused upon the one part of the world where it had succeeded and so remoulded their internationalism into a variety of Soviet patriotism.

The USSR itself was not in form a national entity, but the dropping of the word 'Russian' from the state's title was a poor concealment of the fact that the republics of the periphery were subordinated to the central locus of the regime's power, namely the Great Russian nationality, and that some of these republics, notably Ukraine and Georgia, had had Soviet power forced upon them contrary to their will. This was in spite of a Bolshevik analysis of nationality which insisted on the importance of national rights and the necessity of respecting national sentiments.[10] Lenin, though he had approved these forcible incorporations, (disingenuously justified by the alleged will of the respective proletariats) had nonetheless denounced from his deathbed the 'Great Russian chauvinism' which he saw reviving within the framework of the Soviet state.[11] It was not that the major Soviet leaders were consciously nationalistic in their outlook, but rather that they were acutely aware of the need to retain the outlying areas of the Union (with their constitutional right to secession) under Moscow's tight control; they suspected separatist tendencies – suspicion which became endemic under Stalin's rule. To preserve that control they depended upon a bureaucracy which was mainly Russian in its composition and remained infected with a nationalist, not to say imperial, virus.

At the same time the political and constitutional fictions of soviet power helped to confer legitimacy upon a multinational state which was not a genuine voluntary union, and they did have the real implication that an individual from any of its nationalities could ascend to the highest levels of the regime via the career ladder of the party, which, unlike the state, *was* based upon a formally centralised structure. What had been created by the late twenties was a party-state which had acquired its own institutional momentum as well as deriving its purpose from the international revolutionary mission for whose sake it had been founded. It need occasion no surprise that the latter had come to be identified with the interests of the former, and in particular with the elite which ruled it, supposedly proletarian but drawn from diverse social origins and processed through the party mechanisms into a coherent, distinctive and self-reproducing group spanning the social hierarchy but with its own particular institutional identity.

The state, of course, was not ruled by the party as a whole, only by its upper echelons, and in the last analysis only the Politburo possessed real overall power, though naturally that small circle of men could not altogether disregard the attitudes, feelings and demands generated at other levels of Soviet society, particularly among the party rank and file, for it depended upon them to get its policies implemented, to explain and justify to the citizenry the direction of events and policies. To what purposes did the Soviet rulers rule on the eve of the Stalin transformations? Evidently the continuation of their own power and authority was not absent from their considerations, nor the material benefits which accompanied their situation, highly significant when compared with the deprivations afflicting the average Soviet worker or peasant – though it has to be said that in absolute terms these privileges were meagre and that by comparison with their counterparts in other states the Soviet elite lived ascetically.

They remained transfixed by a vision of communism, to which both their long-term aspirations and their day-to-day endeavours related. The name of the party was intended to proclaim the aspiration. The goal was understood to require a two-stage process. The putative first phase was, in the official vocabulary, termed 'socialism' and implied the essential preconditions of the overthrow of the exploiting class, eradication of capitalism, common property in the means of production and a sufficiently advanced level of general output to assure a high material standard of living in goods and services to every member of the society. Nevertheless, this (utopian enough) perspective still represented a lower stage. Productive forces would still be too limited and social consciousness not yet sufficiently developed to permit the free distribution of both necessities and luxuries, together with the abolition of money. Distribution must continue to take the form of return for labour output on the part of all citizens capable of it, with exemptions only on grounds of age or infirmity. Moreover, a coercive state must remain in existence to repress the unreconciled remnants of exploiting classes, to regulate social interactions and to defend the socialist territory against hostile capitalist powers.

The 'higher stage', or communism proper presupposed the 'society of abundance' where productive forces had advanced to the level that all could draw freely whatever they needed or wanted from the common stores, work was done not out of necessity but for enjoyment, understanding and self-motivation ensured that no one abused those paradisial potentialities and both money and the state had been consigned to the museum. Of necessity, this would only be possible on a planetary level or nearly so, for so long as powerful capitalist states continued to exist, socialist societies would remain in danger of subversion and attack.

In 1924–5 the Soviet leaders had quarrelled publicly and noisily over whether even the initial stage would have to be a global phenomenon, requiring as a precondition workers' power in at least several advanced states, or whether it could be achieved in just one large entity, namely the USSR itself (admittedly over a lengthy period).[12] The outcome was one more instance – indeed the key instance – of the covertly national agendas towards which individual communist parties were beginning to slip. The uncompromising internationalism of the revolutionary period, upheld by Trotsky, was defeated. 'Socialism in a single country' was proclaimed as the official and unquestionable doctrine. Not that there was any question, in anathematising Trotsky's version,[13] of repudiating the world revolution, the foundation charter of the Soviet state, or the institution established to promote it, the Comintern. Rather, in pursuing its own particular interests the Soviet Union would simultaneously enhance revolutionary prospects abroad and act as a yet more inspiring beacon to oppressed proletariats and nations. Bukharin, the principal theorist of 'Socialism in a single country' and now part of a duumvirate with Stalin, was elevated to the Presidency of the Comintern following Zinoviev's disgrace.

The project envisaged a long haul, unless the global revolutionary wave should rise again. The USSR of 1925, despite its Marxist pretensions, remained a primitive and shattered society only just regaining the level of output which had been attained in 1913. Bukharin's conception was intended to take this reality into account: it envisaged a slow process of building up industrial capacity and infrastructure by gently siphoning off and investing the surplus generated from a prosperous peasant economy. In the meantime international revolution was on hold: the Soviet state aimed at diplomatic normalisation and correct relations with bourgeois states. This was especially true in respect of states which were held to contain a progressive element of anti-imperialism, such as Ataturk's Turkey or Chiang's China, and the interests of the indigenous communists in these states were sacrificed to diplomatic necessity as viewed from Moscow. It also applied, however, to Britain, the very epitome of imperialist rapacity, and a careful distinction was maintained between the Soviet trade union federation which offered financial assistance during the General Strike and the

Soviet state or even the Comintern, which eschewed public involvement. Most of all, intimate and friendly relations were sought with the German state, which had been the principal instrument of frustrating the international revolution, because the pariah status of both in the international order gave them joint interests, and specially close collaboration was cultivated with the German army command to the military satisfaction of both parties.

It is clear that ten years after the event the particular form of revolutionary dynamic which had erupted in 1917 was exhausted, both in the USSR and the parties formed under the Comintern aegis – although a different dynamic, no less revolutionary in its own manner, was coming to supersede it. The elemental and protean workers' revolt organising itself through spontaneously formed councils and only loosely guided by a revolutionary party was replaced by tightly structured, bureaucratically controlled oppositional forces exercising quasi-military command over their members. They carried the communist name in western Europe and looked for leadership to a country where state power was exercised along similar lines. In the parts of Asia where the Comintern had established a presence the focus had shifted away, in reality if not in theory, from the urban proletariat to peasant movements led by intellectuals, struggling to find a form of organisation which could survive military repression and devise a strategy to attain ultimate state power. Proletarian internationalism continued to furnish the Comintern's day-to-day rhetoric, but the actuality had shifted in several dimensions.

Stalinism

To this process Stalin's rise (with very little constitutional underpinning) to supreme authority in the USSR was neither central nor incidental. The relationship of Leninism to Stalinism has been a much disputed issue and has generated great quantities of heated partisan polemic on both the right and the left. There are strong reasons to believe that Stalinism, in the sense of an unaccountable, ideologically inspired autocracy devouring civil society, represented a less than improbable outcome of Leninism in power. At the same time specifically Russian traditions undoubtedly accounted for a good deal, and the shattered condition of Soviet Russia following the Civil War for still more, so that in more favourable circumstances the phenomenon might have been avoided. Finally, the particularly cruel and paranoid cast of Stalin's own personality undoubtedly made what we term 'Stalinism' in the hands of this individual a good deal more bloodthirsty and ferocious than it would have been if overseen by a less unbalanced autocrat.

The institutional character of Stalinism was also hammered out in the course of the twenties during the prolonged conflict of the ruling caucus[14] with various oppositions, and in particular the figure who emerged as the archetypical oppositionist, Trotsky. From the necessity of the ruling group to justify themselves in terms of Lenin's legacy and deny that heritage to their opponents derived the suppression of all honest debate, the emphasis on 'monolithicism' within the party and the rendering down of Marxism and Leninism into the sacralised dogma of Marxism–Leninism – a dogma which was nonetheless sufficiently flexible to be used to justify the most peremptory and dramatic reversals of policy.

Via the authority of the Comintern the foreign communist parties were required to endorse these switches and translate them into their own perspectives and actions. The Soviet regime could not of course exercise physical coercion beyond its own borders.[15] The adhesion of the separate Comintern parties had to be voluntary, but such was the sacerdotal authority acquired by the leaders of the 'workers'' state that the consent was always forthcoming even when it contradicted the particular interests of the foreign parties concerned. These were required, moreover, not merely to accept out of discipline a Comintern decision with which they might disagree, but to convince themselves that the stipulated line must be the correct one. If tne party leadership in any country proved reluctant or unaccommodating, the Comintern headquarters would put the weight of its authority behind a more reliable faction within such party until these protégés had successfully taken over the leadership.[16]

Thus it was that tensions within the Soviet regime associated with the fall of Stalin's last serious competitor, Bukharin, together with the onset of brutal agricultural collectivisation and the breakneck industrialisation of the Five-Year Plan, resulted in a counterfeit reassertion of revolutionary intransigence upon an international scale. It was decreed without any justification in evidence (though the world slump of 1929 provided illusory confirmation) that the capitalist stabilisation of the mid-twenties had come to an end and that international revolution was ready to surge forward again, in this 'third period' of development since 1917. The precondition for success, however, was that the social democrat parties, stigmatised as capitalism's chief support and last hope,[17] must be implacably denounced and relentlessly attacked. The strategy was designated 'Class against Class'.

Its application throughout the international communist movement was everywhere extremely damaging to the CPs involved, and in the case of Germany catastrophic, for the insistence at Stalin's behest of the KPD on treating the German social democrats as their main enemies greatly facilitated Hitler's rise and conquest of power. It is a testament to the strength of Stalin's hold upon the Comintern that this debacle did not shake it in any degree.[18] The experience of 'class against class' (which lasted formally till 1935, though it was modified a good deal earlier) had, apart from what happened in Germany, two principal long-term consequences.

Though no criticism could of course be pronounced against Stalin or his regime, the disaster of the policy left a permanent mark upon the consciousness of the international movement and discouraged thereafter not merely ultra-revolutionary but even revolutionary perspectives on the part of most of its individual parties. It was succeeded by the era of the Popular Front, in which the communists tried to mend their fences not merely with socialists but with democrats of any sort for the sake of opposing further fascist advances, though many of these democrats, not surprisingly, doubted the sincerity of their conversion. Now, being obliged to take more specific national circumstances into account and turn towards nationally-minded political forces, the communists could not fail to find a more specifically national inflection being given to their own strategies and outlooks. The period of 'class against class', however, had also seen the proclaimed miraculous success of the USSR in turning itself into a collectively planned, fully industrialised state at the same time as the global capitalist economy was falling apart. It had therefore become not merely the stronghold of the workers' revolution but the embodied demonstration that socialism worked. Its hold upon the imagination not only of communists, but many others who deplored the anarchic inefficiency of capitalism,[19] was correspondingly strengthened. At the end of the decade Stalin announced that socialism, in the terms sketched above, had been achieved within the USSR.

Nadir and Resurgence

He did so at a point when the searing purges of the Great Terror were tearing apart the fabric of Soviet life and putting its defensive capacity in the most extreme jeopardy while European international relations crumbled. The Kremlin sought to protect its own state interests, as it imagined, by entering relations of friendly collaboration with the arch-fiend in the shape of the Molotov–Ribbentrop Pact of August 1939. Stalin, having despaired of forming an anti-fascist coalition – if such was his intention – had decided on a manoeuvre which would either, depending on the outcome of the imminent European war, enable him to divide control of the Continent with Hitler or else allow his capitalist enemies of diverse colours to exhaust themselves in mutual slaughter.

It was *realpolitik* of the utmost cynicism which appeared to symbolise the degradation into which the regime had sunk. Though loyally endorsed by the parties of the Comintern, who argued that Stalin had brilliantly avoided allowing himself to be used as a catspaw by the Western powers, disillusion was acute among many members and even more among the communists' late political allies of the popular fronts. As uneasy peace slid into military conflict in September, the fortunes of the movement founded amid such confidence twenty years beforehand had reached, even in formal terms, a particular nadir. The USSR survived, but on the regime's own showing was infested with traitors, spies and saboteurs who were alleged to grow hydra-like no matter how often they were purged. Abroad, the perspective was even bleaker. Two Popular Front governments had been formed since 1935, in France and Spain, but both had collapsed, in the latter case in consequence of a civil war which resulted in the installation of an Axis-friendly regime and the annihilation of the country's left. Indeed there were few communist parties anywhere which were even legal organisations, let alone bidding for power, the French party having been proscribed soon after the outbreak of hostilities. Communist parties in Asia were for the most part no more than obscure nuclei and although Mao's guerrillas in the remote fastness of the Chinese north-west controlled considerable territory, they remained peripheral on a world scale. Communist parties existed in the Americas, as also in South Africa, but all of them, where more than semi-legal, had been politically isolated and contained, and represented no threat to their respective governments. The communist movement outside the USSR was all but obliterated as a historic agency. In reality the position was even worse, for the Soviet terror regime of the late thirties, though it might be possible to identify a logic of development between original Leninism and high Stalinism, nonetheless represented a blank negation of all the hopes invested in the October Revolution.

The Second World War transformed the fortunes of international communism and did so in two different dimensions. Until June 1941, while Moscow was a semi-ally of Berlin, the Comintern instructed its member parties to treat the conflict as a clash of imperialisms, analogous to that of 1914, in which the democracies were if anything even more culpable than the Axis powers; to the extent that in some occupied countries the local CP even tried to reach an accommodation with the German authorities.[20] Following the invasion of the USSR, however, the intrinsic anti-fascist sentiments of the Comintern members were able to find unconstrained expression. They turned into the most resolute proponents of a fight to the finish and in occupied Europe (with the exception of Poland) and most of Japanese-occupied Asia, rapidly emerged as the leading element in the Resistance,[21] assisted both by the ardour of their commitment and the organisational capacity which was their trademark. If the events of the preceding decade had moved the individual Comintern parties, without acknowledging the fact, surreptitiously in the direction of adopting national agendas, the developments of the Resistance struggles pushed them in unequivocally nationalist directions – it was clear that CPs attained their greatest popularity and respect when they appeared as the upholders of national independence against an alien occupier as well being the prophets of a new social order. The votes received by European communist parties in free elections immediately after the war marked the flood tide of their electoral successes.[22]

The other dimension was the dramatic expansion of Soviet power and the continuing manoeuvre of the USSR as a state power within the international system. The Soviet–German agreement of August 1939 brought substantial territorial gains – the Baltic republics, eastern Poland, Bessarabia, small but strategic slivers of Finland; following 1945 these were retained, along with Ruthenia and half of East Prussia. The southern part of the island of Sakhalin and the attached Kuriles were seized from Japan, against whom the USSR had declared war only in July 1945. Agreements made between Stalin and Churchill in 1944 and confirmed at the Yalta conference of February 1945 agreed upon the division of influence which the great powers would exercise upon the restored independent states of eastern Europe. The Comintern had become an irrelevance and an embarrassment and in 1943 it was unceremoniously would up with an unconvincing pretence that this was the will of the member parties[23] rather than a matter of Soviet *fiat*. The importance of that event was symbolic rather than practical, for it marked the definitive acknowledgment that internationalism was subordinated to raison d'état. Not that Moscow's control over the parties of the liquidated organisation was lessened in the slightest degree. In the immediate-term Comintern traditions, the exigencies of the war and the USSR's moral standing ensured their willing acceptance of the latter's leadership. Institutionally, a department was created within the CPSU to exercise the political remote control which had formerly been the remit of the Communist International.

After the War

The communist movement which emerged from the Second World War was a strange and contradictory phenomenon. In historical terms it was unique, being the only world political movement ever to have existed which was controlled from a single centre. No organisation has existed which paralleled the Comintern in its capacity to exact voluntary and enthusiastic obedience from a scattered membership. In certain evident respects, however, communism had been transformed since 1939. From a beleaguered and/or persecuted political entity, its power confined to a single state which, though large and economically advancing, was embroiled in paroxysms of bloodletting, it appeared once more, incalculably strengthened, as a potential agent of world transformation.

Elements of continuity clashed with fundamental alterations and were reconciled by traditions of absolute obedience. It was of course the alleged continuities which were stressed, both in public statements and for the movement's internal consumption. The principles of the Soviet state, on this interpretation, remained as Lenin had established them. Stalin was the heir to Lenin's genius and had applied these principles with unexampled wisdom and success – proved beyond question in the 'Great Patriotic War'. Moreover, the USSR remained the mirror of the global future, the social form which all others would imitate sooner or later. The communist parties abroad constituted the political force which would bring about such revolutions; while the CPSU, on account of its successes, experience and superior Marxist insight, was rightfully accorded the leading position within the parties of the world movement.

Discontinuities were no less marked, though markedly less emphasised. The dissolution of the Comintern, though blatantly contradicting in reality the fundamental objectives and meaning of the Bolshevik Revolution, was presented as the natural outcome of growing maturity and experience of the national communist parties. This formal development underlined the implicit shift that was taking place within the movement towards more national orientations. At the same time it was contradicted by the deference that was exhibited towards the USSR and the person of Stalin by every communist party and the unwavering obedience displayed by nearly all of them. World revolution had shifted from being an urgent, immediate priority to a very long-term goal indeed – which is not to say that it had become merely nominal and ceased to have practical significance. It remained the ultimate lodestar and inspiration for communists and there was no difficulty in interpreting events up to 1945 as the world crisis of capitalism working itself out, the Bolshevik Revolution having marked the initial breach in its bastions, with the dramatic extension of communist power and influence in the aftermath of the war representing the current stage. However, the war had been fought by an alliance of the USSR with the leading states of capitalist democracy and it was expected initially that cordial relations under the rubric of 'a secure and lasting peace' would continue into the indefinite future. Hence communism's historic role was not seen as taking the form of further revolutions on the model of 1917.

The notion of a 'united front' dated from Lenin's day, but the conception differed utterly from the strategy which informed the intended perpetuation of the Grand Alliance into peacetime. In 1921 it had meant an alliance of expediency with vacillating or non-revolutionary elements of the labour movement in order to pursue immediate common objectives and to politically isolate incorrigibly anti-communist labour leaders. The US–Anglo-Soviet alliance, by contrast, was a combination of states, including the fortress of the world revolution, and it was meant to last. Stalin needed it in order to gain security on his borders, insure against possible revival of German militarism and gain access to the material resources of the United States to rebuild the shattered Soviet economy. This was to be supplemented with 'popular fronts' of domestic political forces in the liberated states, governmental combinations of communist and non-communist parties. It followed that in the zone of influence allocated to the USSR Soviet hegemony would be embodied in the domination of these united fronts by by the local communist parties, reliable allies of Moscow, while in the zone of Anglo-US hegemony the communists would play a subordinate role.

Whatever the merits or demerits of the arrangement,[24] and whether or not it might have lasted had there been more good faith on both sides, it is abundantly clear that it was a pragmatically conceived project, a reflection of the then balance of power in international relations, bearing no relation to Marxist or Leninist analysis or strategy. Nonetheless, the character of the communist movement being what it was, a theoretical justification was required. The proletariat, albeit as an abstraction rather than a reality, remained central to communist understanding. The communist parties regarded themselves as the only ones which comprehended the real historic interests and destiny of the working class; if that class in particular countries failed to follow the communist party it was because they were more or less misguided. In principle there should be only one party representing the class. If, therefore, communists sustained amicable relations or collaboration in government with rival working-class parties, it was done only on an emergency basis or on sufferance, with eventual amalgamation on communist terms as the desired outcome. Ironically, parties of the peasantry or lower middle class were in principle regarded as possessing greater validity, since they were supposed to represent a genuinely different class interest.

Naturally, when collaboration was being sought these monopolistic principles were downplayed. The communist and social democrat working-class parties of post-war Europe were capable, it was emphasised, of working in harmonious concert. Not only that, but all other parties and social forces untainted by fascist collaboration were also capable of making their contribution to the foundation of the new world order. The enemy was monopoly capitalism and the fascist monster to which it had given birth. Once that was expunged all democratic forces were potentially capable of finding a common path of joint national development. According to the communiqué issued from the allied summit at Tehran in 1943, 'We shall seek the co-operation and the active participation of all nations, large and small, whose peoples in heart and mind are dedicated ... to the elimination of tyranny and slavery .... We will welcome as they may choose to come into a world family of democratic nations.' It was a long way from the early congresses of the Comintern.

The new Bulgarian government – within the Soviet sphere of influence – set an exemplary precedent at the end of 1944 by trying and executing scores of politicians and military and civil officials, including three ex-regents, who had been active Nazi collaborators. On the other hand, where the bourgeois forces appeared to qualify for incorporation in the democratic front the attitude was quite different, sometimes startlingly so. In Romania, under a communist-dominated government, the monarchy was retained in the meantime. The British publication *Labour Monthly*, edited by the impeccably Stalinist Palme Dutt, gave room in its January 1945 number to the Deputy Premier of the Royal Yugoslav Government in exile. The words of the French communist leader Maurice Thorez in January 1945 are also representative: 'We who are Communists should not at the moment make explicitly Communist or socialist demands. I say this at the risk of appearing lukewarm in the eyes of those who are forever using the word "revolution." '[25] The leader of the tiny but not wholly insignificant Communist Party of the USA, Earl Browder, adopted the line with such incautious zeal that he set in hand the liquidation of his party, intending to replace it with a Communist Political Association which would permanently renounce any revolutionary pretensions.

It is evident that the priority for the world movement, for which the abolition of the Comintern made no effective difference in the degree of its subordination to Moscow, remained the security interests of the USSR, in whatever form they might be interpreted by Stalin. One would not of course expect communists in capitalist states to be motivated by 'official' national or patriotic feelings, unless, as during the Second World War, these happened to coincide with their own agendas. The interests of their own working class, however, of which they purported to be the true representatives, would also be treated as secondary – under the rubric of 'internationalism'. This is nicely illustrated by the stances adopted by the British communists during the conflict. So long as it was declared to be an 'imperialist' war its continuation was opposed by the CPGB, which, in line with the Soviet position,[26] agitated for peace negotiations. They refrained from industrial sabotage but were unremitting in their struggle (which achieved some success) to oppose any erosion of workplace rights and conditions for the sake of the war effort. Once the USSR became involved, however, the CP became a fervent advocate of war production at all costs and the sacrifice of any practice which might impede it. The party on occasion even ordered its members to participate in strikebreaking, at the cost of painfully-achieved local workplace reputation. Until June 1944 its central campaign was for the opening of a second front by allied invasion across the Channel, which, whatever its objective rationale, also happened to be Stalin's strategic demand upon his allies.

The Party Culture

No real understanding of the communist movement is possible unless the roots of this mental set are appreciated. The notion that it was a product of cynicism, malevolence or opportunism can be dismissed. At this point few joined the communist parties with careerist intentions. In occupied Europe membership could be a death sentence, frequently accompanied with torture. In the USSR itself, purge victims (of whom communists comprised the most important element) rushed, upon release from labour camps, to assume major responsibilities in the battle lines or the war economy. Communists by and large were self-sacrificing zealots[27] whose thinking and action were inspired by a vision of a transformed world combined with the internal collective culture they experienced as party members. The conviction of imminent world revolution and all the sentiments which accompanied that had become transferred to the one place where the revolution had succeeded, the USSR, and transferred collectively into the organisation, not just into its individual members. It was heightened and reinforced when the Soviet Union, in addition to being the workers' state, became the pioneer of planned industrialisation and finally the avenging angel against fascism.

The collective culture of the movement was related to the organisational structures which held its component parts together. These naturally varied to some degree according to circumstance, especially that of illegality or otherwise, but were all cut to the same general pattern. The basic units of a national communist party might be termed branches, cells or locals, but always comprised a relatively limited number of individuals (it could be as few as three) capable of acting in co-ordination to execute the policies and secure the objectives conveyed to them from a higher level. The degree of independent initiative which they were allowed in carrying through their remit again varied according to circumstance,[28] but the emphasis was always upon centralisation. A hierarchy of organisational levels rose above the foundational units, each managed by a committee which might be either formally elected or co-opted according to circumstance, though in practice it amounted to the same thing. Control from the top was exercised by a central committee[29] which always operated in practice as a self-perpetuating oligarchy, whatever democratic forms might be employed. Even this, however, did not represent the full extent of centralisation, for the central committees were themselves controlled by an inner core, entitled in imitation of the Bolsheviks the Political Bureau, more commonly rendered as Politburo. As a rule the leading position within the organisation was that of General Secretary, a reflection of the role of Stalin's position within the CPSU[30] – though this was not invariably the case; a few of the parties followed a different procedure, among them, significantly, the Chinese.

The organisational framework was essentially a command structure, designed for adaptation to either open or underground conditions of political struggle, enabling the party to gain leadership of working-class and democratic struggles of every kind. It was supposedly designed also for revolutionary leadership, to put the party at the head of the masses whenever a genuine insurrectionary opportunity presented itself – though except in Russia, it had never proved very successful in the latter respect. Corresponding to this kind of apparatus there existed what can only be termed an organisational ideology; it was known as 'democratic centralism'. As ostensibly presented this sounded innocent enough. According to the theory, it simply meant that while a policy or a line of action remained under discussion, opposing viewpoints and argument could be freely debated, but once the decision had been arrived at every party member was bound to uphold, argue and work for it with full and active commitment. Obviously in underground conditions open debate was out of the question, it had to be replaced with trust in the leadership's good faith: nevertheless, public discussion was to be preferred whenever possible.

The implication that all decisions must be accepted and pursued unanimously was that any grouping within the party advocating an alternative line was strictly outlawed, and to try to form one, whether publicly or covertly, was to court summary expulsion. Such activity was stigmatised as factionalism and regarded as the gravest possible sin against party rules. It had not always been thus. The ban on factions had been introduced into the Soviet party as late as 1921, supposedly to cope with an immediate and pressing crisis – it seems unlikely that Lenin intended it to become a permanent feature – he continued to encourage dissidents to express their dissidence provided they did not organise themselves. However, under the New Economic Policy economic relations were to be liberalised. This would inevitably regenerate bourgeois relationships and attitudes, against whose infection the ruling party must be protected in the meantime by tightened centralisation. In the event, the rigid interpretation of democratic centralism was to become embedded and have the long-term effect of turning the collective which, with Comintern approval, formed the Politburo of any communist party into effectively unchallengeable autocrats and an oligarchy which selected its own successors.[31] It should be understood that this set-up did not prevent vivid polemic and debate whenever a new line was propounded, but such debate was in essence unreal, as whichever policy was formulated in the Kremlin was the one certain to be instituted with greater or lesser alacrity by all other communists. Moreover, once it became clear (via the organs of the Comintern) what the requirements of the Soviet leadership were, foreign communists, and especially ones in leadership positions, were expected to render not merely a disciplined obedience but to convince themselves that the

line being imposed upon them was the right one and to internalise
it with enthusiasm.[32] Unanimous votes became the routine conclusion to discussions at committees and congresses.

Composition

Ideology and ardour, combined with its organisational principles and
practices, made the international communist movement in countries
where it was well established into a formidable political reality. Not
even the Pope could pretend to such a complete and far-reaching command over his faithful as Stalin enjoyed. The great victory had resulted
in a tremendous expansion of numbers, and elements of every social
class were attracted, though not of course in equal measure. In the
USSR itself the party's composition remained in its majority working-
class, though this did not mean a great deal, as the CPSU had been
virtually annihilated in the great purges and could scarcely be said,
except in its leadership inner circle, to have been the same organisation that it was ten years beforehand. Whatever virtues its rank-
and-file membership possessed, capacity for independent thought was
certainly not among them, and its apparatchiks constituted, as they had
since the state's early days, a bureaucratic layer which had entirely
lost contact with its social origins.

Among the communist parties of Europe on the morrow of
the liberation, membership remained predominantly working-class,
though a significant admixture of intellectuals was present, recruited
from the white-collar and professional middle class, the proportion
of whom rose as the organisational hierarchy was ascended. It has
to be acknowledged, however, that the full-time employees of the
communist parties, their 'professional revolutionaries', maintained a
much closer relationship with their working-class constituency than
was the case with their social democrat rivals or the ruling party in
the USSR.

In Asia matters were very different. In general, the industrial working class in that continent, with the exception of Japan, was small in
number and insignificant in social weight. The only part of mainland
Asia where communism had achieved any appreciable working-class
strength was in the coastal cities of China. That base, however, had
been lost in 1927 when the urban party was virtually exterminated
by its former ally, the military apparatus of the Guomindang, the
Nationalist Party under Chiang Kai-shek. Communist agitation, perspectives and the image (if not the reality) of the USSR, however,

found a substantial response among dispossessed and mercilessly exploited peasants tormented by landlords, tax-collectors and money-lenders. By the outbreak of the Second World War most Asian countries possessed indigenous communist parties, mostly tiny; but in areas of China, where it had regrouped on peasant foundations after the 1927 catastrophe and likewise in Indo-China, sustaining a degree of rural support. There were, however, scarcely any peasants in the leadership of any of them; they were organised and led by intellectuals[33] and occasionally industrial workers from the urban circles in which they first emerged.

On the African continent communist parties, all of them small and fragmented, existed along the Mediterranean littoral and at the opposite end, the Communist Party of South Africa, once it had adopted popular front stances, had succeeded in establishing some trade union presence, though not in the country's centrally important mining industry. Latin and Caribbean America, an overwhelmingly peasant-dominated region, did nevertheless have communist parties established legally or illegally in most of its twenty or so republics. Invariably they were small and largely ineffectual, founded and led by middle-class professionals and intellectuals, such support as they enjoyed among the masses being confined to the relatively tiny[34] urban proletariat. As a survey of world communism published in 1973 notes, neither Lenin nor Stalin showed much interest in Latin America.[35]

The same text uses the phrase 'era of good feeling' to characterise the state of international relations as it affected the communist movement immediately following the allied victory. That may be something of an exaggeration, but it is apparent that Moscow, communists in every country – and indeed most of the politically informed public – expected that the nations were entering upon an epoch of mutual friendship and goodwill. The world-revolutionary hopes of twenty-five years earlier were thoroughly buried,[36] or sustained a spectral presence only as an imagined long and peaceful journey towards the ends that Lenin had envisaged. Nor is there is any reason to doubt that co-operation was at first sincerely sought by Stalin on the one hand and the major Western powers on the other,[37] though in each case, of course, upon their own terms. According to Churchill, 'We were hampered in our protests because Eden and I . . . had recognised that Russia should have a largely predominant voice in Romania and Bulgaria, while we took the lead in Greece. Stalin had kept very strictly to this understanding.'[38] 'Understanding' in a broader sense, however, was the rock which holed allied unity, for what was regarded as a proper and legitimate expectation on the one side was perceived as an intolerable provocation on the other. The tensions and rivalries pressing towards conflict and hostility in the post-war world were not the product of contingent or accidental decisions but were inbuilt and structural. The USSR expected the acceptance of its historic legitimacy together with the respect and deference due to its new superpower status, particularly the hegemony in its own security sphere that was accorded to the USA in the Americas: its quondam allies believed that to concede these things would damage their own vital interests. Matters were complicated even more by the aspirations and hopes of the non-Soviet CPs, which, however willingly subservient they might be to Stalin and the USSR, had agendas of their own which they would not readily forget, with all the enthusiasm and confidence they had gained as a result of the war. Consequently the stage was set for the resurrection of an ersatz version of the global revolutionary project with which the communist movement had begun.

2

Cold War and Colonial Revolution

Not even the most absolute dictators are free agents. It is virtually impossible to rule by terror alone, and even in such a case the dictator must calculate how reliable the terror apparatus is and whether he (up to the present there have been only male dictators) may not get his own fingers caught in the wringer. In practice every dictatorship will stand upon the foundations of some social group which it directly benefits and be able to secure the acquiescence at least of most others. The dictator will therefore have to ensure that he keeps the benefits flowing and calculate how far public acquiescence can be relied upon.[1] He also has to take into account the factions within his own entourage, manoeuvre among them, play off one lieutenant against another and ensure that they do not combine against him. When the dictator is also the leader of a global movement with a large proportion of its members outside his powers of direct coercion but for whom his enemies nevertheless hold him responsible, his range of choices may turn out to be very limited indeed.

These considerations applied with great force to Stalin in 1945. The country he ruled had risen to become an international colossus, but a severely crippled one. For all the enforced conformity, absence of organised dissent and cult of personality immeasurably reinforced by wartime leadership, the regime was in danger unless the gigantic armies could be efficiently demobilised, war damage restored, the economy redirected towards civilian production and the long-suffering peoples of the Union offered some prospect, however minimal or

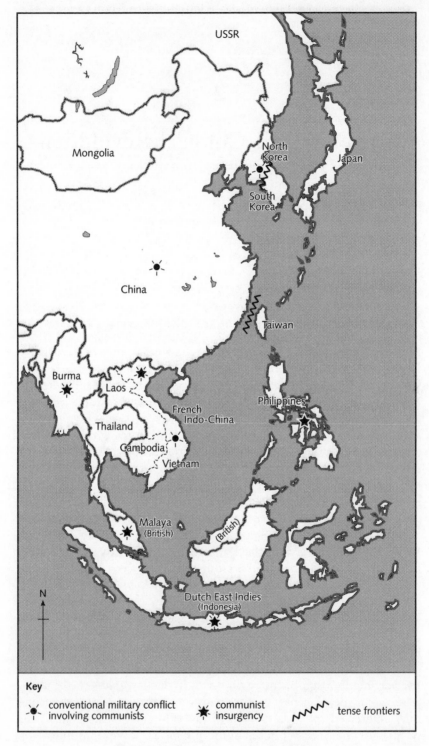

Figure 4 East Asia in the Cold War

remote, of amelioration in the rigours of Soviet existence. Such realities amounted to a powerful argument for the continuation of wartime collaboration with the Soviet Union's immensely more wealthy and less damaged allies, who had the means, in a world of genuine international co-operation overseen by a benign United Nations, to greatly ease their partner's transition to the tasks of reconstruction.

No less pressing, however, were issues of international security. Total defeat of Nazi Germany and its allies had created an enormous power vacuum on the USSR's most sensitive frontier. Territorial expansion along the length of that border, the incorporation of the Baltic states and parts of pre-war Germany, Poland, Czechoslovakia and Romania had eased the difficulty, but any great power in the situation of the USSR at the time, regardless of regime, would have been concerned to ensure that the neighbouring states in the area displayed an amicable posture. It was in these circumstances that what Isaac Deutscher in his biography of Stalin termed the 'dialectics of victory' came into play.

In his dealings with states in the Soviet security sphere and with the Western powers Stalin had two particularly invaluable assets. The first was the informal agreement of Yalta, in February 1945, confirming his arrangement with Churchill the previous year, which conceded such a sphere of Soviet influence and was translated into material terms by the presence of the Red Army on the ground throughout eastern and central Europe. The second was the communist movement itself, which could be employed as the foundation for a security structure within the Soviet sphere and a means of forwarding the objectives of Soviet policy in other parts of Europe.

All over Europe (other than in Germany) the communist parties of the belligerent states had emerged from the war with unprecedented standing and prestige. The pattern, however, was a complex one, for their size and degree of popular acceptance varied greatly from country to country. Some, having led or been prominent in the Resistance struggle, had grown to become mass movements, incorporating substantial armed formations. This was especially true in Greece, Yugoslavia, Albania, Italy, Czechoslovakia and France. Others, like the British, the one European belligerent never invaded, had remained small, or, as in Hungary or Romania, scarcely existed as indigenous forces and were in effect re-established by Soviet influence following the liberation.

Those in the former category would naturally want to exploit their advantages, either to make a bid for power or to dominate any coalition of anti-fascist parties which might emerge, and pressure from their rank and file would push the leaders in that direction regardless of any caution on their own part. They might also reasonably expect an attitude of Soviet benevolence, if not positive encouragement, in asserting their claims. Stalin, by contrast, was particularly concerned to control the activities of such CPs in the Soviet interest, and from his point of view relations with the West constituted the immediate priority. Attempted, let alone successful, communist revolution in France or Italy would fundamentally destabilise the balance of confidence and mutual trust between the wartime allies.[2] The Italian and French party leaders Togliatti and Thorez (who returned from Moscow at the end of the war) were strictly instructed to restrain the impatience of their followers; commands which may in any case have accorded with their own inclinations, not least because in Greece such a conflict actually came to pass.

At the time of the German withdrawal in 1944 a communist-led partisan army with widespread if not overwhelming popular support was in control of the country. The British government however, regarding Greece as a vital interest and the key to the eastern Mediterranean, was determined to restore the pre-war royal regime. Following abortive negotiations full-scale civil war supervened, in which the royalist forces, thanks to military assistance first from the British and later the US, finally prevailed. Greece having been allocated to the British sphere, Stalin resolutely refused to render any assistance to his embattled fellow-communists. and the lesson was not lost upon the leaders of the other major communist parties. The PCI and the PCF therefore obediently joined coalition governments of a 'popular front' variety as very junior partners to bourgeois parties backed by the Western powers. They accepted the disarmament of the partisan and maquis units which they controlled and disciplined any of their subordinates who resisted the demand. They did their best to damp down any manifestation of labour discontent or industrial action and urged the workforce, in France especially, to spare no effort for the sake of patriotic reconstruction.

This may indeed have been the only sensible policy: it is altogether too crude to assume that it was followed merely at Stalin's dictate, much as it fitted in with his strategies. Had the French or Italian communists at large been totally convinced of their ability to win it is certainly possible that neither the Kremlin nor their own leaders would have been able to hold them back. The large communist parties of western Europe therefore represented from the Soviet standpoint both an asset, in terms of their capacity to influence their national governments in a pro-Soviet direction, and a problem in terms of the danger of them overstepping the mark. These same relationships were magnified in eastern Europe.

It seems most unlikely that Stalin intended from the first to impose a replica of Soviet-style one-party rule upon the liberated states of the region, whether they were former victims of Nazi conquest like Poland, Czechoslovakia and Yugoslavia, or former accomplices like Hungary, Romania and Bulgaria. (In the latter country, where there had been a traditionally strong communist base and some degree of wartime partisan activity, the new regime actually applied to join the USSR as a constituent republic, but was naturally not accepted.) There were a number of good reasons to show restraint.

In the first place, an open and undisguised Soviet takeover would be highly offensive to the West, which Stalin continued to court. Secondly, it would involve the Soviet government having to exercise continuous control over foreign states with their own national feelings, cultures, history and, in some cases, rivalries. Certainly Moscow wanted to secure economic advantage from these countries, especially the ex-enemy ones, but that was quite easily done without having to run their governments for them. Reparations and suitably tailored trade agreements would serve equally well. Finally, and perhaps most importantly, Stalin being Stalin was loath to raise up a platoon of mini-Stalins, which would be the inevitable consequence of putting these states under undivided communist control. They would have to be accorded the formalities due not merely to national communist leaders but ones heading formally independent communist states and might well, especially if they had been built up as anti-fascist heroes like Dimitrov in Bulgaria or Tito in Yugoslavia, be tempted to get ideas above their station.

It should not therefore be assumed that the popular front governments established in eastern Europe were merely tactical ploys, intended as platforms from which a full-blown communist monopoly would be instituted as soon as practicable. Much more likely what was anticipated was a somewhat tighter variant of the model employed in Finland – the foreign policies of these states would be closely monitored and directed from Moscow and their internal regimes would be ones with which the USSR felt comfortable, but they would remain capitalist in their economic and social structures and would not be led by communists alone. It is well known that this scenario generated immediate trouble between Stalin and the Yugoslav leaders. The latter, feeling that they had independently defeated the German occupiers (as well as the armed royalist elements, the Chetniks) and carried through a social revolution in the course of the fighting, were far from inclined to share power with anyone, much as Stalin urged Tito to accept back the royal pretender in a nominal role in the meantime and get rid of him at some convenient date thereafter.[3] The Yugoslavs did not publicly dissent but, loud in their protestations of Stalinist loyalty, quietly ignored the course that was being urged upon them, other than to to take a few non-communists temporarily into a token popular front, while abolishing the monarchy and proclaiming Yugoslavia as a socialist republic. The largest of the Balkan states therefore came under an avowedly communist regime, but against Stalin's will, not in compliance with it. The dictator himself, though offended, was obliged in the circumstances to accept Tito as the very paragon of communist revolutionary achievement and accord the Yugoslav party a special status among its east European counterparts.

The reluctance to replace an informal hegemony with full-blown Sovietisation did not mean, however, that the leading position of the local communists in these popular front administrations was not made tightly secure. Where they did not hold the premiership itself the key ministries of defence and internal security were in their hands. In addition they penetrated the higher levels of the non-communist coalition parties, many of whose ostensible leading figures were in fact unacknowledged communists or in agreement with the CP on all important issues. The regimes set about destroying the social base of the forces hostile to communism and the USSR, which conveniently fitted in with the social revolution spontaneously desired by the populace at large. The ruling classes of the ancien régime, which had provided the local reactionaries, fascists and collaborators, were driven out and dispossessed. Landowners and capitalists lost their property, which was, respectively, distributed to the peasantry or nationalised. Plans were laid to surmount by projects of industrial development the economic backwardness and dependence on primary production which had hitherto characterised eastern Europe.[4]

Bipolar World

This is not the place to examine the development of the Cold War as a superpower contest, but only how it impacted upon the communist movement. As confrontation escalated the unstable balance in both eastern and western Europe described above became untenable. The establishment, as it proved, of a bipolar world characterised by grim hostility and permanent threat of war necessitated a far-reaching regroupment of political forces and institutional consolidation of developments implicit since 1945. Without any doubt Stalin believed that his former allies had reneged on the *realpolitik* agreements struck during the closing stages of the war and, and regarding the security of his regime as the ultimate priority, preferred to reverse his previous stances and incur their enmity rather than pursue any *modus vivendi* that acknowledged a position of inferiority.

In the course of 1947 the proclamation of the Truman Doctrine in March, which in essence offered US aid to any regime resisting communism, followed by the announcement of the European Recovery Programme or Marshall Plan, marked the definitive breakdown in post-war relations. Marshall Aid was offered to all European states, including the USSR, and a number of the eastern European regimes, particularly Czechoslovakia, were keen to accept it. The Kremlin reckoned, however, that the scheme did not represent aid without strings but that its purpose was subordination to US economic and political hegemony. This was probably an accurate judgement, for there was a genuine fear among the Western leaders that economic distress might push the masses in western Europe towards communism and the aid was designed at least in part to avert this. The USSR rejected and denounced the offer and the states under its tutelage were commanded to do likewise.

Stalin was now ready once more to identify aggressive capitalist power as a mortal threat – and to hint at international revolution as an appropriate response (though such specific Leninist terminology was studiously avoided). To this end he set about mobilising the international movement to counter the danger. It was done for motives that pertained to the state interests of the Soviet regime, but was the easier to accomplish in that it could seem to correspond to genuine processes of social upheaval and transformation taking place throughout the world – the liquidation of the power of the traditional European ruling elites; an anti-colonial revolution and the end of European global hegemony. The effects which followed upon the European communist parties were immediate and profound and defined their futures for the remainder of their existence. Those in the east, after more or less traumatic processes – which in the case of Poland involved a low-level civil war – imposed themselves as monopolist ruling parties with terror as the backstop of their dominance, forcing their former partners into amalgamation or retaining them as fig-leaves in spurious 'national fronts', purging the 'bourgeois' or social democrat leaders who declined to co-operate. Nevertheless the façade of the immediate post-war system was retained and 'most communist states opted for legislatures of a rather conservative formal design, based on European parliamentary traditions'[5] instead of soviets. The CPs of western Europe were meantime ejected from the coalition governments in which they had participated and all of them – subjected to intense official media campaigns of denigration and vituperation, and forced into political and social isolation – were turned into pariahs within their respective political cultures.

Although at that point still the unquestioned head of international communism, Stalin must have regretted the precipitate dissolution of the Comintern as an agency to co-ordinate the global communist struggle, now back on the agenda. This was especially true at a point when a major reorientation was being imposed upon him and when rank-and-file communists at large, accustomed for over a decade to the slogans and tactics of the Popular Front fortified by the experience of the war and liberation, were liable to find themselves confused and at a loss.[6] Accordingly a new agency was created in late 1947, though without any formal executive powers, not based in Moscow, and with a membership that embraced only European CPs (including the USSR), and not even all of those.

The Communist Information Bureau (Cominform) was explicitly not a re-creation of the Comintern, though for the parties which were its members and for other European ones which were not, it fulfilled very similar purposes to the International under Stalin. Membership, apart from the CPSU, comprised the ruling parties of eastern Europe, less Albania, together with the French and Italian. There was a logic behind this apparently arbitrary composition, though not one which could be openly stated. In interpreting it the omissions are as significant as the presences. No Asian CP was invited to the founding conference, though some of those had grown to become major forces in their own countries, including some which were prosecuting armed struggles with reasonable prospects of victory, such as the Malayan, the Philippine, the Indo-Chinese and above all the Chinese, already in control of territory and population larger than Europe. Nor were there any representatives from the African or American continents.

The at first sight surprising European absences included that of Greece, at that stage engaged in a ferocious civil war against the Western-backed royalist government. Stalin, however, had already written off this struggle; the fact that the KKE had not already liquidated it was a small indication of the limits of his control. The Albanian Party of Labour, though empathically a ruling party, was excluded because the Yugoslav government aimed at the eventual inclusion of Albania in the Yugoslav Federation, and the Yugoslav

Communist Party, as an ostensibly model Stalinist party, was to be accorded a particularly distinguished role in the new organisation; indeed, its headquarters were to be sited in Belgrade. It would have been tactless to include the East German party both for the reason that this still remained the Soviet occupied zone of Germany with reunification as the formal expectation, and because the Socialist Unity Party (SED) was òn paper not a communist party at all but a reunification of the KPD and the SDP with a supposed joint leadership. The Finnish CP, in spite of its considerable strength, was left out because the position of that neutral country was satisfactory in Stalin's eyes. The two western CPs were brought in purely for their size and political and industrial muscle; they were to act as the information conduit for the other western parties.

The founding conference, which took place in Poland in October 1947, included the traditional communist practice of castigating the most zealous executors of the former key strategy which was about to be reversed. The French and Italian delegates (the party leaders had wisely stayed away) were censured severely for their complacent and accommodating attitude to bourgeois forces in the popular fronts and particularly towards right-wing social democracy, now designated as the catspaw of an aggressive US takeover of Europe. The world, they were informed, had become split into two camps, the anti-democratic imperialist and the democratic anti-imperialist, and their mission was to extend all their efforts to save western Europe from becoming irrecoverably integrated into the former camp. The circumstances of the Cominform's formation, its character and the objectives which it adopted suggest that Stalin had not yet wholly abandoned all hope of reaching a compromise with the West. The Cominform ostentatiously ignored the theatres of armed conflict involving communists, and was careful to stress that general war need not be inevitable. Its focus was not merely Eurocentric but significantly took no account of the northern and southern peripheries of that continent. Taken together these realities are best explained as an agenda for a sharper assertion of communist political strength in the European theatre alone, consolidating Moscow's power in the states it 'rightfully' dominated according to the wartime agreements while demonstrating that it could also strike back at US hegemony in the western part, in the hope that this calculated but not excessive show of strength would bring the West into a more conciliatory frame of mind.[7]

If so, he was to be speedily disappointed, for if the Truman Doctrine can be regarded as the effective declaration of the Cold War, the

Cominform's establishment and its language was viewed in Western capitals not as a negotiating gambit, but as the acceptance of a challenge to an all-out contest for world supremacy. Over the course of the next six years relationships between the two superpowers and their respective satellites grew steadily more acrimonious, more than once reaching the edge of a full-blown shooting war involving atomic weaponry. The west European parties achieved no success whatsoever in fulfilling their Cominform mission through propaganda, demonstrations and industrial action; if anything their efforts were counterproductive and only accelerated the consolidation of the Western bloc and its military arm, NATO, and by trying to disrupt US economic salvation through Marshall aid, drove themselves into deeper suspicion and disrepute within their own societies. Nonetheless, the best endeavours of official, commercial and voluntary propaganda agencies, including the not inconsiderable presence of the Catholic Church, were unable to break the ideological grip which the PCF and the PCI exercised upon the labour movements and the working classes in France and Italy.

Tito and the Purges

The Cominform, however, had been in existence for scarcely half a year before it was disrupted from within, tearing the first hole in the fabric of Stalinist unity. The schism was the more traumatic and embarrassing in that involved the party which had been held up as the exemplar of leadership in the 'people's democracies' and allocated the honour of hosting the Cominform HQ. The breakdown in relations between Belgrade and Moscow may not have been inevitable, but the potential for it was certainly very great. The communist movement, on account of its very nature, could never function simply as the quasi-military structure of unthinking zealots to which it was sometimes compared, and which was undoubtedly a part of its reality, but never more than a part. However tightly entrenched was Stalin's infallibility as the ultimate authority, reserving to himself all innovations in theory, yet disagreement and argument over tactics, strategy and even the interpretation of theory (or dogma) were not only ineradicable but even part of the movement's tradition. Dissident currents, no matter how hidden, always existed in every communist party, as well as differences between the leaderships of respective parties, even in the era of monolithic public unity.[8]

As noted above, Stalin's realism had swallowed Tito's infraction of discipline in the latter's assumption of undivided power at the end of the war, and allowed the propagation of his image as a model communist. With the breakdown in East–West relations and formation of the antagonistic blocs, any likely friction arising from Tito's actions had in any case disappeared and Yugoslavia was even more extravagantly commended. Stalin nonetheless expected to treat the communist leaders of the bloc states as he would have treated the heads of the constituent Soviet republics and command not only their general line of direction, which, given their backgrounds, they would have been pleased to accept, but the detail of how they ran the governments they were in charge of. More specifically, he wanted a co-ordination of economic policies that would be most beneficial to Soviet industry and not necessarily advantageous to the individual states of the bloc, who were in effect forbidden to concert economic policies between themselves and obliged to work in one-to-one relationships with the USSR. He was no less insistent that the security apparatus of these states should be controlled by Soviet 'advisers'.

These things the Yugoslav communist leaders were not prepared to agree to, and they even had the temerity to suggest a Balkan federation incorporating Bulgaria (led by another renowned figure, Dimitrov) and themselves – or even a federation of *all* the People's Democracies – which would certainly have constituted a power bloc not to rival but to stand comparison with the USSR, something certain to inflame Stalin's paranoid sensibility. In the past, achievement or prestige had proved to be no protection against Stalin's enmity, as Trotsky's fate had dramatically illustrated, but matters turned out differently in 1948. It was not a question of Tito alone (or as the Cominform preferred to express it, the 'Tito–Rankovic clique'),[9] for Tito was representative of virtually the entire Yugoslav leadership – only a very few of them followed the conditioning of their communist pasts to accept Moscow's diktat as the last word.[10] Although the rank and file of the Yugoslav Communist Party were not involved in taking the decisions, only endorsing them after the event, there is no reason to imagine that their real feelings were in opposition to the leadership or their approval motivated by fear.[11] So far as the population at large were concerned, many of them had reason enough to dislike Soviet arrogance, and harboured feelings of resentment at the behaviour of the Red Army troops who had entered Yugoslavia in their wartime advance westward. Tito and his colleagues were in a position to mobilise without difficulty Yugoslav national feeling and pride against Soviet pretension and attempted dominance. No less

importantly, unlike all previous communist oppositions, they had control over a state, and one that could, if necessary, be defended against
military attack.

The dispute was immediately presented in ideological terms, but
what had clashed, in fact, were the conflicting interests of two states,
or more accurately those of their governing elites. The Yugoslav
leaders could afford to be comparatively frank about this, though of
course they presented their position as one reflecting the popular will,
which in this instance it undoubtedly did. The Kremlin could not, of
course, make any such admission, and indeed to legitimate its position was obliged to take refuge behind the fiction of the Cominform
as a free association of communist parties.[12] It was from this source,
hastily transferred to Bucharest, that the anathemas were pronounced,
not Moscow.

The initial accusations directed against the Yugoslav regime, in
the shape of a Cominform resolution, were that it had seriously devi-
ated from Marxist principles and had ordered its secret police to
harass the Soviet advisers and Cominform executives working in the
country. When the Yugoslavs, instead of prostrating themselves and
acknowledging fault, defended their position, the level of vituperation escalated, culminating in assertions that Tito's regime was both
Trotskyist and fascist, as well as being the principal agent of Western intelligence services and governments aimed at subverting the
People's Democracies and returning them to capitalism and Western
control. Most of the Cominform propaganda and its echo in that
of the non-Cominform CPs was of course fanciful invention, and
no effort was ever made to explain why a regime whose alleged
faults were becoming clear well before October 1947 should have
been awarded the formal leading role in the Cominform. Nevertheless, reading between the lines of the polemical verbiage, it is possible to establish what the Soviet fury was actually about and the
relationship in the Cominform's mentality between theoretical and
pragmatic considerations.

The original sin, from which all subsequent crimes, ideological
and practical, were alleged to spring, was that of a deviation towards
bourgeois nationalism, covered up by populist demagogy. In consequence the Yugoslav Communist Party had been downgraded, its
working-class membership had been deliberately kept small and it
functioned as a semi-secret organisation, assimilated and dissolved
into a broader People's Front filled with unreliable class elements,
while all real power was concentrated in the clique around Tito.

They practised the 'military method' of Party leadership . . . Party elections at all levels ceased. Leaderships were organised by co-option. Internal discussion was discouraged. Criticism [was] suppressed. And Rankovic . . . [took] ruthless disciplinary measures against party members who dared to discuss or criticise the dictates of the ruling clique . . . . Meetings were hastily summoned in which all those criticising the . . . leadership were ruled out of order, after which many were expelled from the Party . . . . Hand-picked delegations were dispatched to the Party congress which . . . was transformed into a series of bitter harangues.[13]

These were the standard techniques of control used in any communist party, and particularly by the Soviet Stalinists in the 1920s campaigns against Trotsky. The Yugoslav leaders naturally used the methods they were accustomed to. In castigating the Titoites in this fashion, the reader might almost wonder whether the Stalinists had a sense of humour.

A further major indictment concerned the Yugoslav peasantry. Tito and his associates were berated for basing the regime too much upon this class. Tito had declared in 1946, 'We tell the peasants that they are the firmest basis of our state . . . because they really constitute such a basis.' Following on from this, the regime failed to be suspicious of and discriminate against the wealthier peasantry 'On the one hand Tito and Kardelj liked to regard the peasantry as a single undifferentiated entity. They rejected the Soviet example. They coined slogans about the peasantry, not explaining the class structure of the peasantry, and the difference in attitude and role of poor peasants, middle peasants and rich peasants (kulaks).'[14] Or, in effect, the Yugoslavs had refused to implement the programme of compulsory agricultural collectivisation upon which the other states of the bloc were currently embarking in imitation of the Soviet example – and with comparably disastrous outcomes.

What the denunciations boil down to behind the phraseology is that the Yugoslav communists were failing to enforce a tight top-down party control in the Soviet interest, and were underpinning their defiance by inciting populist nationalism. The most interesting question and biggest puzzle in relation to these developments is why Stalin, via the Cominform, should have chosen to provoke the issue and bring matters to a head. In this case he did have a choice. The Yugoslavs certainly did not seek the quarrel but returned civil, though uncompromising, responses to the initial charges and indeed at that point went so far as to appeal to Stalin against the Cominform. The regime could have been retained as a Stalin-applauding loyal member of the bloc with its own social and political peculiarities, such as they were, and it would have been very much to Stalin's own pragmatic advantage that this should have been so.

Though we do not have positive answers to the question, two linked explanations suggest themselves. Stalin had grown accustomed to treating all other communist leaders as his vassals, although as a rule he had enough sense to recognise when there were limits to that authority, as with China. However he did not tolerate insubordination unless he had to, and by obstructing Soviet demands, Tito was showing himself to be insubordinate. Worse still, if he was permitted to get away with it, the example might spread. However, Stalin was not in the habit of engineering direct confrontations unless he had made sure of winning them in advance, so it must be presumed that he imagined there were sufficient pro-Stalinist forces inside Yugoslavia to bring the regime to order once the Cominform had given the signal. Despite the control which Tito and Rankovic kept over their own party it is not impossible that, other things being equal, he might have turned out to be justified, but other things were not in any sense equal and the difference was made by national sentiment, the first occasion in which it had proved decisive in Communist affairs. In this the Cominform resolution did actually though distortedly identify the crucial issue at stake.

There was some speculation at the time that Yugoslavia might emerge as the centre of a new and more authentic international revolutionary movement, a hope that was actually voiced by certain Trotskyists, elated by this break in the Stalinist monolith. The European communist party leaderships outside the bloc were certainly worried and expended a lot of effort, mostly with success, to insulate their own memberships against the contagion.[15] There was, however, no real prospect that such a thing would occur, given that the Yugoslav regime had nailed its colours so firmly to the national mast. Though it might expand its critique of the USSR to attack the Stalinised interpretations of Marxism which constituted communist orthodoxy, declare that it intended to commence the process of the state withering away[16] and experiment with new forms of economic management, fundamentally it did not have anything very new to offer. The principle on which the regime in its new dress was established was not global revolution, but opposition to interference in its internal affairs.

Additionally, it was now obliged to turn the Cominform accusations into self-fulfilling prophecies by having to lean towards the West, seek Western economic assistance and keep open the possibility of Western military support in the event of a Soviet invasion if Stalin pushed matters to that length. The West naturally was delighted to observe the breach created in its enemy's bastions and the mere existence of Tito's dissident regime was ample return for the resources supplied to him, but he was in a position to provide a more concrete pay-off by easing the West's problems in Greece. The embattled Greek communists, engaged in a desperate guerrilla conflict, had loyally cut their own throats by joining in the excoriation of Yugoslavia, and so provided Tito with ample pretext for withdrawing the logistic and military support with which the Yugoslavs had hitherto supplied them. Friendly relations were established between Belgrade and Western governments but special efforts were put into wooing the anti-communist and rigidly constitutionalist social democrat parties, in the hope that socialism, even of a very different variety, would provide some common ground. These relationships, about which the Yugoslavs, if they wanted to preserve their independence and their lives did not have much choice, were an additional insurance against their regime becoming a rival revolutionary focus to the one in Moscow. If 'socialism in a single country' had been the primal Stalinist slogan, the same was now to be attempted independently by Tito within yet smaller dimensions.

For Moscow, Belgrade's successful defiance represented not merely a first-class humiliation but realisation of the nightmare thought to have been exorcised in the twenties, of effective challenge to the ruling bureaucracy from within the communist movement, a tear liable to spread uncontrollably if not promptly stitched. It could be viewed as doubly dangerous in that it put in jeopardy the USSR's vital geopolitical interests at the height of the superpower contest.

Very likely Stalin was genuinely convinced of the existence of a massive plot centred on Yugoslavia and masterminded by the Western intelligence agencies – it was the fashion according to which his mind worked. In rooting it out he would not have been much concerned with who or who was not actually involved; he followed the principle that it was better for a thousand innocent people to suffer than for one guilty one to escape. The technique was to trawl a dragnet through the institutions, decimating the categories which were likely to harbour the culprits so that in the process their capture might be assured.

The frenzied Cominform diatribes against Yugoslavia set the stage; the leadership of every east European party had been obliged to contribute, none wished to fall under suspicion themselves or be seen to be behindhand in detecting potential Titoites within their own ranks. It was always the presumption, later confirmed with concrete evidence, that the inoculation of the Eastern bloc against the Titoite contagion was organised directly from Moscow (where less publicised purges were taking place simultaneously) and directed on the ground by Soviet security personnel – though this may be qualified some-what in the case of the Albanian trial (the first one), where Cominform considerations were intercut with an internal power struggle and anti-Yugoslav resentments. The purges affected every eastern European state (and also East Germany which, in 1949, was raised to the dig-nity of statehood as the German Democratic Republic [DDR]), though not all of them did so by means of spectacular show trials.

The terror which now supervened throughout the People's Demo-cracies was to define their political character during the subsequent five years and to resonate in their societies for four decades. The model used in staging the theatrical performances of the trials in the countries where they took place was derived, though with certain variations,[17] from the three show trials of the Soviet Great Terror in the thirties. The principal victims were drawn from the highest reaches of communist party and state. They were induced to confess, by ill-treatment, torture, threats to their families and – preposterously – appeals to their communist loyalty, to the most extravagant and unbelievable plots and crimes; to have been agents of the pre-war fascist security forces and to have betrayed countless colleagues, to have wormed their way subsequently into the highest reaches of their parties where they conspired with Yugoslavs, local Titoites, Zionists, British and US intelligence to overthrow the People's Democracies, assassinate their Stalinist leaders and restore capital-ism. 'The confessions recited by the possessed communists,' writes Fernando Claudin, 'bear a strange resemblance to the exorcisms of the Middle Ages.' Stalin, of course, had once been trained as a priest. By an Alice-in-Wonderland logic it was assumed that the parties and party organisations which had demonstrated the most monolithic loyalty and unanimity and with least apparent reason to give con-cern, must in reality be the ones most permeated with concealed treachery and deviation. By a particularly hideous irony, some Com-inform loyalists who had fled Yugoslavia at the time of the break were drawn into the web and indicted as Tito's spies who had falsely pretended to oppose him in order to carry out their nefarious work. Again, as with the Soviet model, the show trials were an iceberg tip beneath which middle-ranking and rank-and-file party members were summarily disposed of. One estimate puts the purged in all the parties involved at a figure of around 2.5 million, with up to a quarter of a million imprisoned and an unknown number executed.[18]

The Albanian trial noted above was not all that much regarded in the West: the first to make a major impact on international consciousness took place in Budapest in September 1949. The leading defendant was Laszlo Rajk, former Interior Minister and prior to his arrest, Foreign Minister of the republic. The Interior Ministry, as Claudin notes, was a particularly dangerous place to have been or to be, and it was largely a matter of chance whether a minister or official there was likely to end up as accuser or accused. Rajk may also have been singled out for his German ancestry. The proceedings followed the regular script for occasions of this kind: the accused made their abject confessions at length and in detail, giving substance to the vast spider's web of Titoite conspiracy, all were convicted; a number, including Rajk, sentenced to death and the remainder to lengthy prison terms. The next trial opened shortly afterwards in Sofia and proved to be unusual in two respects.

Firstly there was only one death sentence in this instance, upon the chief accused, Traicho Kostov. Kostov was one of the founders of the Bulgarian CP and had been its General Secretary when arrested. The second and sensational novelty was that from the dock he forcefully repudiated his previous confession and held his ground thereafter, the only purge trial victim either in the USSR or the bloc ever to do so.[19] There is no way of knowing whether Kostov might have been spared along with his co-defendants if he had capitulated; possibly he saved his honour at the cost of his life.

Romania, Poland and East Germany escaped show trials, though not purges.[20] The most ferocious of these charades was reserved until the last and was instituted as late as 1952, in Czechoslovakia. Once again, as in Bulgaria, the chief victim was the party's highest official, its General Secretary, in this case Rudolf Slansky, who had himself been responsible for conducting the previous lower-level purges in the country. This trial, moreover, was distinguished by its anti-semitic overtones, an unusual proportion of the accused being of Jewish extraction and the emphasis on contacts with international Zionism being particularly insistent.[21] It resulted in eleven death sentences; one of the survivors, Artur London, was later to provide a particularly detailed account and analysis of the techniques used to extort the confessions.

Stalin's death came too late to save the condemned men and it is clear that had he lived much longer the Prague trial would have been neither the last nor the most spectacular. All signs indicate that a purge of even more extravagant dimensions was being prepared at the beginning of 1953 in the USSR itself that would have destroyed Stalin's remaining veteran associates – its intended overture was the Kremlin 'doctors'' plot (again with anti-semitic overtones) – and was averted only by the tyrant's own demise in March of that year. It is scarcely necessary to add that the communist parties outside the bloc were obliged, taking their line from the Cominform and the CPSU, to mobilise all their publicity resources to applaud and justify the trials, endorsing their unmasking of a supposed imperialist plot with endless ramifications.[22] The surprising thing is that among communists outside the reach of Stalin's security agencies there was little sign of questioning and rejection – the fervour of the official party campaigns in crushing incipient dissent and their own embattled situation in the Cold War may have accounted for that.

The monolithicism being enforced from Moscow amid an atmosphere of unconstrained terror and a parallel suffocation of any independent initiatives in culture or the sciences did not exclude, so far as the western parties were concerned, the cultivation with Stalin's blessing of national postures of a sort – provided they were directed against the USA. The latter was portrayed as leader of the camp of anti-democratic imperialism, bent upon subordinating Europe as a bridgehead for military assault upon the Soviet bloc and meantime drowning national cultures in a swamp of debased commercialism. The Yugoslavs had been anathematised for, among other things, proposing 'national roads to socialism' distinct from that of the USSR, but once the European frontiers of the Cold War had solidified and the USSR had acquired atomic weaponry Stalin had less to expect or demand from the Western CPs; their national stances might still prove marginally useful against the USA and watered-down versions of nationally-orientated socialist strategies could be allowed to develop, as, because of the national organisation of the communist movement they were inevitably bound to do unless impeded by stronger forces. In 1951, with Stalin's blessing, the CPGB produced a programme under the title *The British Road to Socialism*. The Prague trial the following year emphasised, however, that such distinctiveness was for non-bloc parties only.

Storm over Asia

The Comintern had among its earliest demands the dissolution of all the colonial empires and national self-determination for their inhabitants. At the close of the twentieth century, with overt colonialism entirely extinct, it is difficult to appreciate what a profoundly revolutionary demand this was in its time, when the British and French empires had just attained their widest geographical extent.

With the important Chinese exception, Asian communist parties when the Second World War began were invariably tiny and invariably persecuted. By the time the conflict ended the position had been transformed. Unlike its Axis partner, defeated Japan saw its communist party, emerging from the underground, grow into a mass force, working amicably for a time with the US occupation authorities. In certain Indian regions, notably West Bengal and Kerala, though not consistently throughout the country, a similar expansion took place. In Malaya and Vietnam conditions were equivalent to those in Greece and Yugoslavia, the communists having secured very widespread popular support and having emerged in control of formidable military forces in leading resistance to the occupier, though their social base of support was different in the two countries.[23] A comparable development had occurred in the Philippine archipelago and to a lesser degree, but still significantly, in the former Japanese colony of Korea. The position in the Dutch East Indies, with rival independence-seeking movements, was more complex, and in Burma enormously more so, but in essence communist parties in these countries had become in the course of the war significant and armed political forces. And at the other end of the continent, though not large, they had reached the stage of being able to exercise some influence among the urban masses in the Arab Middle East and Iran.

Although the Bolsheviks in their early days had looked primarily towards Europe, Lenin had been acutely conscious of the implications for European politics of developments in the colonial empires.[24] The masses of the east – for Asia was primarily in mind – were viewed in this light as a reserve army for the European proletariat. If the revolution was stalled meantime in Europe (thanks to the treachery of social democracy and its misleaders), it might yet find an indirect route to victory through the subjugated nations. The Comintern exerted itself to nurture communist parties in colonies and semi-colonies.

The combination of Comintern organisational methods with anticolonial aspirations proved in time to be a potent mix.[25] The initial development of Asian communism was both tortuous and imperilled, but the circumstances of world war and European defeat by Japanese power between 1941 and 1945 presented the opportunity which enabled its intrinsic advantages to be exploited with enormous effect. At the same time – though this was far from clear to contemporary observers who interpreted matters either positively or negatively within the old framework – the agenda had changed. The Asian revolutions were not an auxiliary support to European communism but an autonomous force. Where they were successful and led by communists the latter, though they might express due deference to Stalin, were determined to exercise power on their own terms within their own societies.

These CPs were also affected by a profound contradiction. In terms of formal Marxist ideology they were workers' parties with their foundations in the proletariat and labour movements of those countries or colonies where they were located. There was nothing exceptional or contradictory in this conception taken by itself. The working class was assumed to be the social layer most firm and resolute in the independence struggle as well as the one capable, through its most advanced party, of comprehending the general world movement and the connection between the two things. However, it did imply that since such proletariats were small in absolute numbers and tiny in proportion to their general populations, the communist parties based upon them would also necessarily be small. The original Comintern conception accorded with this circumstance – they were to act as a leaven for the general mass movement and hopefully lead it in the independence struggle, but not to be in a position to bid for power upon their own account. Long before that issue emerged in practical terms it was expected that the international revolution would have occurred, after which the former colonies would rapidly produce social structures corresponding to the historic European norm but in conditions enormously more favourable to their working classes. If the notion of long-continuing Bolshevik regime in an isolated Soviet Russia was unthinkable to Lenin and his immediate successors, even more so was that of communist regimes in yet more backward states within a still-capitalist world.

Close alliance of the Asian CPs with the independence-minded 'national bourgeoisie' was therefore viewed as the immediate necessity. That conception came under great strain when in China in 1927 (where up to that point the conception had appeared to work brilliantly) the political representatives of that bourgeoisie turned upon their communist partners and massacred them, very nearly achieving the annihilation of Chinese communism. Moreover, time made it clear – and here again China furnished a clear example – that the national bourgeoisie was not necessarily interested in independence in the sense which the communists understood. Finally, as indicated in the previous chapter, the working-class character of these parties had become by the time of the war no more than nominal, a theoretical construct. Their primary appeal, where it took root, was above all to the peasant masses. That appeal combined nationalist objectives with a social programme, a call for the creation of a new socially just order as the fruit of independence, an order whose principal element would be the the redress of timeless oppressions inflicted upon the peasantry, with land redistribution as the priority – not forgetting severe punishment for the social culprits. Colonialism and the integration of peasant societies into a single world market centred on Europe and America intensified the economic pressures on basic producers and speeded up social differentiation. When combined with resistance to a rapacious new foreign invader, who had demonstrated nevertheless that Europeans could be beaten like anybody else, the communist message was one for which millions in east Asia were ready.

It would be an oversimplification to conclude that Asian communism took on the character of a gigantic peasants' revolt; nevertheless it is certainly true that that was where it found its main component and driving force.[26] As such it had advantages and potential not available to previous episodes of that kind. The organisation, discipline and political doctrine of the Leninist–Stalinist tradition was certainly one of them, though, paradoxically, never intended for a peasant movement. The existence of the USSR as an example and source of moral and material encouragement was of course vital, and the Marxist–Leninist ideology enabled the individual struggles to be perceived as part of a general unstoppable world process rather than separate and isolated rebellions. Perhaps most importantly because Moscow regarded the priority remit of these communist parties as freeing their countries from imperialist rule, they were able to stress nationalism as much as they liked without falling under suspicion of heresy and (provided they made the right gestures) enjoy a degree of political freedom not available to their European counterparts.[27]

Much as those of European CPs under the occupation, their prospects were transformed by the war, though in a manner never foreseen at the time of their formation. Apart from Yugoslavia and Albania the post-war revolutions which had taken place in Europe, though they had some indigenous basis, had succeeded only under the patronage of the Red Army and its actual (or in the case of Czechoslovakia implicit) presence. Elsewhere on the Continent socialist revolution remained stalled and bourgeois democracy (under the patronage of the Western powers) reasserted itself. Asia instead became the storm centre of successful indigenous revolution as the colonial empires crumbled and the neo-colonial regime in China fell to pieces.

Mao's communists had acquired immense popular approval and military experience from their prosecution of the war against the Japanese and for the equity, honesty and reforming zeal of their government in the large area of northern China which they controlled. They had also acquired huge supplies of military equipment captured by Soviet forces from the Japanese in the closing stages of the war. Stalin supplied this, in the expectation that Mao would use it as a bargaining counter with the Guomindang government, not as a means of conquest, for his sights were fixed on accommodation with the Guomindang's sponsors, the USA, and his attitude to China in 1945 was similar to that towards Yugoslavia on a bigger scale. The Indian CP leader, B.T. Ranadive, a Kremlin loyalist, even publicly denounced Mao in July 1949.[28] Stalin's embassy was ostentatiously the last to leave Chiang's capital, for even though by that point the Cold War was joined, Stalin was still aiming to confine it to Europe and resolve it on agreed terms.

It was clear to Western observers in China, however, that no long-term conciliation was possible between Mao and Chiang, for the two represented absolutely incompatible social forces. When their uneasy wartime truce inevitably broke down and the communist forces went on the offensive it became rapidly apparent that the Guomindang was finished despite substantial US aid, being destitute of popular credibility and support. In 1949 its remnants fled the mainland to Taiwan and Mao was able to proclaim the Chinese People's Republic in Peking (Beijing) that October. Stalin grudgingly, and the western CPs with greater sincerity, heralded it as the second greatest revolution of the twentieth century after the Russian. Historical perspective may yet show it to have been the more important one.

The Chinese upheaval was reflected elsewhere throughout eastern Asia. In various countries of the region communist-led independence movements controlling substantial armed forces found themselves, through a quirk of historical fate, in a power vacuum, where they were poised to take over power from the defeated Japanese and against the former colonial rulers not yet securely re-established. From a Marxist standpoint they were caught in an anomaly, for unlike China, the essential preliminary bourgeois revolution had not been accomplished and they were in fact unwilling to pursue bids for undivided power on their own behalf, preferring to merge into some form of nationalist front in which they would be strongly positioned behind the scenes, resembling the original popular front governments of eastern Europe.

Had the former colonial powers conceded independence without further ado or continuing interference and had the Cold War been avoided, the purely nationalist agendas of these parties, in the absence of forces pulling them together and towards Moscow, would have been greatly strengthened. The Cold War imposed an illusory coherence upon the communist movement in eastern Asia as imperialism, now directed by the USA, appeared to behave according to Leninist criteria. The returning imperial powers (including the USA in the Philippines), impelled by considerations of prestige, politics or economic imperative,[29] attempted to reassert their authority, and colonial war in the form of communist-led guerrilla insurgencies was not long in breaking out in British Malaya, French Indo-China and the Philippines. There was conflict also in the Dutch East Indies, where the Indonesian republic was proclaimed, but in this instance the main independence movement was not communist-led and indeed in 1948 massacred its communist rivals.

Only the Chinese communists attained rapid success. Results elsewhere of the Asian revolutions were mixed and in fact most of them suffered defeat in their communist form. After a lengthy struggle the British prevailed against the Malayan guerrillas. The Americans did the same in the Philippines. The Korean peninsula was divided between a communist regime supported by the USSR and China and a fiercely anti-communist one backed by the USA. In Indonesia the communist party, though it revived, remained subordinated, while the Burmese party was fragmented and marginalised. The case of French Indo-China was exceptional: with the assistance of British Forces the returning French administration succeeded in imposing itself upon the main cities but was unable to subdue the countryside, where the communist-led Vietminh was strongly entrenched. So commenced a thirty-year-long war which was to resonate for a time as the dominant issue of world politics and to culminate eventually in total communist victory, though at incalculable cost, both human and material, to all the participants. Armed conflict in Asia at this time involving the communist movement was not confined to the east of the continent. The negotiated Indian independence and partition are best remembered for the bloody communal conflicts they provoked on the Indo-Pakistan border, but it also saw a communist uprising of considerable dimensions in central India, led by elements within the CPI who regarded Nehru as the Indian Kerensky and thought to stage an Indian rerun of the Bolshevik revolution.

The above developments in no sense added up to a co-ordinated push for communist hegemony in eastern Asia or anywhere else. Though issuing in common from the experience of colonialism and the crisis of the global imperial system brought on by the Second World

War, each had its own particular and autonomous reality. Inevitably though, in the circumstances the separate episodes were structured into a unity by the evolving Cold War. Mao's victory occurred in the same year that the Soviet Union succeeded in detonating an experimental atomic device and breaking the US monopoly a decade ahead than predicted. Conjunction of the two events convinced Western public opinion that it was facing a concerted global threat emanating and tightly controlled from Moscow. The strains and confrontations which had characterised the European scene up to that point were now extended to Asia. With the Guomindang's defeat US business realised that it had lost for the foreseeable future the potentially largest single market in the world, and US politicians the client regime which had purported to rule that immense country and population. Demagogues such as Joseph McCarthy gained credibility by envisioning in lurid terms a satanic conspiracy whose tentacles were spread deep within the USA itself and which had been responsible, through spying activities and the penetration of government agencies, for the success of the Soviet atomic programme and the 'loss' of China.

The emergence of a bipolar world with the principals engaged in atomic confrontation, together with the creation of a Cold War frontline in Asia, pushed Stalin and Mao into what was more of an alliance of convenience that a genuine attachment and harmony of two Marxist–Leninist leaders. A treaty of friendship and co-operation was signed in which the USSR exacted high recompense for its material assistance. They proclaimed themselves to stand resolutely behind the peoples of the region resisting an imperialist offensive, with America backing up the old imperialist powers,[30] to deprive them of their independence and plunder their economies. Thus Asian affairs, no less than European ones, came to be viewed in Manichaean terms, with compromise ruled out. It was of course the case that the Western powers, and the US especially, with its formal anti-imperial credentials, was far from lacking indigenous support in prosecuting their anti-communist endeavours. Without it, indeed, they could not have hoped for as much success as they achieved.

Many sectors of east Asian society were wholly antipathetic, and with good reason, to finding themselves governed by regimes led by communists, whether avowedly or at one remove in a national bloc. Landowners and their dependants especially, together with the moneylenders who had preyed upon the peasant population, had nothing to hope for except dispossession and very possibly death. Even the better-off ranks of the peasantry had reason to fear the resentments and ambitions of their less well-off neighbours, among whom communist support was concentrated. All those who had been connected with the former imperial power in whatever capacity, though they might survive and be integrated into the new regime, were scarcely likely to find their prospects improved, and if they had been policemen or tax-collectors, were likely to face an uncertain future at best. Businessmen, whether large or small, though their contribution might be ostensibly welcomed if they had shown themselves to be patriotic and 'progressive', would be watched with suspicion and probably expropriated and 'liquidated as a class' once the opportunity offered. Being literate, they would probably know at least in outline what had happened to their counterparts in the USSR. Religious and traditionalist sentiment was likely to be offended on a large scale by Marxist–Leninist ideology. This was especially true in Vietnam, where many had converted to Catholicism, especially among the upper income levels. Ethnic group conflicts were also part of the equation, again true of Vietnam, but most strikingly in Malaya, where communist allegiance was entrenched among (though not confined to) immigrant-descended Chinese rubber plantation workers, distrusted and disliked by their indigenous Malay neighbours and separated further by the cultural divide of the Malays' Muslim religion; a relationship which was reproduced to some extent in Indonesia.

Thus the Western powers, apart from their formidable technological arsenal and total control of sea communications in the Pacific theatre, had plenty of potential local support upon which to base their counter-attacks, and it is scarcely surprising that the subsequent conflicts were protracted and sanguinary. The Korean example was in many respects both symbolic and defining. The evidence suggests that the communist regime established in the north of the country out of the anti-Japanese resistance was popular both in its own territory and in the south, where a rickety and brutal regime, based upon the landlord classes and Korean functionaries of the former colonial administration, survived precariously with US backing. When Northern troops crossed the border in June 1950, almost certainly with Soviet acquiescence rather than encouragement, the southern regime would have been swept away very rapidly but for massive Western, principally US, military intervention. The North, in turn, was on the point of being subjugated by the weight of American power when the Chinese government in its turn intervened as the fighting threatened to reach its frontier and install a hostile regime there.

The significance of this war – apart from the total devastation of Korea and its population – was that it was the only occasion in the classic phase of the Cold War in which the great powers became militarily involved and the only one ever in which they actually fought each other. Stalin refrained from committing Soviet military forces, as he could well afford to do: the war, although it hardened still further the anti-communist climate and appeared to provide incontestable proof of aggressive communist intent, was much more inconvenient to his enemy and also made Mao more dependent upon Soviet goodwill. It also raised acutely the possibility of escalation into atomic conflict: the limits which were set defined thereafter those of superpower confrontation – both sides were aware of how far they dared to go. Finally, and pertinent to the health of the world communism as it then was, there is no sign that the US[31] occupation of most of North Korea did anything to uproot pro-regime sentiment – the invading forces were regarded as oppressors, not liberators, and the devastation brought about by US air power generated especial hatred. By contrast, the Southern regime experienced great difficulty in suppressing disaffection in its own territory and succeeded only by resort to mass executions.

The Cold War, intertwined as it was with colonial revolt, political terror and social transformation, exercised a contradictory effect upon the communist movement as a global phenomenon. On the one hand it witnessed a dramatic expansion in the territorial area and populations ruled by communist regimes – the 'Socialist Sixth of the World' expanded into the 'Socialist Third of the World'. On the other, that expansion occurred in areas which took the movement even further away from the perspective envisaged by Lenin and the Bolsheviks – the conquest of power in the most advanced countries. The new members of the communist family were the more economically backward and war-ravaged states of Europe and the more backward still of China and North Korea. If the endeavours at 'socialist construction' in the USSR or bloc states gave rise to major frictions and spawned unaccountable dictatorship, the dangers were likely to be multiplied further east. The Cold War cultivated within communist governments and parties a siege mentality, a conviction of being under unrelenting threat and attack, which was reflected in the constant reference of their literature to opposing 'camps' and reinforced their most regressive and discreditable features, such as to close ranks around Stalin. Linked to that, and perhaps the most important consequence of all, the wartime and immediate post-war advances of the movement in numbers and political influence within the developed world were brought to an abrupt stop. The western parties were thrown on to a permanent defensive from which they were never afterwards able to break out.

3

Destalinisation

The Stalinist Universe

Stalin's seventieth birthday fell in December 1949. It evoked an eruption of adulation in the Soviet media and the publications of foreign
communist parties such as to make the term 'Byzantine' hopelessly
inadequate. He was hymned as a transcendent genius, not only in the
spheres of politics and military affairs, but in science and culture to
boot. The embalmed Lenin was still accorded formal precedence, but
it was formal only, and any unauthorised Soviet citizen who took
too close an interest in the lives and ideas of Marx or Lenin was
asking for trouble.

According to Trotsky's analysis, which became one of the central
doctrines of the Trotskyist tradition, Stalin was no more than the
typical and necessary representative, the 'outstanding mediocrity', in
Trotsky's phrase, of a bureaucratic caste which had usurped power
in the workers' state established in 1917.[1] Its success in doing so was
attributed to the social and economic underdevelopment, further
exacerbated by civil war, of the Tsarist empire where the revolution
had been victorious, combined with its failure to spread to the more
advanced nations of Europe. It was erected, Trotsky maintained, on
the foundation of working-class defeat both inside and outside Soviet
Russia. Universal scarcity and squalor, authoritarian traditions, rudimentary and simplistic educational and cultural standards furnished the
soil for bureaucratic proliferation. When consumer goods are scarce, as

Trotsky expressed it, queues have to be formed, and when the queues grow very long policemen (who may well be corrupt) are required to keep them in order. That in essence was what Soviet bureaucracy and Stalinism, on this interpretation, was supposed to be about.

Undoubtedly this encapsulation illuminates part of the truth about Soviet developments in the 1920s, although Stalin was far more than an uncultured bureaucratic mediocrity, and Trotsky's consistent underestimate of his opponent reveals the extent to which he misjudged both his personality and his social significance. The main problem with such an explanation, however, is that it fails to suggest any adequate reason for the virtually unopposed imposition of Stalinist principles and practices throughout the international communist movement, for which the prestige and standing of the Soviet state alone, though important, is hardly a sufficient explanation. Stalinism, in fact, for the historic circumstances in which it developed, possessed a very strong rationale, as well as being able to find justification, real or spurious, in Leninist precedents.

It is important to appreciate that the overwhelming majority of communists, including their leaders, believed fervently in the ideology they had embraced, often enough at considerable risk to themselves.[2] The experience and necessary compromises of leadership might make the leading functionaries more cynical in detail, but seldom in principle – and the very accounts and justifications of defectors at all levels of the movement reinforce this point. Within the framework of a quasi-religious belief system directed towards secular ends the emphasis on organisation,[3] intense commitment and military-style discipline was indeed a highly effective way of getting things done, whether in carrying through centralised economic projects, resistance activities or trade union organisation.[4] Stalin and Stalinists had always made great play with their practicality and down-to-earth understanding of reality compared to the woolliness and abstraction of other currents on the left.

Communist parties everywhere were the living embodiments of Stalinist *praxis*, whose official designation was Marxism–Leninism. If one takes the standpoint of around 1950 and accepts, as communists at that time universally did accept, that Marxism–Leninism constituted as single unbroken continuity from at least the emergence of Bolshevism in 1903 with Stalin as the latter-day Lenin, the record (or perhaps in an appropriate use of more modern terminology, the narrative) of its achievement could be viewed as truly titanic. The model Marxist–Leninist party, having overthrown capitalism in the world's geographically largest country in spite of the worst that imperialist-supported counter-revolution could do, had gone on to frustrate various internal oppositions whose stupidity or malevolence had threatened the newly established workers' state. It had then embarked upon and successfully accomplished the industrialisation of the country in the space of ten years, breaking forever its age-long cycle of underdevelopment and achieving the project of socialism in a single country, while meantime destroying an immense conspiracy of defeated elements in league with hostile foreign powers. Following that it had, at incalculable cost, defeated the Nazi assault, saving Europe and the world from fascist barbarism, then served as the protector and guarantor for the emergence of further Marxist–Leninist regimes, especially the one in the world's most populous nation. In doing so it had also defended the anti-colonial revolution against imperialist comeback and repulsed the general anti-socialist assault of imperialism manifested in the Cold War.

It was easy, too, for a communist activist, from the perspective of the late forties, to view events since 1938 as a projection forward in time of the triumphal political progress celebrated in the *History of the Communist Party of the Soviet Union (Bolsheviks): Short Course.* This remarkable publication, which came out in October 1938, was intended to embody in concentrated form the essentials of Stalinist doctrine for the entire communist movement, relate it to historical development and make it the lodestar of the future. It had long been Stalin's technique to unscrupulously derive and justify his immediate political expedients from alleged Marxist principles, and the *Short Course* brought the practice to a fine art. In addition, every chapter was followed by a 'Brief Summary' to highlight the essential message. Eric Hobsbawm has described it as being, in Stalinist terms, a pedagogical triumph.

Paolo Spriano, in *Stalin and the European Communists*, devotes a chapter to its discussion. He points out that its circulation dwarfed that of the *Communist Manifesto*, with 34 million copies in 200 editions and 62 languages by 1948.[5] It was the basic textbook for a generation of communists vastly expanded by the post-war intakes and was studied among them no less intensively in Asia or Latin America than in Europe. This was in spite of the fact that the text concentrated almost exclusively upon Russia and the Soviet Union and had virtually nothing to say about the international dimensions of Bolshevism's formation or about the Comintern (which the relevant 'Brief Summary' doesn't even mention). The narrative is a moral fable; the inevitable triumph of the correct party line, embodied in Lenin and Stalin, over vacillators and deviators to left and right, before, during and after the revolution, thereby enabling the CPSU(B) to lead the Soviet masses to its historic accomplishments by 'storming heaven': 'the party's evolution is portrayed as an autochtonous process with respect to society and external circumstance alike'.[6] The correct line itself comes across as a platonic abstraction, eternally present in the consciousness of Lenin and/or Stalin prior to delivery to the party, not something that was defined and worked out through debate and the conflict of opposing standpoints. The party is revealed as invariably acceptive of its guides, casting aside weak or alien elements, advancing with unflinching resolution and preordained success towards its goals. Spriano writes that 'to read, distribute and study the *Short Course* was to absorb the very essence of "Bolshevism" as an iron, centralised and self-assured form of organisation'[7] – in which fallibility or weakness was as much a crime as malign intent.[8]

Resemblance between this paragon and the actual Bolshevik party of history was, it need scarcely be said, little more than nominal, but the book is valuable for quite a different reason than historical accuracy – as a revelatory insight into the Stalinist mentality (Stalin himself supervised its composition and wrote some of it). Stalinised Marxism lacked any hint of subtlety or nuance, all relationships are portrayed as clear-cut connections, all *praxis* as straightforward conjunctions of theory and practice, good or bad, all differences in Manichaean terms as stark opposites. When suddenly and without warning, in the middle of the *Short Course*'s narrative, a section is introduced on 'Dialectical Materialism' – the 'world outlook of the Marxist–Leninist party', Hegel is briskly dismissed as a significant influence on Marx's development. The essence of dialectics is that 'Development is the "struggle" of opposites' and the practical application follows that 'Hence we must not cover up the contradictions of the capitalist system. But disclose and unravel them; we must not try to check the class struggle but carry it to its conclusion . . . . Hence, in order not to err in policy, one must pursue an uncompromising proletarian class policy.'[9] Marx's renowned contention that 'It is not the consciousness of men that determines their being, but, on the contrary, their social being that determines their consciousness' is quoted and immediately translated into the political–practical conclusion that 'Hence, in order not to err in policy, in order not to find itself in the position of idle dreamers, the party of the proletariat must not base its activities on abstract "principles of human reason".'[10]

It is often asserted that in Stalin's hands Marxism was degraded into nothing more than a set of formulae employed to provide bogus consistency and justification for whatever arbitrary shifts in policy or unprincipled actions he might decree. That this was one side of the story and that such an intellectual system, if one can use the term, was riddled with contradictions and could attain a simulacrum of plausibility only by suppressing and constantly rewriting its own history, goes without saying. Nonetheless it is a mistake not to recognise that at its foundation there was a consistency of sorts, even though that too embodied an extreme contradiction. The Stalinists interpreted Marxism mechanically; socially, in terms of 'base' and 'superstructure', with developments in the 'superstructure' of social, political, cultural or intellectual relations always following on from changes in the economic 'base'.[11] Even the recognition of interaction incorporated in the word 'dialectical' was mechanistic – there were old, moribund ideas whose time was past and served only to hamper historic progress, and there were new, advanced ones which helped to propel it along.[12]

A form of extreme determinism was implied in these conceptions, with no space remaining for human initiative or agency classes and members of classes fulfilled their appointed roles in the metahistorical scheme. If taken seriously, passivity and waiting upon events might appear to be the appropriate response, allowing the river of historical evolution to follow its appointed course, but that would be in serious contradiction to the extreme activism of the Bolshevik tradition, the tradition of decisive intervention in historical processes, 'storming heaven' in the teeth of incalculable obstacles. Extreme determinism was thus crudely conjoined to no less extreme voluntarism, and the contradiction resolved by locating historic agency in the party guided by the science of Marxism–Leninism–Stalinism, which did not of course choose its objectives arbitrarily but according to the tasks placed on the agenda by the class struggle locally and internationally. The communist movement could thus be viewed as the source of historic agency in an otherwise determinist universe, not quite as the demiurge of contemporary history, but certainly as its indispensable midwife.

The Marxist–Leninist miracle was not only one of theory but of action, and the ability to act was perceived to depend upon Bolshevik norms of organisation. In their Stalinist guise these were ones of extreme hierarchy and subordination, lightly covered by formal gestures towards discussion, criticism and 'self-criticism', with the outcome of the 'discussion' proving to be invariably what the higher level wanted it to be.[13] Thus Stalinism (and Trotskyism resembled it in this respect) was characterised by a passion for leadership – the Comintern and the individual parties after all existed for the purpose

of leading the working class. A policy instigated by the Comintern or
by the Soviet Politburo could not be wrong – if it failed in its objectives that could only be because the party members had neglected to
pursue it with sufficient energy and skill – a failure of leadership –
and in that case their failure must be due to inadequacy on the part
of their 'cadres'[14] and top leadership.

When the logic of the Stalinist approach to historical development is pursued to its limits it is seen to be even more voluntarist
than appears at first sight. The masses and the working class decide
nothing – they are capable of responding only to rhythms of development in the economic base – their behaviour and consciousness is
naturally 'economistic', a 'trade union consciousness' which has its
place but can never be an autonomous historical force. The political
embodiment of this consciousness, social democracy, may occasionally fulfil a positive role in collaboration with communism, but is
generally reactionary. The class enemy decides nothing either, since
the progressive role of the bourgeiosie, both economic and political,
is exhausted and it can only endeavour to retard and obstruct the
march of progress, which it does as if by conditioned reflex. At most,
some healthier and more far-seeing elements can find historical salvation by accepting communist leadership. These perspectives constitute
the determinist side of the equation.

Only a communist party (whose guiding principle is its attachment to the Soviet regime) really possesses the power of determin-
ing historic outcomes whenever objective conditions are favourable[15]
(though it may of course on specific occasions, if insufficiently steeled
in Bolshevism, fail to effectively employ that power). But no communist party at large decides anything either – the decisions are made
by its top leadership (and by convention they were made in secret)
before being communicated to the membership, whose job (after
'discussion') is to implement them, whether the party is in power or
opposition, by leading the mass organisations in which the working
class and other progressive social elements are incorporated. This mode
of operation certainly had its precedents in Leninism, but Lenin had
envisaged a much greater degree of flexibility and interaction between
masses and Bolshevik Party, and was on occasion prepared to go over
the head of the latter to appeal directly to the revolutionary workers.[16]

It is interesting that Stalin naturally depicted his opponents as being
unable to behave in any other manner than his own style:

> Naturally the Trotskyists could not but hide such a platform from the
> people, from the working class. And they hid it not only from the

working class, but also from the Trotskyists as a whole, and not only from the Trotskyite rank and file, but even from the leading group of the Trotskyites, consisting of a small handful of thirty of forty people . . . .[17] It is such an 'unprincipled gang' that the Titoites are today. Their platform, known only by an inner ring.[18]

It went without saying that in the USSR or bloc countries problems in economic development or social organisation were never to be accounted for by the nature of the difficulties faced, and seldom by honest errors or routine incompetence, such as complex machinery handled by untrained rural draftees, but nearly always by sabotage and wrecking activities on the part of malevolent enemies organised by Trotsky or Tito. This indeed was the universal excuse produced during the time of the purges for setbacks in socialist construction. The very philosophical bases of Stalinism bred a conspiratorial mentality.

The conspiratorial mentality was likely to be enhanced and superheated by the doctrine which was treated as Stalin's star contribution to Marxist theory (that of 'socialism in a single country' was mendaciously attributed to Lenin). The doctrine was that as workers' power was stabilised and the building of socialism progressed with increasing success, the overthrown exploiting classes, far from accepting defeat and being absorbed into the new society, would redouble their efforts and grow more frenetic in their determination to undo the progress, achieve counter-revolution and regain their power. The repressive apparatus of the state, far from being dismantled,[19] must therefore be reinforced and vigilance intensified. It provided a theoretical gloss for the unaccountable police regime with which the dictator sustained his power and for the uncovered 'plots' of the purge trials.

Political opposition had of course been outlawed inside the USSR from the early twenties, along with any overt public criticism of the essential bases of the Soviet regime. Nevertheless the period between 1921 and 1928 is renowned as a period of relatively open artistic creation and cultural speculation provided that sensitive political topics were avoided. With the 'Stalin revolution' of collectivisation, the Five-year Plans and the industrialisation drive, all that was to change beyond recognition. Social science and culture were also to be mobilised to reflect the requirements of the regime and to see their principal duty as the promotion of its objectives. Not merely the history of communism but the pre-revolutionary history of the Russian state and society became subject to official prescription. What was known as 'socialist realism' was made the only legitimate approach in the arts: these were, in their various ways, to portray 'positive heroes' who would serve as inspiration to the public, or unspeakable villains without subtlety or ambiguity who would evoke their hatred and contempt. It meant outlawry for any forms of literature or painting other than the pseudo-naturalism inherited from the nineteenth century[20] and especially the proscription of abstract or modernist styles.[21] When an art form, such as music, was inherently non-representational it was nevertheless required to be inspirational. It was easy enough for Soviet officialdom to dismiss all except the approved socialist realist style as bourgeois decadence. With the onset of the terror in the later thirties the penalties for even unintentionally violating the rules became horrendous. Artistic malpractice was never in itself formally an arrestable offence, but to indulge in it was certain to bring charges of political crime.

The exigencies of the war brought about a degree of relaxation at the margins when basic loyalty to the state or nation and willingness to fight or work on its behalf were the overriding priorities. By late 1946, however, even before the full onset of the Cold War, which was a cultural as much as a political–military conflict, Stalin's cultural overseer, Andrei Zhdanov, the Leningrad party boss, was denouncing artists who failed to measure up to the strictness of socialist–realist criteria. Some, such as the world-renowned composer Dmitri Shostakovich, found themselves obliged to offer humiliating self-criticisms. The new rigour which accompanied the development of the Cold War, the establishment of the Cominform and the Yugoslav breach affected the natural sciences as well as the human ones.

With the world supposedly divided between imperialist and anti-imperialist camps it occurred to the Stalinist mentality that if there existed bourgeois and proletarian politics, bourgeois and Marxist economics, bourgeois and proletarian interpretations of history, bourgeois and proletarian culture, there ought to be in addition bourgeois and proletarian science. Ensteinian relativity theory and quantum mechanics, with their indications that the world 'is not only queerer than we know but queerer than we can know', were cited as instances of the former, although the Soviet scientists working on nuclear projects were able to evade the implications of this decree. The biologists were less fortunate. An agronomist and ambitious scientific charlatan, Trofim Lysenko, persuaded Stalin that the central principle of Mendelian genetics, the non-inheritability of acquired characteristics in any organism, was mere bourgeois obscurantism. Practical implications were involved, for Lysenko claimed that he could enhance crop yields by the application of techniques purportedly based on his claims. These were officially endorsed and Soviet biologists who were remiss in subordinating their scientific judgement to political requirements were purged.[22] The matter did not end at the borders of the Soviet Union or the Soviet bloc, for the entire communist movement was required to pronounce its agreement with Lysenkoist genetics and in the process lose the adherence of some eminent Western scientists. The Lysenko affair was easily the most notorious instance of the subjection of scientific knowledge to Stalinist ideological imperatives, and brought upon the communists of the time a unique degree of discredit.[23]

As noted previously, a national agenda was implicitly present in every communist party, and if the party attained power it quickly came to the forefront unless restrained by Stalin's iron straitjacket. In the state which he himself ruled, it could of course flourish unrestrainedly and be identified for form's sake, however incongruously, with the needs of the international movement. A tyrant to all under his rule, Stalin's tyranny was not, however, equally apportioned. The Soviet nationality on which his regime was principally based was that of the majority of Great Russians, the nationality from which the leading cadres of the regime were disproportionately drawn. The non-Russian nationalities, though officially equal partners, were in reality subordinate to the main one and suffered even more severe repression.

Stalin though, paradoxically, as he himself was a Georgian and his first state appointment was as Commissar of Nationalities, might well convince himself that the record of the Russians was incomparable. The Bolshevik Party had been nurtured especially in Great Russia and the Bolshevik Revolution had been a Great Russian affair, later exported – often unwillingly[24] – to the other provinces of the former Empire. The nationalist tone was noticeable as early as the thirties with the rehabilitation of the 'great' tsars, such as Ivan the Terrible and Peter the Great, who had constructed the Empire. The Soviet Union, from the Kremlin's viewpoint, had stood alone against fascism in the thirties and had during the Second World War rescued the world from fascist enslavement, but Stalin also believed and openly stated that the victorious outcome of 'the Great Patriotic War' – a significant title – had depended principally upon the Great Russians, whom he singled out at its end when praising all the constituent republics. In the closing years of his rule this attitude reached obsessional dimensions, though no doubt there were plenty of Russians all too eager to pander to it. Not content with the real achievements of Russians in statecraft, war, science and culture, propaganda began to insist that an entire catalogue of scientific inventions and discoveries

– radio transmission and powered flight, to mention only two –
which had been attributed hitherto to western scientists and inventors,
were in reality the work of Russians. Whatever the intention behind
this, it was certainly not much help to the Western communist movement, which in addition to its political isolation was made to look
ridiculous by being compelled to reproduce these fantasies along with
Lysenkoist twaddle.

'Them'

There are few occasions on which unrepentant high-level Stalinists
in government have frankly, uninhibitedly and without ulterior purpose documented their behaviour and their motivations. Even when
acts of that kind became possible all their political training and
experience militated against anything in the nature of 'true confessions'. Khrushchev, after his dismissal, did secretly produce a set of
memoirs and these are certainly revealing, if not very reliable. Some
of the other leading apparatchiks, such as Mikoyan and Gromyko,
produced complete or fragmentary memoirs,[25] but while interesting
information could sometimes be gleaned between the lines, these were
exercises in concealment rather than revelation, with delicate subjects
either avoided completely or else blandly covered over.

A source therefore that is very nearly unique of its kind is the
collection of extended interviews made in the early eighties by Teresa
Toranska, a journalist connected with the Solidarity movement,
covering five individuals who had led the Polish CP and state between
the end of the war and 1956,[26] and including Edward Ochab, who
had been second in the leadership and largely responsible for defusing the invasion-threatening crisis of October 1956. At the time of
the interviews they were living comfortably, though in political disgrace because of their Stalinist roles, despised and shunned by the
general public. When in power they had been referred to as 'Them'
(in Polish *Oni*) an index of their sinister importance and the fear they
provoked: hence the title of the volume reproducing the interviews.
Toranska did not act as a dispassionate interviewer but argued with
her subjects and induced them to answer on the discreditable aspects
of their pasts, thus eliciting explanations, excuses and statements of
motive which would never have featured in a standard memoir.

For all that they have in common, the five (there is only one
woman) come across as distinctive personalities, and while they do
not emerge as very admirable individuals, neither do they betray

themselves as monsters in human form. Before their elevation to power some of them had distinguished records in the underground pre-war Polish labour movement and the wartime resistance. Some had lost close relatives in the Nazi extermination camps. They congratulate themselves in having averted show trials in Poland following the Yugoslav rupture, in limiting the number of secret death sentences and in obstructing the pace of collectivisation. They do not remain classic Stalinists in the sense of continuing to approve or deny the crimes and injustices committed under Stalin's hegemony, rather they bracket them off as contingent errors that were not implicit in the system, regrettable excrescences which did not invalidate a basically sound form of politics.[27]

> We waged a victorious war against fascism, and there were some bad things. But the victorious war compensated for all the bad. And anyhow if you have to choose between the party and an individual, you choose the party, because the party has a general aim, the good of many people. But one person is just one person.[28]

Their revelations of the practices and thinking at the highest levels of Polish communism while they were politically active are fascinating, but more interesting still is the consistent theme that is followed in the arguments and justifications of every interview and which combines internationalism and nationalism.

> *I'd like it if Polish communists concerned themselves with the affairs of their own nation rather than with the world's.*
>
> Then they wouldn't be communists. We are working people and we should unite ourselves throughout the world. We look after our own country but we also reach out to other workers, regardless of their nationality. The revolution has to win on a world scale.[29]

A new society was being built in the post-war years, they claim, under the leadership of the pioneer regime, the USSR, and to be part of that project was the most worthwhile thing in the world that anybody could do.

> *What about your private friends?*
>
> We didn't have any. There wasn't time for that. Minc was at the Planning Commission every day until midnight or one in the morning . . . . Work was our enjoyment . . . In those times we had order and discipline and people worked instead of gabbling on to no purpose.[30]

Even at the time of the interviews, when, after the eruption of Solidarity and the exposure of the political system's complete bankruptcy, 'barrack socialism' seemed to any outsider utterly degenerate, they persist in regarding it as superior to western models of development and its problems as ones of growth and adjustment. 'I assumed that the terror of the Great Purge was a side effect of the Soviet Union's extremely difficult international situation, and possibly also a result of Stalin's own internal struggles and contradictions.' They regard the country's vassalage to Moscow therefore in a positive fashion, justified in the light of historic progress, and indeed as a service to the nation as well as humanity. At the same time they justify it by the argument that not only was the USSR Poland's guarantor against German revanchism and the possible loss of the territories gained in 1945, but – implicitly contradicting the previous argument – that they had failed to play along, then Poland, like the Baltic states, might have been annexed to the USSR as a constituent republic. The international and national perceptions come together in the following comment: 'For me Stalin was victory incarnate. He bore upon his shoulders the whole burden of the war with Hitler *and he was the hope for the changes in Poland of which we expected so much*' (emphasis added).[31] It was a point that might have been made by any communist anywhere in the world around 1945. It is interesting to compare this with the afterthoughts of a Czech communist with some responsibility for the purges in his own country:

> I firmly believed it was in the sacred interests of the Party. They entrusted the jobs to me because they knew that I would always and in every way obey the Party. And even if they had told me: 'Put your head in the gas oven, we're going to gas you. It's in the interests of the Party,' I would have obeyed, I would have put my head in the gas oven.[32]

Stalin's Death and Aftermath

There have been suggestions that Stalin hoped to emulate the alleged feats of some of his Georgian countrymen by living well into his second century. Whether or not there is any substance to these stories, old age and failing health brought no inclination on his part to relax the relentless grip he exercised upon both state and party in the USSR and upon the international movement which was loyal to it. As his seventieth birthday was celebrated amid frenetic adulation, *For a Lasting Peace . . .* informed its readers that Hungarian workers had resolved to work extended hours in honour of the event. Stalin remained both General Secretary of the CPSU and head of government. He extended his scientific expertise to the field of linguistics. At the 19th Party Congress held in 1952 he did not make the Central Committee report for, in the words of Roy Medvedev, 'The cult of Stalin's personality had reached such heights by this time that it would have been strange indeed to expect him to explain himself, as it were, in front of the Party and the people.'[33] His speech to the delegates appeared to diminish the importance of the party in comparison to that of non-party state employees – as indeed it had already been in practice ('For example the Party had no control over the punitive agencies.')[34] Following this congress the party leadership bodies were reorganised in such a manner as to suggest that several longstanding colleagues were facing his displeasure. The 'Politburo' title was dropped – perhaps with symbolic significance – though the reality remained.

All the signs during Stalin's last months pointed to an impending purge of exceptional ferocity, which would remove the remaining members of the dictator's entourage who had any familiarity with his career prior to and in the years immediately following the revolution. 'At the plenum session of the Congress Stalin attacked Molotov and Mikoyan and indicated his lack of trust in them. They defended themselves, but they were considered by many to be doomed men.'[35] Near the beginning of 1953 a number of doctors serving the high Kremlin dignitaries were arrested on charges of plotting to murder their patients. The Jewish origin of most of these victims was remarked upon.[36] It was apparent to any outside observer that the unfortunate physicians were pawns, and that once interviewed at length by Beria's secret police, would implicate high political figures in their 'plot'. It is an interesting speculation as to how the communist movement at large would have reacted to another Soviet blood purge, especially one incriminating figures they had been taught to revere for two decades as Stalin's most loyal lieutenants,[37] but Stalin's own death supervened at the beginning of March.

His close colleagues (with the possible exception of Beria), whether or not they were in good standing, were only too relieved to be rid of their master's suffocating presence. On the other hand, popular grief and apprehension for the future throughout the USSR was intense and genuine and it is alleged that tears were spilt even in labour camps. Stalin had succeeded in imposing his image as a severe but benevolent and virtually irreplaceable father-figure who had prevailed in the greatest military contest in history, saved the nations of the Union from enslavement and turned a prostrate and backward state into a superpower – though it was a very long way indeed from the hopes and aspirations of 1917. Paroxysms of mourning took place through-out the bloc as well as in the non-ruling parties and the *Vozhd* (boss) was embalmed and placed in the mausoleum beside Lenin, follow-ing a funeral ceremony during which large numbers of people were crushed to death.

His successors were conscious both of the need to ensure their own future safety, and of the fact that the system of generalised terror applied to every individual in a responsible post was proving increas-ingly counter-productive in a society of growing technological and economic complexity, as fear stifled initiative and willingness to take responsible decisions. They were conscious, too, of the desirability of some degree of détente with the West and access to its trade and technology. At the same time, they could not simply abandon the heritage in which they had been formed, whether in its rhetorical aspects of declining capitalism and global socialist advance or the realities of single-party rule and centralised economic planning, all embodied in the ideology of Marxism–Leninism.

Accordingly there was no immediate direct criticism of Stalin or of his heritage. Nonetheless, even a not particularly acute observer would have noted the emphasis on 'collective leadership' pronounced from the Kremlin, condemning by implication the style which had pre-vailed up to then. The same observer would have observed that the funeral obsequies in the Soviet media were terminated with unusual rapidity. Most significantly of all, charges were dropped against the Kremlin doctors, who were all released. The reverberations of this event were profound, if unstated, for it constituted an implicit admis-sion that they had been framed by the security services, something that would previously have been unthinkable and which must have dropped the initial seeds of doubt into the consciousness of many a communist activist, most especially in the West, where the implica-tions were spelt out in the bourgeois media.

If the liquidation of communists and Soviet citizens now ceased, the ruling group turned its attention to liquidating the principal areas of conflict with the Western powers. The two most acute of these were the ongoing war in Korea and the continuing tension over Germany and Berlin. Though the Kremlin had no official locus in the Korean war it was able to use its influence behind the scenes so that in the course of 1953 a grudging and precarious armistice was agreed at Panmunjon. Germany was even less easy, for it represented a cardinal security issue for Moscow and one in which Soviet con-cessions would have to be matched by the West. The incentive which Moscow was willing to offer was withdrawal from East Germany and reunification (within the post-1945 borders): what it demanded in return was agreement to neutralise the reintegrated Germany as a military power along the lines that were being projected for Austria and which were in fact achieved there the following year. NATO, however, and the United States in particular, were determined to incorporate West Germany or united Germany into the Alliance, and consequently unwilling to contemplate the country's military neutralisation.

In any event schemes and projections of this sort were overtaken by events upon the ground. In June Czech workers, sensing the change in political atmosphere and provoked by a currency reform which had wiped out their savings, took strike action and demonstrated, escalating their protest into one against Communist Party rule and Soviet vassalage.[38] This upsurge was suppressed with comparative ease, but almost immediately a much more serious defiance erupted in East Germany, where the former Soviet Zone had been elevated since 1949 as the German Democratic Republic to the status of a 'People's Democracy' with full membership of the Soviet bloc. It was led by Walther Ulbricht, an unquestioning Stalinist and professional survivor of the purges which during the Great Terror had decimated foreign communists resident in Moscow. Doubtless he objected to the veil which was being partially drawn across Stalin's memory and to the implicit criticisms which were beginning to seep out of the Kremlin – no doubt he objected even more to the exhortations directed towards all the bloc parties that they too should adopt norms of 'collective leadership'.

Most objectionable of all, however, were the clear indications emanating from the Soviet leadership that the GDR was expendable for the greater good of improved international relations and Moscow's purposes in central Europe. The proposed trade-off of German reunification for neutrality meant the end of Ulbricht's political importance. The GDR in 1953 was no great economic asset. Prior to 1945 most of it had been among the less industrially developed parts of the country, and since then greater part of the industrial plant that it did have and which had survived the war had been stripped and transported to the USSR as reparations. Ulbricht's strategy was to rebuild and develop the industrial base so that the GDR would emerge as a major supplier of manufactured products to the USSR and the bloc. Thus he hoped to protect his own position and the future of the new state. The threatening diplomatic manoeuvres proceeding over his head increased the urgency, and consequently more severe production targets were imposed upon the GDR's industrial workforce.

The result was that in June 1953, possibly inspired by rumour of what was happening in Czechoslovakia, East Berlin building workers downed tools, to be followed by other workers throughout the country. As in Czechoslovakia, the strikes were accompanied with political demonstrations, which in some locations assumed insurrectionary proportions. Ulbricht's own forces proved incapable of putting down the the revolt – or unwilling – and it was finally got under control only by means of Soviet tanks and considerable bloodshed.

It might have been expected that the debacle would have ended in Ulbricht's disgrace, but in fact it confirmed him in power and his regime for another thirty-six years. He was able to divert the blame from his own intransigence and mismanagement and cast it upon the slacking of discipline and loosening of control inspired from the ruling circle of the USSR itself. Ulbricht and his counterparts in Eastern Europe well knew, of course, that the Politiburo[39] was divided. The rulers who paid the price for the East German events were the proponents of (relative) liberalisation, consumer concessions and of far-reaching negotiations over Germany. These included Georgi Malenkov, who had succeeded Stalin briefly as head of both party and government, although he had demitted the former position within a week in favour of N.S. Khrushchev. He was not toppled by the German crisis – and other lesser strikes, including in the USSR itself – but his position as premier was comprehensively undermined and he was replaced and demoted at the beginning of 1955.[40]

The other principal leader it undermined did not escape so lightly. Exactly how Beria was regarded by his colleagues at the time of Stalin's death is impossible to guess, but they certainly had reason to fear him, considering his record and the vast police apparatus he controlled, including heavily armed formations. It may well be that they decided to make sure by disposing of him as soon as opportunity offered. Rather astonishingly, and contradicting all his past career, he emerged along with Malenkov as the strongest advocate for a degree of relaxation in domestic affairs both in the USSR and throughout the bloc, as well as for rapid détente with the Western powers. Very likely, on Beria's part, these stances were tactical, for he was doubtless intelligent, as well as being a mass murderer and unspeakably depraved in his personal life, and could appreciate the necessities of the times. The German events however, for which he primarily was held responsible, showed the policy to have run out of control and supplied the pretext needed to destroy him. With the aid of the military leaders, who resented as well as feared him, he was arrested that same month on charges of being a Western agent (since

1919!) and executed later in the year following a secret trial at which he was not allowed to be present. With Beria safely dead, advantageous use could still be made of him as a catch-all scapegoat for the disreputable aspects of Stalin's rule in his later years, since the latter remained exempt as yet from direct criticism.

Nikita Khrushchev, the First Secretary (the title of General Secretary having been dropped), consolidated his own power, making sure that when Malenkov was replaced he was succeeded as premier by the rather colourless Marshal Bulganin. Like Stalin in the twenties, though in a vastly altered context, Khrushchev was viewed as pursuing a middle course and occupying the centre ground, in his case *vis-à-vis* the too advanced liberalisers such as Beria and Malenkov on the one side and unrepentant Stalinists like Molotov and Kaganovitch on the other. It is some credit to the abilities of the Soviet rulers that they did succeed after a fashion in coping with the accumulated tensions throughout the bloc that began to surface once Stalin's personality and the fear that it inspired were removed from the scene – even if the reconciliation was a short-term one and planted the seeds of later disruption. A cartoon of the time shows Malenkov as a bather on a choppy sea astride an inflatable horse representing the bloc, with leaks springing all over its body.

However, 1954 and 1955 looked like years of recovered stability, on a basis that discarded the worst aspects of Stalinist governing methods while retaining the essentials of the system. The Soviet *nomenklatura* and their counterparts in Eastern Europe got what they wanted most of all – removal of the threat of death or imprisonment for any political infraction or failure in attainment, or for no reason at all. The security services were downgraded in importance and brought under political control. That, doubtless, is where most of them would have wished to stop. The process once begun, however, acquired a momentum of its own. Economic planning and production targets acquired more realism. With the removal of the sacerdotal interpreter, Marxism–Leninism, rigid and dogmatic though it was, once more became open to varying and disputable exegesis. Though there was no official rejection of 'socialist realism' greater, albeit still cautious, experimentation became possible in the cultural and creative fields. The worst scientific scandals were disposed of; Lysenko was discredited and removed from his principal offices and his surviving opponents quietly rehabilitated – though he continued in lesser positions, still unrepentantly proclaiming his notions. Political prisoners began to be released from labour camps and some dead purge victims to be rehabilitated, though still slowly at this stage.

Fences were mended with Yugoslavia when in 1955 the Soviet leaders travelled to Belgrade and more or less apologised for Stalin's behaviour. The Cominform was wound up in the same year, further implicit confession of political error. An important index of the changed climate was to be seen when Malenkov, evicted from the premiership, was not only allowed to remain at liberty but even to retain a government post.

In fact Khrushchev, supported initially by Stalin's old guard as more traditionalist in inclination, soon emerged as far more daring, innovative and disruptive that ever Malenkov might have been, pressing ahead with dramatic changes in both internal and diplomatic postures that soon alarmed and dismayed his former sponsors. Again the element of personality cannot be discounted – Khrushchev possessed an ebullience, earthiness and impetuousness quite foreign to the standard Kremlin apparatchik. His successful ascent through the hierarchy and his survival can only be attributed to the fact that under Stalin he also kept these qualities well under control and channelled them unquestioningly towards fulfilment of the dictator's requirements[41] – even when these involved massive repressions and bloodlettings. At the same time it is clear that Khrushchev was responding to and trying to control pressures appearing on all sides from the Soviet equivalent of 'civil society' emerging from its long nightmare,[42] but which in the circumstances of the Stalinist inheritance, where the CPSU had swallowed civil society entirely, could only be reflected through the Party.[43] Nor could Khrushchev in his new role afford to be neglectful of the international movement, whether ruling or non-ruling parties. These too were trying to keep their feet amid the currents and eruptions of the new phase and their leaderships were all Stalin's protégés. Dominated though they were by the CPSU, their attitudes for or against particular initiatives in the fields of theory or communist history might nevertheless have weight in support of one side or another in a Kremlin power struggle.

The 20th Congress

Political tensions within the Soviet party finally exploded at its 20th Congress held in February 1956. Once again, the decision to undertake a dramatic exposure of Stalin's reputation was, it appears, largely driven by Khrushchev himself and opposed by the overwhelming majority of the Presidium. That was the reason why it was not incorporated in his formal report but confined to a secret session which the

Presidium could not prevent, because technically its existence was suspended pending re-election by the Congress. As to the First Secretary's motivations, it can be surmised that he felt it essential to settle two sorts of accounts. The first and less important was the memory of the slights and humiliations he and others had endured from the dead leader, which undoubtedly continued to rankle and which could only be posthumously revenged. More important were the growing contradictions between the processes of liberalisation occurring in Soviet life and the heritage which Stalin had left to to the state. Some resolution appeared to be necessary if ideology was not to drift too far out of conformity with reality.

It is important to note that Stalin was not condemned comprehensively. His leadership was defined as having been positive and necessary in the inner-party struggle of the twenties against Trotskyism and Bukharinism and during the industrialisation drive. Nor was there any suggestion of rehabilitating the victims of the show trials.[44] Stalin's 'violations of socialist legality' (the term 'crimes' was avoided) were supposed to have commenced once he broadened the purges and started persecuting Stalinists, or 'loyal communists' (oppositionists were disloyal by definition). These 'errors' could be attributed to the malign influence of his successive police chiefs, Yezhov and Beria, under whose spell Stalin had fallen on account of his morbid suspiciousness and the inherent vanity fostered by the 'cult of the individual'. Thus 'collective leadership' had fallen into disuse and terror had run riot. Nonetheless all the structures of the Soviet state and party instituted in Stalin's time remained sound and healthy, only needing the unwelcome accretions to be brushed off and the distortions rectified. After all, socialism had been built during those years. As a political myth to close the account and permit the move to the next item on the agenda it was not very convincing, but, even though 'a crude attempt to find a scapegoat for a history of terror which damned the whole system',[45] probably the best that could be done within the constraints of Soviet politics to forestall a greater explosion later on. Khrushchev was subsequently to conclude with satisfaction:

> The Twentieth Congress restored justice, eliminated distortions, and emphasised the great role of the people and the role of the Party . . . . The Congress instructed the Central Committee to implement consistently necessary measures that would ensure that the cult of the individual was completely overcome, that would eliminate its consequences in all fields of party, state and ideological work, and that would bring about strict observance of the norms of party life and the principle of collective leadership elaborated by Vladimir Illych Lenin.[46]

The 'Secret Speech' was delivered in a closed session with all the
fraternal delegates of foreign parties excluded (though some especially important leaders were given either a transcript or a summary),
but not surprisingly, its content soon became generally known. In any
case, delegates on their arrival could note the absence of Stalin's por-
trait around the Congress and the absence of favourable references
to him in the opening speeches. Soon Mikoyan, to the consternation
of those present, condemned Stalin's abuses in open session, though
largely without mention of his name and without the wealth of detail
that Khrushchev was to deploy.

The 20th Congress represented a watershed in the international
movement, and, if the Yugoslav episode is omitted, the real beginning of its fragmentation. Intrinsic to the communist belief-system up
to that point was the conviction that whatever incidental misjudge-
ments had occurred along the way Lenin's party could not be wrong
in any matter of importance and that it had been led since his death by
an infallible superman. The events of the three years between Stalin's
death and the Congress could not have failed to erode that belief-
system for anyone who had eyes to see; the Secret Speech shattered
it forever and 'broke the spell in which the whole Communist movement had been caught'.[47] It was rather as though the Pope had declared
St Peter to have been a rogue.

The party leaders from Eastern Europe were certainly shattered, and
not simply because Stalinism's exposure and the inevitable accusations of complicity which would now be directed against them put
their futures into question. Such evidence as exists suggests that at
least some were genuinely devastated. Stalinism had been up to that
point the foundation of their existential being, and they viewed with
horror the pillars of the temple crumbling around them. A particular case was Boleslaw Bierut, the leader of the Polish CP (formally
the Polish United Workers' Party) and Stalin's faithful apparatchik,
although on one occasion Beria had explicitly and to his face threatened
to have him arrested for enquiring about disappeared Polish communists. According to the evidence of 'Them' (who had no occasion
to lie in this regard), Bierut appears underneath his Stalinist carapace
to have been a sensitive individual, anguished by the things he was
forced to do, and the Khrushchev revelations to have killed him. In
any case he died before he could return from Moscow, and there is
no suggestion that his death was other than natural.

Other bloc leaders were more hard-boiled, and if they even in
their own minds acknowledged the Stalin had been a criminal (and
that they were as well), contented themselves with the thought that

his crimes counted in the scale of human progress no more than the existence of slavery in ancient Athens. Two particularly notorious examples were Walther Ulbricht in the GDR and Matyas Rakosi in Hungary, who, though they did not argue with the revelations (and Ulbricht even supplied some examples of Stalin's supposed military incompetence), did their utmost to obstruct, and in Rakosi's case sabotage, any moves towards destalinisation in their own particular fiefs. Some party leaders, both inside and outside the bloc, dug in their heels more firmly still. The Albanian Enver Hoxha,[48] though his regime, like Tito's, had come to power by means of partisan warfare rather than Soviet intervention, had particular reason to be grateful to Stalin. The Cominform break with Yugoslavia in 1948 had saved Albania from likely incorporation into Yugoslavia, and in reaction against its neighbour, had made it into a particularly fervent partisan of Moscow's most hardline policies. Hoxha, not surprisingly, was highly alarmed at the new leadership's developing rapprochement with Yugoslavia, and these diplomatic considerations, together with his Stalinist disposition, set him on a course that was to lead before long to rupture with Moscow and the uninhibited celebration in Tirana of Stalin and all his works.

The reaction of communist leaders and parties outside the bloc was a sign of how diverse international communism was actually in the process of becoming. The Italian Communist Party (PCI) had, ever since the Comintern, combined formal deference to Moscow with a highly flexible and individual political strategy in relation to its own country.[49] In this it had achieved outstanding success, having in alliance with the Italian Socialist Party (PSI) just failed to win outright the parliamentary elections of 1948. It was a mass party of over a million members with even larger trade union and other associated organisations, and apart from its substantial parliamentary representation, controlled numerous local authorities with impressive reputations for honesty and integrity. Its General Secretary, Palmiro Togliatti, was easily the most intelligent and perceptive of all the communist leaders. To most of the Italian leadership the revelations must have come as little surprise, and indeed they were presumably welcome for bringing the issue out into the light with a Soviet imprimatur. Togliatti responded by calling for a thorough Marxist analysis of the Stalin regime, though this was going too far for the CPSU, which publicly censured him in June.

A very different state of affairs was in evidence across the border. The French Communist Party (PCF), like its Italian counterpart, was a mass organisation (not so large or strongly placed as the PCI, though its presence can be gauged from the fact that in 1955 it produced no less than fourteen daily newspapers), and for the same reason – its Resistance record. Unlike the PCI, however, its members, with the onset of the Cold War, 'retreated back into a citadel they had been able to leave during the Resistance'.[50] Its style and outlook therefore contrasted markedly, being much more 'workerist', secretive and intolerant. The General Secretary, Maurice Thorez, was a dedicated Stalinist who had been imposed on the party by Stalin's Comintern and encouraged a cult around his own person. 'The major quality of Maurice Thorez was the docility with which he reacted to directives from the secretariat and representatives of the Third International. He would execute orders most painstakingly, continuing to do so until fresh orders were issued. If these were reversed he quickly complied.'[51] Thorez made a point of standing and applauding Stalin's name when it was (rarely) mentioned in the open sessions of the Congress and, along with others of his stamp, hoped that Khrushchev would soon be overthrown and the Secret Speech repudiated. It is claimed that before its publication in the Western media one of his subordinates challenged him regarding it. Thorez at first blandly denied its existence, but when it became clear that the subordinate had got hold of a copy from Eastern Europe, remarked that it would not continue to exist for very long.[52] Such was also the attitude of R. Palme Dutt and other unreconstructed Stalinists in the British Communist Party. At the other extreme the CPUSA more or less broke ranks and not only accepted but amplified the content of the revelations. Its paper, the New York *Daily Worker*, went on to print fresh details of anti-semitic persecution in the USSR.

The Khrushchev speech did not only produce different reactions from party leaderships, it resulted in deep divisions within the different Western parties, setting members in many cases in embittered antagonism towards each other. Among the communist parties in a position to do such a thing none, not even the PCI, engaged in a fundamental reappraisal of its past, nor did any of them sever fraternal relations with the CPSU on the grounds that such a deeply corrupted body could never have been restored to health by a partial (and ostensibly secret) confession. Among rank-and-file members of these parties there were few if any to be found willing to shrug and retort, 'Well, we knew that all along, how else do you expect a Leninist revolutionary leader to behave?' On the contrary, the almost universal reaction appears too have been one of stunned shock that the supposed lies of the bourgeois media had turned out to be true after all. It does make clear that these individuals were not cynics consciously delivering themselves over to evil, but well-intentioned individuals insulated by the counter-culture of the communist parties' belief systems against truths acknowledged by everybody else.

The consequential actions fell into three broad categories. There were firstly a minority indignant that Stalin's pygmy successors had dared to denounce their hero and who either refused to accept the truth of the revelations or else regarded them as much exaggerated and his actions as wholly justified by extreme circumstances, principally the fascist threat. The majority, however shocked and stricken, went along with the Soviet line that he had indeed had his bad points but these had to be viewed in the perspective of the USSR's and the movement's historic achievements, and that fundamental principles had not been corrupted in either case. So far as their own parties were concerned, they were anxious above all to put the episode behind them and get on with the fight for socialism as they saw it. Another minority felt that their good faith had been outraged and abused and demanded a historical accounting both internationally and in their own parties – demands which the leaderships, understandably fearing the uncontrollable consequences of submitting to them, were able to suppress with the support of the majority membership.[53]

Outside Europe and North America the impact of the Twentieth Congress appears in the main to have been less severely felt. Certainly none of the parties of southern or south-eastern Asia suffered major convulsions over it (or over the subsequent Hungarian events), possibly because their perspectives, as largely peasant-based organisations and not involved in the Cominform, were less intimately bound up than the Europeans' with the standing of the Soviet Union or the significance of Stalin's memory; at any rate they experienced nothing approximating to the ruptures that were to occur six years later. The position with the Chinese communists, however, was somewhat different. Their leaders might possibly have cause to respect Stalin's memory, but little reason to revere it. He had tried to discourage their victory in 1949 and when they had triumphed in spite of his obstructions he had driven a very hard bargain in return for Soviet aid. All the same he had, however grudgingly, done his internationalist duty, and he was at least an authentic revolutionary and colleague of Lenin. Like Thorez, the Chinese delegates to the Congress had ostentatiously applauded his mention.

At first though, the denunciation was not a major issue between the two parties. CPC statements dutifully noted certain flaws in Stalin's relations with itself, and the matter might have subsided. What was to keep it on the boil and eventually make it part of a cauldron of vituperation in which relations between the two largest communist parties became immersed, was Chinese suspicion of Soviet state intentions, fears of their continuing subordination, and Mao's growing determination to succeed Stalin as the acknowledged theoretical leader of world communism and establish a continuity through him with Marx, Engels and Lenin. In these developments the principle of 'my enemy's enemy is my friend' became operative, even though the 'friend' had been dead for several years.

The East European Revolts

By and large the turbulence that followed in Eastern Europe was at first contained: the mechanisms of the police states and the institutional structures controlled by 'Them' in the individual countries of the bloc continued to function, but it soon became clear that popular expectations created by the 'thaw' both within and outside communist parties were running ahead of the marginal liberalisations envisaged by the rulers. In the GDR, Czechoslovakia, Romania and Bulgaria, not to speak of deep-frozen Albania, such restlessness was soon repressed, but in Poland and Hungary it found an outlet.

The differences are accounted for partly by historical circumstances, but may also have had something to do with the fact that while in the majority of those countries the unrepentant Stalinists continued to dominate their parties' governing bodies, in Poland and Hungary they were more equally balanced with liberalisers. In Hungary an easing of cultural control led to the formation in Budapest in March of an intellectual club called the Petofi Circle (after a renowned Hungarian poet), which initiated debates that attracted enormous audiences and at which the regime was openly attacked. It was soon closed down, but in July the Soviet government, conscious of the deadlock in the Hungarian party, sent Mikoyan to Budapest to compel Rakosi to resign as General Secretary – unfortunately to be replaced by his no less hardline alter ego, Erno Gero.

In the meantime the Polish Stalinists, probably in secret consultation with Moscow, were struggling to regain the upper hand and demanding that the ferment of discussion erupting in Warsaw (copies of the Secret Speech were said to be on sale in the market-place) be closed off.[54] They controlled crucial positions, including the Ministry of Defence, but the carpet was pulled out from underneath them by an insurrectionary outbreak at the end of June in the large industrial city of Poznán. Strike action by railway workers over unpaid work escalated into a general strike and thence to armed revolt during which a police station was stormed and a policeman lynched. It required tanks and two days of considerable bloodshed to put down the rising – in full view of visitors to a trade fair. The reformers now had the initiative, for the Stalinists' policies were blamed. Bierut's successor, Edward Ochab, limited the repression once the revolt was under control and moved to bring the enormously popular Wladyslaw Gomulka back to the centre of affairs.

Gomulka was exceptionally fortunate to be alive in 1956, for of all the Eastern bloc leaders in the years after 1948 he had been the nearest thing to a genuine Titoite, a 'right-wing nationalist deviationist', to a far greater extent than the accused who perished in the show trials from 1949 onwards. Though dismissed before long from state and party responsibilities, he was arrested only in 1951 and his survival was due only to the way his colleagues used such scope as they had to resist Moscow pressures. Had Stalin lived beyond March 1953, however, it is unlikely that he would have survived much longer. From his imprisonment – he was released, under restriction, only in 1954 – he had become a folk-hero and a symbol of Polish identity.

At the beginning of October the imminence of Gomulka's restoration to the position of First Secretary alarmed the high Kremlin leadership to the extent that they flew in person, uninvited, to Warsaw to intervene, while Soviet armed forces took up threatening positions in and around the country. The situation constituted a first-rate crisis, the more so when it became clear that the Polish leadership would not back down tamely and that the Polish armed forces, despite being under the command of a Stalinist loyalist, Marshal Rokossowski, would forcibly resist Soviet military intervention. In the event the stand-off was resolved by compromise which was in reality a Soviet backdown, for what the Poles conceded was a renewal of their commitment to the Warsaw 'Mutual Defence' Pact signed the previous year and the preservation of the single-party system, neither of which they had any intention of repudiating. The Kremlin, on the other hand, conceded Polish control over Polish affairs within that framework, and the removal of its watchdog, Rokossowski, shortly afterwards. It appears that the Poles' position was strengthened by a message to Khrushchev from Zhou Enlai informing him that the Chinese CP strongly opposed armed intervention.

The reason why the Polish crisis was resolved by agreement and the simultaneous eruption in Hungary was not has to be put down to the fact that popular pressures in the former country were successfully channelled into supporting a party leadership which was able to

retain its unity as it negotiated with the Soviets, while in the latter they
proved to be uncontainable. The sinister star of the Hungarian crisis,
Matyas Rakosi, had been removed from office earlier in the year but
his influence still dominated its government. Rakosi[55] himself provided
a case history of how a seemingly well-intentioned individual with
admirable, even heroic, qualities could develop into an abominable
tyrant. Braunthal describes him as 'a strong personality and a master
of political manoeuvre[56] – a very considerable understatement. Having become a communist as an Austro-Hungarian prisoner of war in
Russia, he had subsequently served both as a minister and a military
commander in the short-lived Hungarian Soviet of 1919. Arrested on
a clandestine visit to Hungary in 1922, he was sentenced to death and
saved only by an international campaign, after which he spent fifteen
years in the jails of the semi-fascist Hungarian state. When he became
a member of the post-war Hungarian government he was regarded as
an exemplary communist, almost on a level with Dimitrov. Possibly
his experiences of imprisonment may have warped his personality, for
when from 1947 he began to dominate Hungary he established what
may well have been the most terroristic of all the Eastern European
regimes. Nor did he confine his oppressions to Hungarian citizens.
Edith Bone, a stringer for the British *Daily Worker*, was arrested
secretly, knowledge of her whereabouts denied, and imprisoned under
atrocious conditions. She was convinced that only her stubborn refusal
to 'confess' saved her life.

In 1953, following Stalin's death, Moscow had insisted on tne
appointment as prime minister of the reforming Imre Nagy, a survivor
of the forties purges with a communist record as long as Rakosi's.
The latter, however, remained as party leader and directed his efforts
to sabotaging Nagy's reform programme, which mirrored that of
Malenkov with the addition of de-collectivisation in the countryside.
By 1955 he had prevailed upon Moscow to get his rival removed
again, and at the end of the year spitefully had him expelled from
the party. These episodes made Nagy, like Gomulka in Poland, the
focus of popular hopes and regard. Public anger, particularly among
young people, intensified and was not appeased when Gero replaced
Rakosi in the summer of 1956. Hence in this instance too, the dead
were called in aid when at the beginning of October Laszlo Rajk's
rehabilitation and reburial with honour were announced in the hope
of conciliating popular feeling.

An enormous demonstration accompanied the reburial and from
that point the level of protest, no longer under the control of
the authorities, escalated steadily, fuelled by reports of what was

happening in Poland. When the secret police opened fire on demonstrators in Budapest, fighting spread across the city and public build-
ings and communist party premises were stormed. In panic, the party
leadership on the night of 23–24 October decided to reinstall Nagy
as prime minister and call in the Soviet military to quell the disorder.
As Soviet tanks arrived in the course of the day, fresh provocations
by the security police escalated the fighting and occasioned a massacre
of demonstrators in front of the parliament building. Revolt then
exploded across the country, power on the ground being seized in the
capital and provincial towns by revolutionary committees of workers
and students. Barricades went up, the insurgents armed themselves
and were joined by the soldiers of the Hungarian army, though not
as a cohesive military formation.

Even at that point the possibility of a Polish solution was not yet
entirely out of the question. The key Soviet leaders, still anxious to
pursue détente, were not unconscious of how adversely Western
opinion would be affected by draconian intervention. As the crisis
developed they sought to defuse it. Mikoyan, the most flexible of the
Soviet leadership, arrived in Budapest and arranged the replacement
of Gero as General Secretary (which the Central Committee had
neglected to do). His successor was Janós Kadar, also a well-reputed
figure, for he too had suffered persecution in the purges. The first
moves of the new administration were relatively cautious, but as the
fighting continued a coalition government was announced as well as
the dissolution of the secret police, whose members were receiving
summary justice on the streets wherever they could be found.

These lynchings were among the later publicly quoted pretexts for
the Soviet re-invasion, but it is hard to imagine that Khrushchev and
his Presidium were much exercised over the fate of a few hated and
discredited functionaries. What tipped the balance was Nagy's radio
announcement on 30 October of the abrogation of the single-party
system – the communist party had in any case dissolved at its base –
the formation of a new coalition government with reduced communist
representation, and above all the stated intention of this new administration to withdraw from the Warsaw Pact and assume Austrian-
style neutrality. The invasion with which Khrushchev responded was
given the flimsiest of political cover by enticing Janós Kadar to break
ranks with his colleagues and form a counter-government under Soviet
protection, asserting that Nagy's administration had fallen under the
influence of counter-revolutionary elements. The Hungarians resisted
desperately but hopelessly until overwhelmed by superior military
power, with much of Budapest laid in ruins. To defuse the continued

resistance Kadar at first purported to treat the rising as legitimate and the intervention to have been provoked only by Nagy's 'excesses'. For about a month he negotiated in amiable style with the workers' councils which had seized control of the enterprises, until their morale was exhausted and they could be liquidated early in the new year.

Reform was demonstrated to have its limits. Without any doubt the Polish events would have ended in a similar fashion had the Poles been so bold as to attempt what Nagy had done in the liberalisation of the internal political system or the redefinition of their country's international role. To look at matters momentarily from the point of view of Khrushchev and the Kremlin reformers, whether or not they themselves favoured invasion as a last resort, they must have considered that they had little choice. For one thing, there were undoubtedly genuine fears of profound damage to the Soviet security system if one of the bloc's front-line states defected, even if it promised not to join the opposing camp. Possibly even more alarming, a successful internal revolution against a communist regime would have profound repercussions for the system's ideological credibility, the more so as the revolution was led and dominated by left-rather than right-wing anti-Soviet elements.[57] Last, but certainly not least, acceptance of Soviet defeat in Hungary would have undermined fatally the position of the reforming group in the Kremlin vis-à-vis the still-entrenched Stalinists – Molotov, Kaganovitch and Malenkov, who, in spite of his earlier 'liberalism', had rallied to their side.

The unreconciled Stalinist leaders in Eastern Europe, dissatisfied in any case, would have redoubled their efforts to undermine Khrushchev and support his rivals. The Chinese regime would also have been alienated, for although it had encouraged the Poles to assert national autonomy within the communist system, trying to break from it was a different matter. Beijing congratulated Moscow on the action taken. When the critical choice had to be made, virtually all the non-ruling communist parties also endorsed it, even the Italian (though its trade union arm, the CGIL, refused to do so). There were a few excetions. The Communist Party of India protested at the intervention, as not surprisingly, given its stance over the Khrushchev revelations, did the CPUSA. In Europe, the Danish communists, led by a veteran from the thirties, Axel Larsen,[58] opposed it strongly, and likewise the Icelandic CP, which had close associations with the Danish. In all the other parties oppositional currents emerged, denouncing Soviet behaviour with greater or lesser vigour, but all of them were successfully controlled and the individuals involved expelled, driven to resignation or reduced to silence.[59] The traumatic events of 1956, though immensely consequential in the long term, did not lead to any immediate fissure within the movement. The CPI's protest remained an isolated action and was not followed up in any manner. In the USA a pro-Soviet faction succeeded in regaining control within a year, though at the cost of a great haemorrhage of members. In Denmark, though the majority was with Larsen, CPSU intervention established a loyalist minority as the official representative of Danish communism.[60] As a result of the events, all the Western parties lost members in considerable numbers. Though membership had been steadily declining since 1945, an acceleration is clearly visible in most of these parties between 1956 and 1957. Beyond that, the admission of historic fallibility and the spectacle of popular revolt in a 'People's Democracy' meant that the movement could never recover the unthinking confidence that it had previously enjoyed.

New Roads for Old

However if 1956 had shattered one ideological universe it also, by breaking the falsely imposed image of communist continuity between 1917 and 1956, opened up opportunities for the movement to embark on new and more profitable directions. When the smoke had cleared, both literally and figuratively, the defeat of a 'revisionist' challenge was pronounced, but this did not signal a return to hardline postures.

Soviet forces, acting in concert with Kadar's regime once it was consolidated, rigorously repressed continuing opposition in Hungary. Mass arrests occurred, and in early 1957 it was made a capital offence to incite strike action. In 1958 Nagy and his closest associates were executed. He had taken refuge in the Yugoslav embassy but having been tricked into leaving, was kidnapped. It says something about the state of affairs in Hungary that the secret 'trial' and death sentences were carried out in Romania – in defiance of even the most remote conception of legality.[61]

Once all resistance had been thoroughly crushed, however, Kadar switched to a strategy of concessions, to the extent that Hungary proceeded much faster and farther than Poland along the road which the latter had pioneered. The concessions took two forms, the symbolic and the material. In the former case, the insignia of the old regime were not restored, the red star, for example, being removed from the centre of the national flag. More importantly, the abolition of the Rakosi secret police, the AVH, proclaimed by Nagy, was confirmed and most (though not all) prisoners rounded up during the suppression were released once they presented no further danger. In the longer term, the highly centralised system of economic management typical of all Stalinist regimes was abandoned, agricultural collectivisation dismantled, consumer provision made the central economic priority and a large measure of market flexibility allowed in the distribution of consumer goods. Hungary in the sixties became the model example of a new-course communist regime, 'goulash communism', as it was to be termed after a remark of Khrushchev's.

The notion of varying 'national' roads to socialism had been around in the immediate post-war period, and it was indeed for taking the notion too seriously that the Yugoslav communists had been excommunicated. Even so, while insisting that the model of the USSR was the only valid one, it still could not be denied that the bloc regimes (and the Chinese) owed their origins to different processes from that which had given birth to Soviet Russia. On paper the former were 'people's democracies' rather than soviet states, and in that form allegedly progressing from capitalism to socialism. China, too, was following its own individual path. Even Stalin became more tolerant of the principle (if not the practice) of variation, and exemplified this by his endorsement in 1951 of the programmatic document produced by the British Communist Party under the title *The British Road to Socialism*. The title itself made a point:[62] it had been used earlier for a chapter in a pamphlet by the party's leader Harry Pollitt, published before the Cold War closed down. The content was more innovative still, for it postulated a British revolution achieved without significant violence and by means of parliamentary processes – a suggestion that would have been regarded as the most damnable heresy in the days when Leninism was taken seriously. The significance of this programme, however, was not in the implausible scenario it sketched for the transformation of Britain but that it could receive the Kremlin's imprimatur. It might be concluded that Stalin by that time was not too concerned with the theoretical political perspectives of the Western parties so long as they stayed devotedly loyal. Following his death and the partial reconciliation with Yugoslavia in 1955, the potential was yet further strengthened for every individual communist party to develop and extrapolate its own outlook for its nation's future, and the events of 1956 emphasised that this could apply to ruling parties as well – provided that they kept inside certain limits which were, to be sure, prescribed from Moscow. It became possible for the Italian party leader Togliatti to elaborate the concept of 'polycentrism'.

In Moscow itself Khrushchev resumed his reforming course after the traumas of 1956, though not without opposition. Colleagues who distrusted and feared the direction in which events were moving combined against him, aiming to overthrow him and denounce the Report as a 'tissue of lies and infamy'.[63] These were pre-eminently the old gang of Molotov, Kaganovitch and Malenkov, but they added recruits to their faction, including even the premier, Marshal Bulganin. In June 1957 they secured a majority against Khrushchev in the Presidium (Politburo), but unprecedentedly this was overturned by the Central Committee – theoretically the superior committee, but in practice always in the past the obedient instrument of its subcommittee.[64] According to Medvedev, the Central Committee members were frightened of renewed repression if Molotov & Co. prevailed. Instead it was the conspirators who lost their jobs – though not their heads. Khrushchev was only able to mobilise his Central Committee majority in the emergency because of the sympathetic attitude of the military and the secret police chiefs, who transported the pro-Khrushchev members to the meeting – an interesting comment on the way in which these matters were settled in the workers' state. Khrushchev then became free to develop a new ideological framework appropriate for the international communist movement in the post-Stalinist nuclear age.

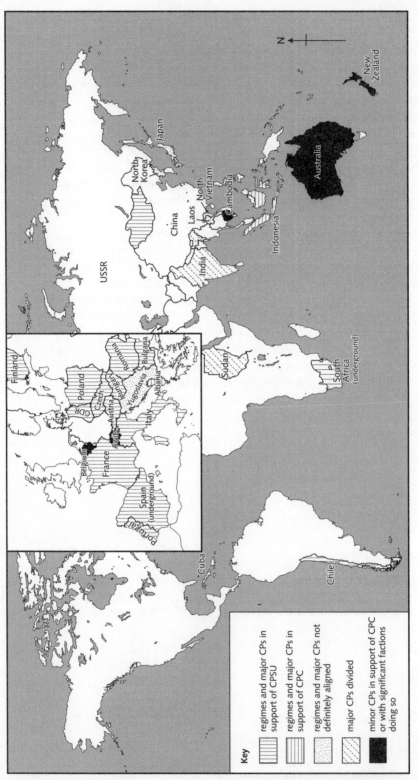

Figure 5 The communist schism, 1963

Key

regimes and major CPs in
support of CPSU

regimes and major CPs in
support of CPC

regimes and major CPs not
definitely aligned

major CPs divided

minor CPs in support of CPC
or with significant factions
doing so

4

'Peaceful Coexistence' and Schism

'Problems of Peace and Socialism'

An acceptable theoretical formulation of the communist movement's self-perception of its role in the world of the late fifties had to meet a number of requirements. Firstly, it had to look convincing – not too far out of accord with the realities of superpower nuclear stand-off and the political stasis of two rival blocs competing for influence in what would soon be known as the 'Third World'. Secondly, it needed an historical narrative relating, however tangentially, what the movement was actually doing at that period to what its purposes had been in its early days. This could not be dispensed with since the movement possessed some of the attributes of a theocracy; its ideological credentials and political legitimacy were grounded in the writings of its founders and the multiple deviations in reality from their perspectives had somehow to be justified and made to appear plausible. Thirdly, and perhaps most importantly, with the power of Moscow to lay down the party line substantially weakened since 1953, it had to be acceptable to the many different communist parties and the increasingly national agendas that many of them were exploring. In the event these priorities proved impossible to reconcile and the movement was disrupted.

The CPSU ideologists elaborated a perspective and tried to win its acceptance at world conferences of communist parties in 1957 and 1960. Whether realistic or not, it did not lack a certain cohesiveness and consistency. It may be sketched as follows. It was recognised implicitly that the expectation of the capitalist economies returning to slump conditions – which had been an important premise in the late forties and early fifties – was unfounded, at least for the foreseeable future. The global 'long boom' of these decades had to be recognised in the East as well as in the West. The socialist economy of the USSR, however, drew such strength from the fact that it was planned and centralised that it might be expected to outstrip that of the leading imperialist state, the USA, before too many more decades had passed. The attractiveness of the USSR would increase all the time that this process continued and become irresistible once it had been accomplished. The desire to imitate such a phenomenon would draw more and more parts of the world into the socialist orbit and away from imperialism – possibly by way of neutralism – until in the long run the working classes of the imperialist countries themselves would insist on proceeding along the same road and take matters out of the hands of their respective bourgeoisies.

In Kremlin terminology this scenario was referred to as 'peaceful coexistence' and 'peaceful competition'. The former term was one which had been used by Lenin though, as might be imagined, with a wholly different connotation. He had envisaged it as no more than a brief respite before a reviving revolutionary storm, not as a permanent condition leading to eventual socialist triumph. For Khrushchev it served as useful shorthand to define his strategy. It also provided fresh justification for the USSR to enjoy pre-eminence in the communist family of nations since it must assume the chief responsibility in applying peaceful competition. Moreover, it justified the practice of the USSR concentrating on developing its own consumer expansion rather than giving priority to sharing its resources with fellow socialist states.

It was accepted, of course, that imperialism would not passively allow itself to be overtaken in this manner and dismantled piecemeal. As its positions became increasingly threatened it would grow more aggressive and might – certainly would – be tempted to stake everything on its trump card, nuclear weaponry, even at the risk of global catastrophe. The 'struggle for peace' therefore assumed a joint paramountcy with the development of socialism. There were three interlocking supports to the protection of peace. The first was the USSR's own nuclear armament,[1] acting as a deterrent to any adventures the US government or its brass hats – or any subsidiary imperialist power for that matter[2] – might be tempted to undertake. The second was a network of agreements and treaties aimed at defusing the nuclear threat so far as possible and the third was the action of the masses, led by labour movements, in the imperialist countries themselves bringing anti-war pressure on their governments.[3] The Soviet ideologists expressed confidence that these deployed in combination could ensure that war would not be inevitable and imperialism prevented from launching an annihilating conflict. In short, the Soviet perspective assumed that, though there was no room for complacency, history was fundamentally on the side of the communist movement and its objectives; which was the source of Khrushchev's much-quoted remark 'we will bury you!' – clearly he did not mean under radioactive rubble. Thus the immediate priorities of the USSR – to give its citizens some relief from constant trauma and allow them to set about improving their material lives – were brought into supposed conformity with the historic aims of Marx and Lenin.

It is worth making the point that, unlikely as it may seem from the perspective of the nineties, in the early sixties it was not only communists who found these perspectives convincing. However comparatively backward the USSR might have still been, its growth rates of the time appeared to outpace those of its main rival. To that impressive record was added between 1957 and 1961 two astounding technological triumphs which stunned the world. The first was the sputnik, the earliest artificial satellite, which heralded the beginning of the space age, and the second was success in the competition to put a man in orbit.[4] Western commentators began to consider seriously whether communism could actually deliver on its long-range promises, or at least the material ones. Marxists sceptical towards orthodox communism, such as Isaac Deutscher, never doubted that once the social powers of collective production were harnessed in a planned manner free of terror and without interruption by wars and crises, the results would be stupendous – though they were also convinced that rising consumer standards and the demands of a better-educated population would undermine the regime rather than stabilise it.

The Soviet ideologists were also quite perceptive in anticipating the approaching collapse of overt colonialism, for in the late fifties, though its dismantling was evidently under way, that still appeared from a Western viewpoint likely to be a leisurely process lasting quite a number of decades – and both French and British governments continued to struggle desperately to hold on to certain of their more valued possessions or else perpetuate the ascendancy of the local colonial elites. The Kremlin foresaw correctly that the newly liberated states would become arenas for contests of influence between East and West and surmised that their own anti-colonial record would work to their advantage in this respect. For the USSR, however, success in attracting the loyalty of emergent nations had a contradictory aspect, especially if close relations with Moscow made these nations *personae non grata* with Washington. In that event the Soviet Union would be obliged to spend resources it could ill afford in supporting and defending its new clients, in addition to the strains imposed by its own defence, which had to try to match Western armaments absolutely from a much inferior economic base.

By and large, however, prospects for world communism in the wake of the sputnik appeared encouraging. Khrushchev, having consolidated his own position and dismissed his rivals, sought to consolidate the unity of the movement around the Soviet perspectives and interpretations of political reality. One means of doing so was the pair of international congresses already mentioned, though in the event these disappointed their convener's hopes. A simpler and more reliable instrument was a monthly journal, aimed at an audience principally of communists and sympathisers, to serve as a common platform for the individual parties so long as they disseminated a viewpoint basically in accordance with Moscow's. Accordingly it was established in Prague, and appeared under the generic title *Problems of Peace and Socialism* (the English language edition was called *World Marxist Review*). It was in formal terms the last ghostly echo of the Communist International. More material ones, however, also existed in the shape of a section of the CPSU Central Committee for dealing with relations with foreign parties, and the secret subsidies which the latter continued to receive.[5]

Cleavages

The restored stability in the movement following the shocks of 1956–7 were not, as matters turned out, destined to last for very long, and although the disruption was contained for a further six years, the signs of fracture were present even as the USSR celebrated its initial space triumph. The essence of the problem was that the perspectives of the CPSU, which continued in the changed conditions to give it a hegemonic place in the world movement and the expectation that the other parties would follow its leadership, conflicted increasingly with the national agendas of many of these parties, especially the larger ones, whether or not they were in power.

The emergent disagreements were, not surprisingly, given the history and character of world communism, expressed in terms of theory and ideology, which may well have been genuinely felt on the part of the participants, but which were certainly intermixed to a substantial degree with considerations of power relations and possibly even ones of personal pique and ambition. The initial frictions which appeared indeed possessed an element of absurdity, for they pitted the USSR against Albania, the smallest, most remote and backward of all the communist regimes.

In the Balkans, Albania was a particularly mountainous and inaccessible region, the Illyria of Roman times. The language and culture of its inhabitants pre-dated the Slavonic migrations of the early Christian era, which had formed the other Balkan countries with the exception of Greece. Prior to the Second World War its virtually illiterate society continued in a basically tribal form, based upon the blood feud and ancient oral law and custom. The majority of its people had (like the Bosnians) absorbed the Muslim religion of the Ottoman Empire (though frequently in revolt against the Sultan),[6] and had been one of latter's last Balkan possessions. Its creation as a modern state was largely the diplomatic work of the Austro-Hungarian Empire, with the intention of denying Albania and its coastline to Serbia following the Balkan War of 1912. During the inter-war years one of the local feudatories had elevated himself to regal status under the name of King Zog, though the central government's authority failed to extend very far into the interior. Much the same remained the case when in 1939 it was seized as part of Mussolini's projected Mediterranean empire.

The terrain was ideal for guerrilla warfare and an Albanian liberation movement, under the leadership of a local communist party founded and sponsored by Tito's partisans and headed by the French-educated former schoolteacher Enver Hoxha, achieved successes comparable to those of the Yugoslavs, having expelled the invaders by 1945. The condition of the country immediately afterwards, with the former ruling elements in flight or subjected to political represion, can be gauged by the fact that there were insufficient literate revolutionaries available to fill all cabinet posts. Despite his formal positions as party leader and commander-in-chief Hoxha was largely sidelined by the pro-Yugoslav faction and, with economic co-ordination well advanced and plans for a joint military structure, up to the spring of 1948, it appeared certain that Albania would be absorbed.

The Stalin–Tito split saved him and enabled him to purge his enemies. Frequent and systematic purges followed in succeeding years, with political debate in the Albanian party[7] taking on the character of tribal vendetta. The relatives of victims were invariably purged along with them: the traditions of the clan system continued to prevail in socialist Albania. The common factor in all of these episodes was the enhancement of Hoxha's own power and personality cult.[8] Since he was not only a zealous Stalin acolyte but a would-be-imitator of the Soviet dictator it is not surprising that he was profoundly disturbed by what had transpired at the 20th Congress, the more so when it was used by opponents, allegedly encouraged from Moscow, to mount another challenge to his authority.[9] Possibly even more threatening was the prospect that if Soviet–Yugoslav relations continued to improve Hoxha's position would certainly become untenable. Albanian propaganda insisted on every possible occasion that 'contemporary revisionism' remained the principal threat to the international movement and that the Yugoslav regime embodied it in a crystallised form. By 1961 the split was out in the open to the extent that the Albanian leadership was being openly attacked from the platform of the Soviet party Congress and a little later diplomatic relations were severed between the two states.

By that time, however, the issues had enlarged immeasurably, though the new dimension had still not become explicit – Albania and Yugoslavia continued to be used as stalking-horses for the two major communist powers. The rift between these was probably unavoidable sooner or later, since neither could endure to concede supremacy to the other in international communist affairs. Occasions for dispute, both the trivial and the portentous, soon multiplied once the initial antagonism was recognised. The way that the Chinese had been patronised by Stalin doubtless still rankled; not so long after his death they found themselves at odds over the perspectives sketched above on the meaning of 'peaceful coexistence', relations with imperialism and the USA, and the character of socialist advance in individual countries and throughout the world generally.

In essence, the CPC leadership objected to what they perceived as the readiness of their Soviet counterparts to seek agreement and understanding with a power whom the former regarded as communist China's mortal enemy, which continued to threaten it with invasion, occupy part of its territory (Taiwan) and exclude the People's Republic from its rightful seat in the UN. Very possibly they regarded war as more likely than not and wanted the socialist community of nations to aim for the maximum state of preparation and certainly to refuse to be intimidated by Western threats. Though the Chinese claimed to favour peaceful coexistence as much as anyone, this must not be at the expense of concessions which would weaken socialism. Mao had generalised his own experience of warfare to the global theatre, convinced that morale and political attitude counted for more than technology and that 'people's war' on the model of the Chinese revolution was the sovereign way to defeat the imperialist onslaught. He and his colleagues definitely did not accept that nuclear weapons would constitute the decisive factor, in the form of mutual annihilation, but maintained that they could destroy imperialism while leaving socialism (especially in China) with sufficient reserves to conquer globally. Hence the designation of imperialism as a 'paper tiger'. The imperialists were presumed to be aware of their inferiority and therefore always ready to back down before a resolute socialist show of force and determination. One consequence of this was that China was resolved to develop her own nuclear programme and expected the USSR to provide the technical necessities.

They thus rejected the entire strategic orientation that the CPSU had developed, and nothing could have appeared more preposterous to the austere Chinese Politburo than the notion of the USSR developing material incentives, consumption and consumer facilities in the hope that the masses within the imperialist countries would thereby be attracted into following the same road. Instead, confrontation should be the watchword and the Soviet Union should provide her allies with every material and moral support that might be available, thus demonstrating her 'internationalism' rather than selfishness. The criticisms of Stalin in Chinese eyes, whatever their factual justification, therefore appeared to them to be made in bad faith, not as a way of correcting abuses, but as an indirect method of diluting and dismantling the revolutionary nature of the Soviet Union and possibly even seeking favourable reactions from Western opinion.

In China, as in the USSR, there were also internal considerations operating. The first seven years of the People's Republic had been ones of overall success. Though still immeasurably low by Western or even Soviet standards, an economy ravaged by forty years of breakdown, revolution and war had been reconstructed and launched on a path of growth. The peasantry, the base of the revolution, had received basic satisfaction[10] and the 'iron rice-bowl' of entitlement to a subsistence minimum for all citizens had eliminated the worst aspects of desperate hunger. The CPC had likewise reversed the trend towards the country's fragmentation and the inefficacy of central rule. Its writ ran throughout the nation and it had an organisational bureaucracy capable of implementing it. It had also demonstrated the new state's military effectiveness, not only in the rapid success against the Guomindang but in the Korean conflict, and had underlined this by bringing back under its authority the long-seceded province of

Tibet. However generally popular the regime might be – and there is no reason to doubt that at this stage it was popular – it was intensely authoritarian in character (although with its own peculiar style of authoritarianism) and considerably more of a 'barrack socialism' than the post-Stalinist USSR. There is, of course, an argument that in view of the country's low levels of development in every respect no other way of governing it was imaginable, and the only real alternatives the immense Chinese population faced were between well-intentioned and malevolent authoritarian rule.

In any state of China's size and complexity, particularly a revolutionary one, it was wholly inevitable that tensions would exist at the top levels of leadership, though up till the late fifties they had been well contained. Here the personality of the party's Chairman and central figure, Mao Zedong, has to be placed in the balance. Although the architect of the Chinese communist party following its move to the countryside, the evidence suggests that he also distrusted it, after it had come to power, as a potential bureaucratic impediment upon the revolutionary instincts of the masses – and also upon his own line of thinking, which he regarded as that of the peasant masses raised to a theoretical level.[11] Notions of consolidation and controlled development seem to have been foreign to his mentality: the history of China under his direction after the mid-fifties was one of constant lurches and abrupt alteration in direction – forced through at terrible human cost. His estimation of his own theoretical competence expanded as well, and there can be no doubt that he intended to be recognised as *the* Marxist authority for the second half of the twentieth century in succession to Marx, Engels, Lenin – and Stalin.

An internal crisis in the CPC and in Chinese society thus coincided with and was linked to developing stress in the international movement. The first attack orchestrated by Mao against his own party structures took the deceptive shape of a dramatic liberalisation, the 'Hundred Flowers' episode, so called from the slogan 'Let a hundred flowers bloom: let a hundred schools of thought contend', launched in 1957. The purpose behind this was not a real freeing of debate and culture but to provide an opportunity for the criticism of officials who were failing to meet acceptable standards and show sufficient dedication. As soon as it had served its purpose and showed signs of running outside the bounds regarded as appropriate by the leadership it was abruptly stopped and the hundred flowers of criticism scythed down, with reprisals taken against their cultivators.

At least those who suffered as a result of the Hundred Flowers were a small elite – it was quite otherwise with the consequences of

the next drive launched under Mao's aegis. The aim was rapid industrialisation, but the methods employed were in defiance of all norms
of economic management, whether capitalist or socialist. For Mao that
was no objection: the conception was that the limitless availability of
China's most plentiful resource, human muscle, could be channelled
into a crash programme of industrial growth provided that the masses
were sufficiently inspired with socialist zeal. The foundation of the
drive was to be the countryside itself, and accordingly the rural villages
were reorganised into communes. This was not an equivalent to the
Soviet collective farms, for the land itself continued to be cultivated
in relatively small units, but the labour force was organised collectively and under more or less military discipline, which extended even
into their personal lives. In effect, if not formally, the peasantry were
deprived of the benefits of the land reform which had followed the
revolution.

There were much worse aspects. New methods of cereal cultivation were insisted upon in defiance of science and agricultural
experience. Mao had added to his adoption of Lysenkoism even
more pernicious fantasies, in which it was asserted that rice could be
grown in much more closely-packed formations than were known to
be viable – because the socialist plants would share water, air and light
instead of competing for these resources, and therefore yields could
be increased enormously.[12] The claims of 'bourgeois science' or feudal
tradition were to be overborne by the enlightenment of 'proletarian
science' as interpreted by Mao via the party. The outcome was the
wholly predictable agricultural disaster, but this was intensified by the
peculiar mechanisms of Chinese communist authoritarianism which
now came into play. Once the official line was indicated, mass initiative was demanded to confirm it. There were of course parallels with
routine Stalinist techniques in other countries, but its combination with
elements of traditional Chinese culture appears to have given it a
peculiar intensity. Communes produced wholly imaginary figures of
rice production to validate the methods of applied 'socialist science'
– but the central government requisitions of grain were based upon
these fantasies. What was already a prime catastrophe, occasioned
not by natural forces but by human dogmatism, was compounded
immeasurably by state action, resulting in a famine worse than any
under the old regime. Exact figures are largely guesswork, but it
appears certain that at least twenty million and possibly twice as
many individuals died of starvation.[13]

Had Mao – and he, the peasant leader par excellence, was unquestionably the driving force behind the calamity – been simply a tyrant

in the old style he would have done his people far less damage. It was China's misfortune that he was also ideologically obsessed. The famine was kept hidden from the world and naturally also from the communist movement at large, which in the mass remained convinced that China was overcoming the obstacles of its backwardness, satisfying the needs of its enormous population and progressing towards socialism. By contrast, the industrialisation programme, designated 'The Great Leap Forward', was given a very high profile and publicised with all the resources of state propaganda. Its symbol was the backyard steel furnace. Instead of constructing large, new industrial complexes, small-scale industrial production would be multiplied throughout the communes to raise overall output. Mao appears to have regarded this as the Chinese answer to the Soviet technological advances of the late fifties. Logistical and technical criteria were altogether neglected and most of the steel that was produced was useless. Incalculable human resources went into the Great Leap and they were not merely wasted but counter-productive. Only Mao's great reputation as a figurehead enabled him to survive after the experiment was ended in 1961 and for a time his authority was shaken and diminished.

The question of differing roads to socialism was therefore no abstraction or question of detached ideology but a matter of profound and even terrifying material consequence, as well as one which interlocked national and international considerations. After the preliminary moves of the late fifties, 1960 witnessed the beginning of serious engagement between the rivals. In that year the CPC published a commemorative pamphlet for Lenin's ninetieth anniversary under the title *Long Live Leninism*, generally regarded as the initial public statement of its differences with the Soviet leaders, though mentioning only Tito when naming names and casting the argument in terms of Leninist principles rather than historical specifics. It asserted the centrality of class struggle, the implacable character of imperialism and the unavoidability of violent struggle, and it contained the lines:

> But if the imperialists obstinately insist on imposing these sacrifices on the peoples of the different countries, we are convinced that, just as the experience of the Russian Revolution and the Chinese Revolution has demonstrated, these sacrifices will have their compensation. The victorious peoples will, on top of the ruins of dead imperialism, establish very rapidly a civilisation a thousand times superior to the capitalist system and, for themselves, a truly radiant future.[14]

It was an implied, though not specific critique of the Soviet concept of 'peaceful coexistence'. Khrushchev's response raised the stakes both

materially and ideologically, for in June the Soviet fraternal delega-
tion to the congress of the Romanian CP circulated criticisms of the
Chinese position among the communist parties present and in the
following month Soviet technicians were withdrawn from China
(allegedly because they were being harassed by the Chinese authorities), leaving many half-finished projects which could not be com-
pleted without their expertise. That was a most serious escalation. A
little later Hoxha claimed to have frustrated yet another pro-Soviet
plot inside his party and now began to voice open attacks upon
Khrushchev.

The course of 1961 saw a number of developments upon the
international plane which were to have significant bearing upon the
progress of the dispute. In the spring of that year the newly installed
Castro regime in Cuba, which had been steadily moving in a left-
ward direction though in antagonism to the Cuban CP, sensationally
defeated at the Bay of Pigs a CIA-sponsored invasion attempt by
right-wing exiles. In consequence the ties between the regime and
the USSR were drawn closer and Cuba began to lean increasingly in
a pro-Soviet direction, though with its individual eccentricities. The
summer brought with it a less happy outcome in the overthrow
and annihilation of Soviet-backed left-wing forces in the newly
independent Congo. The developments here were significant in
that Lumumba's debacle was the responsibility of a United Nations
ostensibly peace-keeping force which in fact acted as an instrument
of US policy. More ambiguous was the construction of the Berlin
Wall in August. It saved the Ulbricht regime in the GDR from a
crippling drain on manpower brought about by its citizens fleeing to
West Berlin, but, taken together with a 50-megaton Soviet nuclear
test in the atmosphere, amounted to wretched public relations for the
USSR and the bloc.

That same year Khrushchev set forth in unmistakable and explicit
terms both the Soviet perspective for the future of socialism and how
the USSR proposed to give the lead. The 22nd Congress of the CPSU,
meeting in the aftermath of the above events, but also of another
spectacular space triumph, the first man in orbit, was second only in
importance to the 20th. It now made public the attack upon Stalin's
record, but more importantly, the First Secretary's report spelled out
the promise to overtake the USA in all branches of economic performance in twenty years and on that basis to institute a regime of
full communism – the society of abundance – thereby making it an
irresistible pole of attraction to the world's masses. A Marxist–Leninist
theoretical gloss linked this future with the present. It was proclaimed

that the Soviet regime was no longer to be regarded as the dictatorship of the proletariat but as a 'state of the entire people'.

The novelty of this formula can only be appreciated in the light of
the Leninist theory of the state, to which all communist parties were
at that juncture formally committed. According to this the state is
everywhere and always an instrument of class suppression, an apparatus of coercion, 'bodies of armed men' through which the ruling class
maintains its supremacy.[15] It is central to the Leninist analysis that
in order to carry through a revolution the proletariat must *not* take
over the existing state but 'smash' it and replace it with its own state,
which will, under the name of the 'dictatorship of the proletariat',[16]
act as an arm of coercion against the defeated exploiting classes trying
to regain their position. The further projection of this theory holds
that when class antagonisms have disappeared and social relations
are harmonious, the 'proletarian dictatorship', the workers' state, will
disappear.

It was fairly clear in 1961 that the Soviet state was evidently not dis-
appearing, so for Khrushchev to declare that it had done so because
antagonistic classes had disappeared in the USSR was a blocked theoretical move. 'The state of the whole people' was in Leninist terms
an oxymoron, but if the USSR was a harmonious society of workers'
peasants and intelligentsia rapidly advancing towards full communism, and with the last remnants of former exploiting classes eradicated,
what further need could there be for dictatorship, even in the Marxist
sense? The answer was that the USSR and the socialist community
still required protection from external enemies in the shape of imperialism, and therefore the state could not as yet be dispensed with, but
having no antagonistic classes to repress, it had now become a 'state
of the whole people'.

Acclaim by the communist parties of Eastern Europe could be
taken for granted; the parties of the West reacted likewise, both
to the Soviet space successes and the perspectives of economic and
consumer development. Khrushchev's public denunciation of the
Albanian regime, however, now made it clear to even the most
imperceptive communist that there was a split in the world movement, though because of Albania's size and marginality it might yet
be dismissed as of relatively minor importance. So long as there was
no official announcement it was possible to deny the reality of the
growing rift between the Soviet and Chinese parties, even though
references critical of the Chinese position were beginning to creep into
the speeches of some communist leaders, such as Thorez, towards the
end of 1961. Speculation and rumours in the Western media could be

ascribed to ignorance or malice – it was assumed that they automatically lied about developments in the 'socialist third of the world'.

The Split becomes Definite

Denunciations of Yugoslav revisionism or Albanian dogmatism were only capable of being used up to certain limits. Sooner or later the reality behind the coded phraseology would have to be brought into the open, and that began to happen in the course of 1962, especially in the latter part of the year (at its beginning *Pravda* was still referring to the Chinese regime in effusive terms).[17] Two episodes in the autumn assisted the process along and strained relations close to breaking-point.

China and India had long been at odds over the delimitation of their joint Himalayan frontier. The border (with Tibet) had been fixed in the days and at the dictates of British imperialism. It was a region of no economic but of some strategic and prestige value. In October, after diplomatic efforts had got nowhere, the Chinese launched an offensive which quickly captured the disputed terrain of mountain and glacier and then, though they could have overrun much more, stopped and consolidated the border they claimed. Moscow was placed in a dilemma. All communist principles required it to give its support to a fraternal party and regime engaged in military conflict with a capitalist (even though neutralist) power. India, however, was its diplomatic ally, and a channel through which it hoped to enhance diplomatic, economic and ideological influence in southern Asia. In the event the Kremlin opted to throw its influence on the Indian side, not surprisingly enraging the Chinese leaders.

The latter were not directly involved in the simultaneous and much more threatening crisis occurring on the other side of the globe, but they nevertheless regarded it as their concern. Khrushchev decided to use the USSR's increasing closeness to Castro's revolutionary regime and its growing dependence upon Soviet economic support to redress the unevenness in the global nuclear balance, whereby the Americans had bases strung around the Soviet borders but the USSR had none close to the USA. Accordingly, nuclear missiles were placed on Cuban soil. It was done without announcement but, when detected by US spy aircraft, provoked the Americans to blockade the island and threaten to invade it. Since Soviet fleets were at that moment en route for Cuba, the possibility of a thermonuclear armageddon seemed all too likely, until resolved by Soviet climbdown and agreement to remove the missiles in return for President Kennedy's promise not to invade Cuba. Attempts by propagandists to present this as a Soviet–Cuban victory of some kind were less than convincing. As emerged later, the Chinese blamed Khrushchev on two counts – firstly for behaving in an 'adventurist' fashion for installing the missiles, and then in a 'capitulationist' one for withdrawing them once the USA threatened force.[18]

Even then there was at first reluctance to be totally explicit. In widening their critique, on the last day of 1962, the Chinese ideologists directed their fire not at Moscow itself but at the most notable of the 'new thinkers' outside the ruling parties, Palmiro Togliatti. The attack came in the form of an editorial in the CPC organ, *Renmin Ribao* (*People's Daily*), under the title 'The Differences between Comrade Togliatti and Us'. Further bridges were nevertheless crossed with the international publication of this polemic in the multi-language propaganda journal *Peking Review*, established at the beginning of 1963, and its yet further dissemination in pamphlet form. Correspondingly, the Chinese language edition of *Problems of Peace and Socialism* was also cancelled (the Albanian edition had met the same fate several months previously).

Nonetheless, at this stage there remained a measure of restraint, even if only for form's sake:

> We have been forced into a public discussion of the major differences between ourselves and Comrade Togliatti and certain other comrades in the Italian Communist Party. It has occurred against our wishes and would not have occurred if they had not publicly challenged us first and insisted on a public debate. But even though we are obliged to enter into public debate, we still sincerely hope it will be possible to eliminate our differences through comradely discussion.

Mao Zedong's world view was clearly formulated:

> The possession of nuclear weapons by imperialism has not changed by one iota the nature of imperialism . . . not has it changed by one iota the basic Marxist–Leninist principle that the masses of the people are the decisive factor in the development of history. When, in his talk with Anna Louise Strong Comrade Mao Tse-Tung first put forward the proposition that imperialism and all reactionaries are paper tigers, the imperialists already had atomic weapons. In this talk Comrade Mao Tse-tung pointed out: 'the atom bomb is a paper tiger which the US reactionaries use to scare people. It looks terrible, but in fact it isn't. Of course, the atom bomb is a weapon of mass slaughter, but the outcome of a war is decided by the people, not by one or two new types of weapons'.

In a follow-up and lengthier extension of the critique, under the title 'More on the Differences between Comrade Togliatti and Us' (4 March 1963) the Chinese stated a central grievance:

> The National liberation movement and the people's revolutionary movement in Asia, Africa and Latin America give great support to the socialist countries . . . . Beyond any doubt, the socialist countries should give sympathy and warm support to these movements, and they absolutely must not adopt a perfunctory or selfishly national attitude, or an attitude of great-power chauvinism – much less hamper, obstruct, mislead, or sabotage these movements.

And further on, Togliatti's doctrinal errors: 'Comrade Togliatti's idea is (1) there is no need to smash the bourgeois state machine, and (2) there is no need to set up a proletarian state machine. He thus repudiates the experiences of the Paris Commune [which was (1871) Marx and Lenin's example of the first "dictatorship of the proletariat"].' In other words, Togliatti is accused of abandoning Leninism.

Rival camps were beginning to form around the two main protagonists, but the common sentiment being expressed at this juncture was that the differences should be resolved, the two major parties be reconciled and the unity of the international movement be preserved. In March 1963 the two parties exchanged letters in civil terms proposing bilateral discussions, and these were arranged for the middle of the year, an agreement universally welcomed throughout all shades of opinion in the communist parties. These cautious feelers towards détente in the ideological polemics were, however, swept away when in July the USSR signed a nuclear non-proliferation treaty with the USA, France and Britain, excluding China from nuclear weapons technology. For Beijing this was the last straw, and its attacks on Soviet policy, Soviet ideological perspectives and the Soviet leaders became wholly uninhibited. The latter began to be referred to as the 'Khrushchev clique'; they were accused of having capitulated totally to revisionism and US global hegemony and then later of reintroducing capitalism to the USSR. The Soviet side for its part responded by portraying the Chinese leaders as ultra-left adventurists (or even crypto-Trotskyists), nonchalantly prepared to destroy the world by starting nuclear hostilities on trivial pretexts, Mao as a megalomaniac tyrant and the CPC as corrupted because its base had been petty bourgeois (peasant) rather than proletarian, and so ripe for descent into national chauvinism:

> Mao Tse-tung described the struggle waged by the CPC leadership against the Soviet Union and other socialist countries as a 'paper war'

and added that such a war does nobody any harm since no-one is killed in it. This in the first place contains a recognition of the fact that the Chinese leaders regard their polemic with the CPSU and other fraternal Parties as a 'kind of war'. Secondly this clearly reveals the supercilious attitude of the CPC leaders to the interests of the unity of the world communist and liberation movement. The communists of the whole world express deep concern for the situation that has taken shape in the international communist movement through the fault of the Chinese leaders. The damage they have inflicted on the cause of the people's struggle for peace, national independence and social progress is evident to everybody . . . . Their struggle against the CPSU, against the world communist movement, against the USSR and other countries of socialism is not a 'paper war'. As regards its fierceness, its scale and methods it does not differ from the 'cold war' of imperialism against the countries of socialism . . . . We are confronted with an openly expansionist programme with far-reaching aims.[19]

With the split out in the open and no reconciliation in sight, the communist parties round the world and their members had to choose which side they were on. Albania, supported by Beijing both ideologically and materially since its initial quarrel with the Soviet leadership, not unexpectedly became China's loyal ally. For the parties under Moscow's control in the Soviet bloc, whether Eastern Europe or the Mongolian People's Republic, there was no option: they were obliged to repeat Moscow's version of events and the anathemas against its opponent. However there was one member of the bloc, less under Moscow's control and in the process of asserting its independence, although not in a noisy manner like Yugoslavia or Albania. This was Romania, which assumed a neutral posture in the dispute and maintained good relations with Beijing. The Western parties of Europe and the Americas, with varying degrees of enthusiasm, all took Moscow's side, although Cuba, which also fell into this category, was a special case and requires to be considered individually.

Matters were quite otherwise in Asia and Australasia. This is scarcely surprising, given that China's political gravitational pull was much stronger in that region. For one thing, Beijing was presenting itself as the champion not only of the underdeveloped nations, but of all those upon whom US imperialism's malign influence was being exercised, their ruling classes as well as their masses (for which naturally Moscow accused it of abandoning a class analysis). This was essentially a diplomatic rather than a revolutionary stance, but with its concurrent, if somewhat contradictory emphasis on the need for resolute class struggle and people's war, appealed to rural militants confronted by repressive regimes.

Neither of the two established Marxist–Leninist regimes in Asia, North Korea and North Vietnam, committed themselves unreservedly, though the former leaned towards Beijing and the latter towards Moscow (which was its main supplier of aid for support to the insurrection against the US-backed South Vietnam regime). Of the other large Asian communist parties the Japanese also leaned towards the CPC, though tentatively, while the PKI of Indonesia, which was the third largest communist party in the world with close to three-quarters of a million members, was the major CP most closely identified with the Chinese position. For the Communist Party of India the dispute proved traumatic, the more so because of the Sino-Indian war. This party had a history of particularly intense factional infighting and the Sino-Soviet dispute crystallised the divisions between its right and left wings. Its veteran leader Ajoy Ghosh died early in 1962 and was succeeded by the authoritarian S.A. Dange, a Moscow loyalist, whose personality was scarcely calculated to avert a split. The split came when Dange committed the party to support of the Indian government in the border war, exactly the same crime – only worse, since on the other side was a socialist state – for which Lenin had damned the leaders of the Second International. The CPI split down the middle, the left breaking away to form the CPI (Marxist), taking probably a majority of the members, together with the largest and most militant region, West Bengal.[20]

The smaller parties of south and south-east Asia, both legal and underground, opted for different sides of the divide, but in general the Chinese one. Those in Australasia were of course located in societies much closer in culture to Europe than to their Asian neighbours. Both, like that in their ancestral British society, were small and relatively insignificant. The CPA wavered and at first seemed to favour Beijing, but in the end came down very firmly in favour of the Soviet position. The New Zealand CP, however, passed into the Chinese camp, the only English-speaking one to do so. Given the small size of these organisations and their separation from the general political culture of their societies, the outcomes in both cases can most likely be attributed to accidents of circumstance and personality. The parties, mostly underground, of the Middle East (including Israel) and such as existed in Africa, were more or less unanimously attached to the Soviet side.

The stance assumed by a party leadership did not necessarily, of course, reflect the opinion of each of its members. The division did not appear only between communist parties but, as in India, within them. For communists it was a bewildering and unprecedented state of affairs. In previous divisions of this sort a unified world communist movement could always be seen as opposing an isolated rebel or heretic, whether that was an oppositional trend in the Soviet Union of the twenties or a stigmatised regime like Tito's in the forties. What was novel about the early sixties was that there were now rival major centres laying claim to Marxist legitimacy. For the majority, the CPSU's lustre (albeit somewhat tarnished) as the party of Lenin, the historic heart of the revolution, decided the issue, together with its greater resources and the increasingly eccentric behaviour and convulsions which came to beset its rival. There were, however, in all the parties which adopted a pro-Moscow attitude minorities attracted by the ostensible revolutionism and anti-consumer austerity of the CPC, and some seceded to establish small rival organisations. The only one of more than trivial significance was in Belgium, where the pro-Beijing dissidents may have had the support of the party's majority (they were nevertheless expelled and the official PCB remained Moscow-orientated). Their spokesperson, Jacques Grippa, neatly summed up the essence of the world ideological division when he stated that, 'The strategic goal of the international Communist movement in our time . . . is and will continue to be the victory of the socialist revolution on a world scale . . . . In this sense, our struggle for peaceful co-existence between states with opposite social systems is a tactical goal.'

By the beginning of 1965 the split had reached the dimensions of an unbridgeable chasm, and the world communist movement was sundered into two bitterly antagonistic camps, each accusing the other of the vilest betrayals in the Marxist–Leninist lexicon. Although the actions of the states which embodied these rivalries might have consequences for the world at large, the ideological dispute itself was at this stage still confined to what would have been referred to in the hostile media as 'card-carrying communists'. Within a relatively short time, however, Chinese politics were to spill over into a much more extensive audience and Maoism, as distinct from the CPC or its Politburo, to define a newly emerged style of revolutionism.

Castroism

The Cuban revolution of 1959 established a complex and contradictory relationship with world communism. It also marked the beginning of a trend, absent since 1917, of the emergence of credible left-wing alternatives to Marxism–Leninism. Fidel Castro, the son of a Cuban bourgeois, together with eleven companions who called themselves the 26 July Movement,[21] began in late 1956 a guerrilla struggle against the local tyrant and racketeer, Fulgencio Batista, which drew on rural support, expanded its scope across the island and in the last days of 1958 overthrew a corrupt and demoralised regime.

The guerrillas were not approved of or supported by the Cuban communist party (PSP, one of the more substantial Latin American CPs), which regarded their initiative as 'adventurist' and unlikely to succeed. Moreover, it was anything but a working-class movement, having been generated in the rural areas and led by intellectuals; was essentially nationalist in orientation – its reference was to José Martí, the hero of Cuban independence, not to Marx or Lenin – and wholly lacking in communist discipline and ideology. In truth, the Cuban communists had been more inclined towards co-operation with Batista, having entered his government for two years in the forties during an earlier phase of the dictator's career. The working class in the cities remained passive until the very final phases of the insurrection.

In this the attitude of the Cuban Communist Party reflected the ones generally prevalent throughout Latin American communism. The parties founded there, which all dated from the days of the Comintern, fitted in well neither with the local political structures nor with the Latin American traditions of revolution. Consequently they were nearly all small and relatively marginal organisations, and where they did possess any modest influence, as in Chile, tended towards moderation and constitutionalism in their practice if not their rhetoric – even latterly the Brazilian CP, which did have some genuine past revolutionary credentials. Neither of the two revolutions of the fifties which aimed at social transformation, the Bolivian in 1952 and the Guatemalan of 1954[22] was led by communists, nor indeed were these local parties much involved, despite US accusations in relation to Guatemala. Every one on the continent or in the Caribbean was wholly loyal, or rather subservient, to Moscow.

The Cuban revolution was, on the other hand, greeted with acclaim and jubilation by the 'new left' which was currently developing in Europe and would soon make its appearance in North America. Castro's revolution was unquestionably socially revolutionary and undeniably left-wing: its rhetoric spoke of social justice, land reform, welfare services, expunging corruption and organised crime, economic development in the interest of the masses. At the same time it was alight with spontaneity and improvisation, consciously informal in style, dispensing with hierarchy and bureaucracy. 'We are neither with communism or capitalism, as Fidel Castro has said. This is a humanist revolution against right and left dictatorship.'[23] The flavour is expressed in the Havana Declaration of September 1960:

> The National General Assembly of the People of Cuba expresses its conviction that democracy cannot exist only in an electoral vote, which is almost always fictitious and manipulated by big landowners and professional politicians, but in the rights of citizens to decide . . . their own destiny . . . .

> The National General Assembly condemns the latifundium, a source of poverty to the peasants and a backward and inhuman agricultural system; condemns starvation wages and the iniquitous exploitation of human labour by immoral and privileged interests; condemns illiteracy, the lack of teachers, of schools, of doctors and hospitals, the lack of protection for the aged in Latin America; condemns the inequality and exploitation of women; condemns the discrimination against the Negro and the Indian; condemns the military and political oligarchies that keep our people in utter poverty; . . . condemns the granting of our countries' natural resources to the foreign monopolies . . . .

> . . . the people of Cuba have acted with free and absolute self-determination and therefore neither the Soviet Union nor the Chinese People's Republic can be blamed for the existence of a Revolution which is Cuba's firm reply to the crimes and wrongs perpetrated by imperialism in America.

The communists, whether in Cuba or internationally, if they were to retain any credibility, could not reject or ignore this electrifying new phenomenon with its attractive style and its intensely charismatic leaders. Conversely, the 26 July Movement discovered in its turn that it could not do without them. The revolutionaries' reforming zeal duly provoked an indignant US response and economic reprisals. Castro turned to the USSR to make good the resources and expertise the Americans were withholding, and expropriated US property into the bargain. The 26 July Movement also lacked political expertise, and the liberal ministers who constituted the initial government of the new regime quickly resigned when its radical programme became apparent. It was logical, therefore, as relationships with the USSR grew closer and especially after a CIA-organised counter-revolutionary invasion was defeated in April 1961, to turn to the local communists to make administrative use of their organisational skills and experience. An Integrated Revolutionary Organisation (ORI) was created out of an amalgam of the PSP and the Castroites, later to become the United Party of the Socialist Revolution (PURS) and after 1965 and from

1965 the new Communist Party of Cuba. It was, however, Castro's followers, and Castro himself in particular, who retained decisive authority in the new organisations. Old communists unwilling to submit to this were purged, including their leader Anibal Escalante.

Relations during the sixties between Castro's regime and its protector were never wholly easy, and not surprisingly it was the object of wooing from Beijing, whose revolutionary outlook appeared to correspond with its own much better than did Moscow's. Castro, however, though he was determined to remain his own master, could not afford to break with the Soviets and was in any case offended by the ideological arrogance of the Chinese. In 1966 he declared that Mao was 'senile, barbarous and no longer competent to stay in office', and China was worse than an absolute monarchy.[24] The regime had an agenda of its own, for both to ensure its own safety and on ideological grounds, it aimed to weaken the American colossus and liberate the oppressed of Latin America by igniting revolutions similar to its own throughout the continent. Havana advocated the pursuit of guerrilla warfare to destroy the open and the lightly disguised dictatorships of Latin America. In the words of Che Guevara, Castro's leading colleague, the objective should be to 'Create two, three . . . many Vietnams!'[25] and although he was thinking primarily in Latin American terms, Africa and Asia were also in mind. Not surprisingly, the magnetism of the Cuban revolution in its early years inspired considerable numbers, principally among the youth, in Latin America to respond to the appeal. Castroism had a modish following throughout the developed world, but in South America[26] it became a political force of some consequence, vying with the established communist parties and the Chinese-inspired groupings which emerged to challenge them.

Unfortunately neither the terrain nor the social structures of South America offered the same opportunities as Cuba to revolutionaries in that romantic mould, especially when the US put forth all its strength to avert a repeat occurrence. Footholds were gained in Colombia and Venezuela but they could not be expanded into victorious campaigns. The communist parties of the continent refused to have anything to do with the Castroite attempts: in this they were probably well-advised, for although communist participation could have made them more effective than they were, ultimate failure would have been the end result in any case. A particularly notable refusal of assistance occurred in Bolivia when Guevara himself arrived there in the hope of repeating the Cuban experience. The party's estimate that Guevara stood no chance and would get no support from the country's Andean peasantry was wholly accurate, and he duly perished at the hands of the US-advised Bolivian military, to become a revolutionary icon for a generation of newly emerging radicals.

The Cuban revolution during the sixties and seventies therefore remained confined to Cuba. For Moscow and the Soviet bloc the Castro regime was probably more of an embarrassment than an asset. Until the mid-seventies brought about a shift in the geopolitical balance, it brought no real economic or strategic gain.[27] For reasons of ideology and credibility, however, it could not be abandoned. Cuba, especially in the sixties, was enormously popular on the left, and this was a left in which Moscow-centred communism was facing competition and rivalry. Peaceful coexistence, on Moscow's own showing, and this applied to Khrushchev's supplanters as much as it did to him, certainly did not imply that the geopolitical map was frozen; on the contrary, it was supposed to provide the framework for accession to socialism by growing numbers of states. Cuba, whatever its peculiarities, was therefore a shining example and its defiance of imperialism, for both communists and the audience they wanted to appeal to, was exemplary. As the sixties advanced, however, another embattled communist regime grew into a more potent symbol for the hopes of the entire movement.

Vietnam

The Vietnam quagmire developed out of the anti-colonial revolutions which broke out at the end of the Second World War. French Indo-China, comprising Vietnam (Annam and Cochin-China), Laos and Cambodia, were French colonial possessions, which, at the time of the Vichy government, had come under Japanese occupation. It was a region of exceptionally complex social structure, the meeting-point of a Chinese-influenced mandarin culture in Vietnam itself,[28] and the ancient Hindu-derived Khmer civilisation of Cambodia. There were in addition numerous hill peoples of primitive cultures and lifestyles. Though the prevailing religion was Buddhism, the colonial era had created a large Catholic element, concentrated in the Vietnamese mandarin class, while to this blend in the urban areas a number of politico-religious sects provided havens for the socially marginalised.

The legendary Ho Chi Minh had founded the Indo-Chinese communist party under Comintern aegis, and its programme and slogans, adapted to the rural poor, found a strong response in the villages of Vietnam, tormented by the usual ensemble of landlords, money-lenders, officials and rapacious merchants. When armed resistance to Japanese rule broke out, the communists were able to take command of what was essentially a national independence struggle.[29] This continued after 1945 when the returning French refused to give substance to their verbal recognition of the Vietnamese republic proclaimed by Ho, after which a war lasting nine years culminated in total military defeat for the French, the only instance of decolonisation brought about in such a manner. Diplomacy, however, deprived the Vietminh of the complete victory they had won on the ground. The great powers intervened, and by the Geneva agreements of 1954, designed as a compromise settlement, as much as anything to save Western face, Vietnam was divided, with a communist-ruled state established in the north, its capital at Hanoi, and the anti-communist forces and population, particularly the Catholics, regrouped in the south with Saigon as the capital. Separate neutral states were established in Laos and Cambodia. The Vietminh were understandably reluctant to surrender half of what they had won, but were pressured by the Chinese and Soviets who were thinking of world stability and the need to limit their external commitments. They were also conciliated by the undertaking that the country would be reunified after three years on the basis of a general election – which Ho was confident he would win.

The elections were never held because the USA established itself as the protector of the vehemently anti-communist regime which emerged in the south, socially based upon upon the Catholic community, particularly the northern exiles and the traditional mandarin ruling classes. Rural social relations were re-established upon their traditional hierarchical foundations and villagers divested of the benefits they had gained from the Vietminh war. Predictably, guerrilla conflict broke out again, the more readily as the Vietminh had left behind an underground network of cadres at the time of the country's division. The corrupt and unpopular southern regime proving unable to contain the insurrection, the US government steadily stepped up its intervention in its client's support, at first with advisers and material, but in the course of the sixties with air power and armies of ground troops, extending its role to the air bombardment of North Vietnam and Cambodia – in the case of the latter this was particularly devastating and accompanied by full-scale invasion.[30]

Three aspects of the Vietnam war are pertinent to the evolution of the communist movement. The first point to note is that despite the tensions existing between the great powers and the strenuous armed involvement of one of them, the war was confined to Indo-China and not allowed to spill over or be linked to nuclear threats. No equivalent to the Cuba crisis of 1962 occurred throughout all the years of the fighting, even when the USA faced humiliating military defeat. Either the USA, the USSR or China could, if it had so wished, raised the stakes to one of global confrontation, but none of them did so. Their self-interest in showing such restraint is obvious, but from the communist standpoint, whether of Soviet or Chinese orientation, imperialism would never voluntarily limit its aggressions. It was there-fore an article of faith among communists that the only considera-tions which kept Washington from using nuclear weapons against North Vietnam or trying to blackmail the communist powers into forcing its surrender were firstly, the armed strength of the socialist regimes and secondly, the oppositional movement which had been evoked in the West itself.[31] Thus 'peaceful coexistence' in general terms was not incompatible with a merciless war being fought in particular locations.

In the escalating and increasing bitter confrontation between the Chinese and Soviet communists after their breach became open, Vietnam was not the prime source of dispute, but it did feature. Each accused the other of being half-hearted in its commitment to the struggle and even of obstructing the other's assistance efforts. According to the Chinese, the USSR, with its nuclear strength, failed to take a sufficiently vigorous stand in deterring US aggression and was also mean-spirited in supplying the material resources that Hanoi needed. In making these accusations Beijing was playing on a sense of unease felt throughout the movement. Party leaderships in the Soviet camp were frequently asked by their rank and file why the USSR did not do more. The answer was usually that all the assistance was being supplied which the Vietnamese requested. Moscow, for its part, alleged that the Chinese refused to allow the Soviets to establish air bases in southern China from which they could have provided air support to North Vietnam.[32] It does appear, moreover, that Soviet supplies destined for North Vietnam and crossing China by rail were held up by the Chinese authorities. As with Cuba, the communist great powers, for the sake of their credibility, had to be seen to be acting in solidarity, but both had their own concerns, internal and external, which they had to balance against their willingness to come to the aid of a fraternal party and regime under attack.

For the communist movement throughout the world the Vietnam War embraced two central concerns. It exemplified imperialism's attack on the socialist world, in the shape of the Democratic Republic of Vietnam, which belonged not only to the socialist community but to the Third World, an attack which would take the form of military assault whenever the opportunity offered. US intervention in the south of the country signified another feature of imperialism, its hostility to national liberation and rabid determination to stop any society anywhere adopting the socialist mode of life which was assumed to be national liberation's natural outcome, and its willingness to use unrestrained violence and massacre to further that purpose. It was to be expected, therefore, that communist parties everywhere would express their support vociferously for the DRV, Ho Chi Minh and the National Liberation Front in the south, and that in Western countries they would do their best to organise anti-war demonstrations and other forms of protest.

What was less predictable was that the war also evoked the passionate involvement in the same manner of many thousands, mostly young people, who were not members of communist parties and not a few of whom were were the communists' opponents on the left.[33] Indeed, within the Western anti-war movement the communists were frequently accused of being insufficiently energetic in their commitment to the Vietnamese cause and the communist powers of seeking a rotten and unprincipled diplomatic compromise.[34] These developments reflected the social, political and cultural radicalisation of Western youth, particularly its educated sectors, during the 1960s. It represented a novelty with which the Western CPs had to deal, and on the whole they did not deal with it too successfully. Although some of this new generation of radicals were attracted to the official communist movement,[35] in the main its traditions of discipline, hierarchy and political caution held little appeal to the new political activists of the sixties and even less to the proponents of sexual or narcotic experimentation.

On the communist side attitudes had changed a great deal since the days of Stalin and the Cominform. No longer was there generalised denunciation and anathema of left-wing rivals. Though the communist parties varied in their approaches, most of them tried to come to terms with the novel phenomenon. Orthodox communist positions were defended vigorously in debate, but the attempt was made to argue seriously with the various currents of the new left (and even with Trotskyism) rather than dismissing it as the latest expression of hostile class manoeuvres. Errors were attributed to naivety and inexperience rather than to malign intent and the expectation advanced that this new force, whose sentiments regarding Vietnam were commendable even if its political judgement was in error, could be won as an ally for the communist movement if not directly recruited to it. That at least was the general position up to 1968–9, though after the communist parties of France and Italy had been severely embarrassed by the new movements (see below) the tone grew much sharper. There was a degree of irony in the fact that the Vietnam War became the central symbol of the new politics of the sixties, given that the object of support was a very orthodox communist regime – but it is significant too that this did not lead to widespread embrace of orthodox communism by those involved.

Trotskyism, Maoism and the Cultural Revolution

It was in the swirl of sixties youth rebellion that the virtually moribund Trotskyist tradition was to experience a new lease of life.[36] Since its formulation in the late thirties Trotskyism had represented an alternative interpretation of the communist experience. As a version of Leninism it shared with the orthodox communist movement an attachment to clearly defined political positions, a metaphysical view of the proletariat as the demiurge of modern history, an intransigent conviction of rightness and historical super-confidence, a readiness to interpret disagreement as expression of hostile class interests and a zeal for discipline and hierarchy.[37] On the other hand, it asserted a revolutionary commitment which the Stalinist-inspired movement was said to have long abandoned in order to seek accommodation with imperialism. This, Trotskyists contended, was done to protect the interests of the bureaucracy which had usurped power in the USSR at the expense of the workers' democracy which the 1917 revolution had instituted and for which the Trotskyists claimed to stand. Their analysis of the USSR concluded that it was a 'degenerated workers' state'[38] in which its socialised relations of production represented something historically progressive, but whose potential could only be released by a workers' *political* (not social) revolution which would return the state to true Leninist and internationalist lines.

In the twenty years following Trotsky's death Trotskyism underwent extreme fragmentation. Since it was in essence a political theology in which correct doctrine was accorded cardinal importance, and since it had acquired no great material assets and no political responsibilities to act as stabilising forces, the usual way in which disagreement, whether over ideology, strategy or even tactical judgements were resolved was by splits in the organisation, the minority

seceding to set up its own rival sect and denouncing its former colleagues as renegades.[39] Such constantly repeated episodes helped to
ensure that throughout the war and post-war years it remained nothing
more than a marginal phenomenon,[40] although in 1956–7 Trotskyist
groups received an infusion of recruits from disillusioned communists re-examining the history of their movement. Most soon departed
again, however, discovering that they had only exchanged one brand
of authoritarian dogmatism for another.

In the sixties, with numerous young radicals looking for a more
authentic and less compromised revolutionary tradition than could
be offered by the mainstream communist movement, Trotskyism
revived, especially in the higher education institutions of the democratic West, and in Italy succeeded in influencing part of the official
communist youth movement. In the thirties and up to Stalin's death
it had been standard practice for communist parties to denounce
Trotskyists as agents of fascism, then of the Western spy agencies.[41]
Once this kind of thing was no longer credible the communist hostility did not abate; the accusation was simply changed to stigmatise
them as 'ultra-lefts', splitters and would-be-misleaders of the labour
movement and the enemies of the socialist states, but by the mid-
sixties it was clear that the phenomenon could no longer be ignored
or dismissed as irrelevant. Critiques of Trotskyism began to appear
that were more than simple vituperation. At this stage it nowhere
achieved any significant influence in the Western labour movements[42]
so the CPs did not have to worry about rivalry in that area; so far
as the students were concerned, their reaction varied – the French
party continued in intransigent hostility and did its best to discredit
and isolate these challengers, the British grudgingly collaborated with
them on occasion, especially on the organisation of anti-Vietnam
War activities.

The Trotskyists, however, were not alone in presenting themselves
as claimants for the supposedly vacated role of orthodox communism
– the revolutionary vanguard which would direct and provide leadership for the spontaneously surging protest movements of the decade
and lead them towards the overthrow of imperialism and capitalism. From 1966 a new arrival appeared upon the scene, a product of
developments which grew out of and yet were separate from the
Sino-Soviet rupture. Maoism is to be identified with this later phase,
when the concepts and claims emerging from Beijing moved out from
being an internal dispute within the world communist movement to
occupy a wider arena and when they became intimately linked to the
ideas and person of the chairman of the CPC.

In the closing months of 1965 the Chinese party's success in assembling support for its stance in the international movement experienced a horrific setback. The adherence to its side of the apparently mighty Indonesian CP, the KPI, represented what was probably its single most striking achievement in its contest with Moscow. The KPI, as noted, was huge in numbers, with its size further multiplied by associated organisations such as trade unions and peasant associations. In addition it had the confidence and the ear of the President, Soekarno, who had gone out of his way to prohibit ostensibly anti-communist political organisations. To all appearances it seemed only a matter of time before a communist regime was installed in Indonesia. Nevertheless the PKI's strength was illusory. It was the outcome of a strategy which had added numbers to the party's rolls and had offended and terrified the more affluent sections of rural Indonesian society, along with the sentiments of the majority religion, Islam, without making preparations for coping with possible violent response. It had also acquired influence with one element of the state, the presidency, while the remainder, the armed forces above all, remained in the hands of its mortal enemies, all the more alarmed by its close relationship with Soekarno.

In October 1965 a bungled coup attempt against the generals by young leftist officers, half-heartedly supported by the PKI leadership, gave the anti-communists their opportunity. The party's protector, Soekarno, was sidelined and subjected to house arrest. Its entire leadership was rounded up and killed. Systematic massacres by the military and the civilians they incited exterminated the grass roots. In all, it amounted to the worst intentional atrocity in the twenty years since the Second World War, with at least half a million murders. Communism was utterly expunged as a political factor in Indonesia and suffered its worst debacle since the extinction of the KPD by the Third Reich. The Indonesian generals, who proceeded to install a particularly corrupt and ferocious right-wing dictatorship, were encouraged and advised by the CIA, and they suffered no wave of outraged denunciation from around the world. The radical movement around Vietnam, which might have mobilised such a reaction, had not yet got into its stride. From the Soviet bloc and the parties which supported it, expressions of repugnance were mild and platonic (Brezhnev voiced a brief and passing expression of indignation in his report to the CPSU's 23rd Congress in 1966). Moscow was more satisfied to see the elimination of one of Beijing's major supports than concerned at the fate of its members. It was also anxious not to interrupt its trade relations with Indonesia or lose whatever influence might be found with the new government. More surprisingly, China did not incite a storm of international concern either. Three reasons may be suggested for this. In the first instance, its own internal problems were approaching boiling-point, in the second, though doubtless regretful over the PKI's extirpation, Beijing too preferred to cut its losses and mend its fences with the new regime, and thirdly, it was concerned so far as possible to protect the large ethnic Chinese community in Indonesia, endangered by association with the PKI.

The following year marked the transition of Maoism from an outlook defining one half of a divided communist movement to an ideological inspiration for sets of newly forming would-be revolutionaries who were to achieve brief if spectacular prominence in the upheavals of 1968. Maoism in this sense was intimately connected to events within China itself, and what began there as an inner-party conflict. In August 1966 Mao proclaimed the initiation of 'the Great Proletarian Cultural Revolution'. It seems clear that the immediate target was the group of leaders who had ended the Great Leap Forward and upon whom Mao was determined to be revenged, but no less clear that his more far-reaching aim was to turn the Chinese administrative system upside down and replace it with a structure animated solely by self-sacrificing collective zeal. With the skill of a practised intriguer, Mao combined shifts and manoeuvres at the top of the party with the incitement and manipulation of mass sentiment, using his own prestige and reputation as the principal instrument to foment and control the social forces which distinguished the Cultural Revolution. Mao's formula for leadership combining, in Westoby's words, vagueness with assertive dogmatism, was to 'take the ideas of the masses', concentrate them by study into systematic ideas, then carry them back to the masses until they were accepted and tested in practice, continuing to do so 'over and over again in an endless spiral'.[43] If the masses were discontented and the leadership divided it represented a perfect recipe for upheaval and turmoil.[44]

The attack commenced against a lower-ranking official, the mayor of Shanghai, for cultural misdemeanours, and then spread to his superiors in the party's central organs, eventually snaring the President of the republic, Liu Shao-Chi, a long-standing critic of Mao (and from working-class rather than peasant background), who was dismissed from his offices, designated as 'China's Khrushchev', expelled from the party and imprisoned to die in confinement, probably of ill-treatment. A further major target was the party Secretary, Deng Xaioping. The striking force used by the Chairman was the horde of 'Red Guards', mostly teenagers devoted to his cult, who, with schools

and universities shut down, travelled around China, transported and
supplied by the army, terrorising party and civil officials, technicians,
(it was held to be more important to be 'red' than 'expert') academics
and cultural personnel, subjecting them to violent and degrading rituals
in front of mass audiences and dispatching those who survived to hard
labour in rural environments.

The Cultural Revolution, however, was not simply a creation
of Mao's will but a product of intense contradictions and tensions
within Chinese society, though detonated by the Chairman's words
and action. It offered the common folk, with encouragement from
the very top, the opportunity for revenge against an arrogant, arbitrary, often corrupt, and previously unaccountable bureaucracy –
though honest and conscientious cadres and officials suffered no less.
The force of the Cultural Revolution was concentrated in the urban
areas, but the structures of the CPC unravelled everywhere. To all
intents and purposes, if not in name, the Chinese Communist Party
was liquidated,[45] and there is little doubt that this was Mao's intention: that he regarded it as having ceased to fulfil a revolutionary
purpose and instead to be strangling the country's revolutionary
potential.

The slogans of the Cultural Revolution, while having little objective meaning and giving an impression of sinister mindlessness, are
nevertheless indicative. During its progress the quarrel with the Soviet
Union intensified dramatically. In 1967 the Soviet embassy in Beijing
was besieged by hysterical mobs of Red Guards, to the danger of the
lives of the diplomats inside. In the same year armed clashes occurred
on the Issuri River frontier. The USSR had come to be defined as the
main enemy, and could no longer be accepted as a socialist regime. In
Maoist propaganda it had graduated from revisionism to the restoration of capitalism. Similarly, the targets of Mao's wrath were indicted
as being 'persons in authority taking the capitalist road'. From his
standpoint, policies or practices that contradicted his vision would lead
inevitably to the restoration of capitalism to China.[46] 'Bombard the
bourgeois headquarters' was another frequently chanted slogan originating with the Great Helmsman – it signified both a military metaphor
and the identification of political disagreement as an expression of
hostile class resistance. Less renowned but equally important slogans
defined the purpose of drive as uprooting survivals of the ideas of
Kung (Confucius). 'Although the bourgeoisie has been overthrown,
it is still trying to use the old ideas, culture, customs and habits of the
exploiting capitalists to corrupt the masses, capture their minds and
endeavour to stage a come-back.'[47] A family-centred ethic of unques-

tioning subordination was, accurately enough, displayed as inimical to the revolutionary mentality Mao was trying to inculcate. The most repeated slogan of all was 'It is right to rebel!' – which was alleged to summarise Marx's teaching.

In the broader sense of culture as an expression of social mentality these developments may have had some rather dubious claim to be defined as attempted revolution. In the sense of culture as the advancement of imagination and discovery, it was much closer to counter-revolution, if not even an endeavour to suppress culture altogether. The fanatical dogmatism of the Red Guards has already been noted. Regarding themselves as armed with 'the thought of Mao Zedong', no other source of knowledge or inspiration was believed to be necessary, and Mao's thought was further reduced to the quotations inscribed in the 'Little Red Book', which the Red Guards treated as a talisman, to be waved as a sort of charm when confronting opponents or victims and the contents of which were to be chanted like mantras – though naturally this 'thought', no less than Marxism, was open to conflicting and antagonistic interpretations.[48] A purported speech of Mao's from around July 1967 reads like nothing so much as senile rambling.[49]

In the wider sphere of Chinese culture, history became very dangerous and suspect ground for any writer to intrude upon. This applied not only to recent history, which was of course reserved for official interpretation, but that of imperial history, no matter how distant. It had long been customary to read into presentations of ancient imperial politics possible coded criticisms of current government behaviour, and in fact accusations of this sort now began to be used extensively against intellectuals writing on historical themes if they incurred the Maoists' disfavour. Creative artistic production or consumption was more or less brought to a dead stop, for virtually all already in existence was held to violate the precepts of the Cultural Revolution, which were of extreme didactic simplification, of unambiguously heroic revolutionaries overcoming hate figures stripped of all complexity. Soviet art was denounced in one case for suggesting that the Red Army soldiers of the Civil War era might have contradictory sentiments about the Whites whom they were killing. Creative artists ceased to produce lest anything they said might be used in evidence against them and lay them open to reprisals. Theatre and cinema were reduced to the constant recycling of a few items approved for revolutionary purity at the highest level, specifically that of Madame Mao, Jiang Jing, who was a former actress and took upon herself the status of a revolutionary cultural arbiter.

Another renowned percept of Chairman Mao was the assertion that 'power grows out of the barrel of a gun'. The Red Guards were not armed and were sometimes forcibly resisted by those whom they had arrived to persecute – including workers in industrial areas, accused of counter-revolutionary selfishness for asking for improved wages or conditions. Ultimately the direction of events depended upon military power and whoever controlled the People's Army. The Red Guards depended upon it not only for transport and supplies, crucial though these were, but for protection and assistance whenever matters got out of hand. The army chief, Lin Bao, who had assumed a political role in addition to a military one, was throughout the episode Mao's faithful accomplice as well as designated successor. In the end, when the activities of Mao's shock troops had brought Chinese society close to paralysis – rival gangs of Red Guards had even begun to fight each other – the army, which was the only institution protected from their depredations, was also crucial in restoring order. Criticisms of excess and ultra-leftism began to appear in the official press, the importance of technical expertise and of uninterrupted production to be re-emphasised. Administrative structures were rebuilt and purged officials and party cadres rehabilitated. The military disbanded the Red Guard formations, put the youngsters back to school or college and restored a semblance of normality. The Cultural Revolution was nonetheless formally announced as having succeeded in its objectives. Mao had effectively destroyed or demoted his rivals and elevated himself to an unchallengeable position of god-like authority.[50] The reconstituted CPC was even less of a popular force and more of a pliable instrument in the hands of whoever might be leading it.

> Though Mao followed what was in many respects a Stalinist course before 1949, his party depended . . . on popular mobilization and was therefore necessarily less repressive. It was only through the succession of crises that punctuated Chinese political life in the 1950s and 1960s that the party lost its ties first to the intellectuals (with the aftermath of the Hundred Flowers campaign), then to the peasants (with the Great Leap Forward), then to the workers and even to the great mass of its own cadres (with the Cultural Revolution).

> . . . 'Subjectivity' is standardised and conscripted by the vanguard, so that the 'masses' exist not in their rich creative individuality, but as a sanitised category of bureaucratic politics.[51]

Despite its assault upon the intellect the Cultural Revolution fascinated and attracted numerous intellectuals in the West; it transformed Chinese politics from a matter of inner (as well as inter)-communist conflict into a model for aspiring revolutionaries hitherto outside the communist orbit altogether. These new partisans of Maoism ignored, shrugged aside or embraced the authoritarian collectivism and irrationalism which characterised this species of politics. For them its central features were the activism of the masses which the Red Guards supposedly embodied and stimulated and the opposition of spontaneity to bureaucratic structures which appeared, through these tinted spectacles, to be driving the revolution.

> Great things have been happening in China during the past three years, where the masses have been taking part in struggles to decide the future of the socialist revolution in their country. An established Communist Party and government structure has been shaken and in places replaced in popular rebellions from below and from the left that have enjoyed the support and encouragement of the Party's Central Committee and are intended to strengthen socialism.[52]

There is a faint echo here of the contrast between pristine Bolshevism and compromised social democracy in the wake of the Russian Revolution fifty years earlier: socialism (or in the sixties case, communism) was imagined to be recovering its soul. That may have been, on the face of things, difficult to square with Beijing's continuing positive evaluation of Stalin, or its tight alliance with proudly and fervently Stalinist Albania,[53] but contradiction of this sort was an integral part of Maoism. Stalin's reality was simply papered over and he was presented mythically in the guise of a populist as well as vanguard Leninist.

Within the Western communist parties,[54] too, new currents were stirred when the Sino-Soviet rupture moved into the Cultural Revolution phase. Their own members, primarily but not exclusively youthful ones, were not exempt from the attractions that accompanied a roseate impression of Red Guard activities. All the leaderships, of small parties as well as large ones, had to take account of Maoist tendencies within their own ranks. These were never permitted to exercise the slightest influence upon these parties' standpoints; and whether they were dealt with by disciplinary measures or simply ignored depended upon how vociferous they were and much of a nuisance they might create. The most highly publicised instance of a prominent CP intellectual luminary influenced by Maoism was Louis Althusser of the PCF, renowned (or notorious) especially for his commentaries in a structuralist mode upon Marx's writings. Structuralism, a philosophical approach originating wholly outside Marxism, was much in vogue at the time, not least because of the application to the

latter which it received at Althusser's hands. That Althusser had
Maoist proclivities is known separately from these obscure and con-
voluted works, for though a Maoist or Stalinist message can be read
into them[55] it is far from evident, and since he was discreet about his
sympathies the PCF leadership imposed no sanction on him.

Western Maoism reached its apogee in the tumultuous years of
1968–9. By the beginning of the year student radicalism in a number
of states had grown to the extent that it escaped the control of the
authorities and of any structured leadership, party political or otherwise. Although the Maoists were not the majority trend in these developments, nor even the largest single influence, they certainly made
their presence felt, though generally more as agitators than as the diffuse leadership on the ground who directed the individual episodes.
With the May events in Paris massive student rioting touched off
a general strike throughout the country and rocked the foundations
of the state. The PCF (see below) was a reluctant participant, so far
as it participated at all, and once immediate demands were satisfied
hastened to use its authority to assist in getting the situation back
under control. The comparable events in Italy were less climactic but
lasted much longer, with student occupations and industrial strikes
frequently accompanied with violence spread over the 'hot autumn'
of 1969. The reaction and behaviour of the PCI in the Italian circumstances was with variations very similar to that of its fraternal party
north of the Alps. In neither case did the small groups of Maoists –
and there were a multitude of different ones – (*groupuscules* was the
term used in France) nor the Maoist sympathisers inside the CPs have
a preponderant or even a major role in the development of events.
The famous slogans of the Paris student insurrection, 'Imagination
to Power!'; 'It is forbidden to forbid!', for example, were anarchist rather than Maoist in inspiration. Maoism's role there was felt
more in the immediately following period, when its organisations
emerged as the most intransigent critics and exposers of state action
and equally of communist behaviour.[56] For a time Maoists achieved
the distinction of becoming the chief objects of persecution by the
French political police.[57]

There were occasional hints or rumours that Maoism might, like
Bolshevism after 1919, assume the shape of a coherent international
movement with recognised parties linked formally to a headquarters
in Beijing. Nothing of the kind occurred, nor was it likely to, for Mao
and his colleagues were not disposed to assume political responsibility
for their followers abroad over whom they had no control and who
might embarrass their diplomatic priorities.[58] In any case the Maoist

grouplets, some of which titled themselves political parties and some which did not, were much too fragmented and at odds with each other to constitute a convincing international movement on the lines of the Comintern.

Remarkably, a Maoist group even appeared within the Soviet bloc: student sympathisers in Hungary, who set up an underground party and condemned the USSR and the Kadar regime for revisionism. They appear to have attracted a considerable following.[59] It has to be acknowledged that the fact that the Cultural Revolution evoked an international response in the way it did argues that Maoism met what was an otherwise uncatered-for need to engage in revolutionary activism in the Leninist, or rather what was imagined to be, the Leninist tradition. Trotskyism's stall displayed similar goods, and of a far intellectually superior quality, its disadvantage was that it lacked a sensational piece of contemporary history like the Cultural Revolution to which it could relate.

Maoism in this phase also had its impact upon the Third World. An established party which had already come under Beijing's influence was the Khmer Rouge of Cambodia, engaged in fighting first the neutralist government of Prince Sihanouk and then in alliance with him against his US-backed supplanter. Following the Cultural Revolution Maoist groupings independent of the previous communist organisations appeared in Asia and Latin America and, given their ideological origins, naturally gravitated towards guerrilla war. Two of them were to achieve a measure of success in this enterprise – ironically in complete organisational and political isolation from the Chinese communists – though neither has been able to overthrow the governments they oppose. The first was the New People's Army in the Philippines, in origin a breakaway from the previous defeated communist guerrilla movement. The other was a wholly new creation, the 'Sendero Luminoso' – 'Shining Path' – of Peru. As with the Khmer Rouge, this latter had been distinguished by an exceptional taste for extreme atrocity and indifference to the degree of suffering inflicted upon the population among whom it operates: especially pathological variants of Maoism. In these two cases historical super-confidence and commitment to 'necessary violence' have produced what can only be characterised as political dementia.

These three movements, however, should be regarded more as inspired by certain notions of guerrilla war and social reconstruction borrowed from Mao's writings rather than Maoist in any strict sense – if strict sense in this case has any real meaning. Maoism's intellectual and ideological incoherence, its identification with little more than the personality who gave it its name, caught up with it very rapidly. When in the early seventies, with the Cultural Revolution over and the older forms of Chinese communist administration reinstated, Beijing began its diplomatic turn towards the epitome of imperialist evil, the USA, Maoism's foundations were knocked from beneath it. By the time of its creator's death in 1976 it too had effectively expired.

5

Orthodox Communism, 1963–1970

During the six watershed years covered in this chapter the Moscow-centred international communist movement evolved both according to the internal logic of Marxist–Leninist ideology and the pressure of the outside forces coming to bear upon it. The latter included the rival versions of communism discussed above as well as the actions of its main political and ideological competitor, the Western bloc and the official liberal pluralist values upheld there (though these could conveniently be ignored by their partisans whenever right-wing dictatorships had to be supported for geopolitical advantage). The year 1963 marked the finalisation of the break with the between Moscow and Beijing and 1969 the final international conference (it excluded the CPC).

For convenience sake the 'orthodox' movement can be divided into the CPSU itself, the communist parties of eastern Europe and the parties and associated organisations outside the bloc, the latter being further subdivided into those of the developed and the underdeveloped nations.[1] During the period in question all maintained the same formal principles, though with great variety in interpretation, and also similar organisational structures and culture, inherited from an earlier phase of the movement's history and paradoxically being more difficult to alter than a party's political perspectives. Although the essential unity of this movement was retained during those years, it was within very definite limits, which to Stalin or the ideologists of the Comintern would not have seemed like unity at all. The CPSU

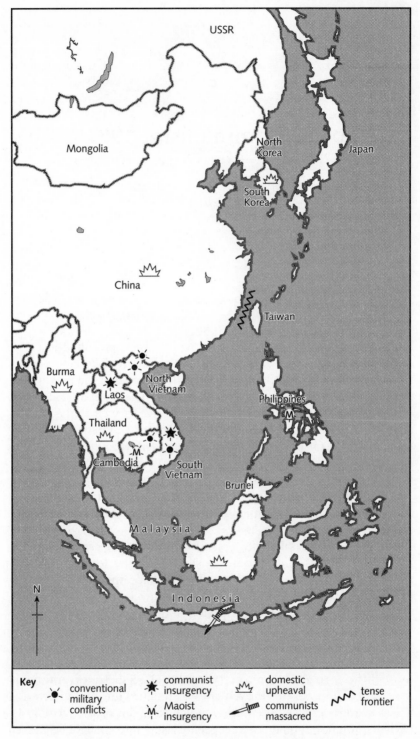

Figure 6 East Asia in the sixties and seventies

would have liked to arrange an international conference to formally denounce the CPC and withdraw its credentials as a genuine communist party – which would merely have formalised a schism that had already taken place – but could not induce the other parties in its orbit to agree.

The bonds linking the parties of the movement to each other became much looser during these years and the ties binding each party to Moscow relaxed very significantly – though for the bloc parties this loosening too had unmistakable limits. For those outside, however, it became possible to criticise Soviet policy and even to condemn individual Soviet actions without provoking a break in relations. Criticism of this sort, when voiced, came predominantly from the parties of western Europe; those of North America adopted stances of unimaginative loyalism that could be classed without much distortion as neo-Stalinism; those in the Third World experienced varied fortunes, but most were very reluctant to adopt critical attitudes towards the state they regarded as their source of inspiration and the protector of their regime if they succeeded in coming to power.

The CPSU, 1963–1967

It did not take long for it to become evident that Khrushchev's extravagant promises at the 22nd Congress could not be fulfilled, and that the Soviet economy, though growing, was accelerating at nowhere near the rate required to overtake the USA within twenty years. If the disappointed hopes of Soviet citizens could be discounted, at the same time the failure could not be other than a source of embarrassment abroad, for foreign parties had made the 1961 Congress a central feature of their publicity, as exemplifying what socialism could achieve in contrast to moribund capitalism. It was partly under these pressures, as well as the diplomatic ones and those of the Chinese conflict that the First Secretary's own behaviour grew increasingly erratic and incoherent. Correctly enough, he had identified the state of agriculture as a critical problem, but his solutions were not thought through. His project for opening up the Siberian virgin lands for grain cultivation was flawed through failing to take due account of soil and climatic conditions.[2] His attempt to decentralise planning ministries was likewise nugatory and signalled a possible threat to the interests of the party nomenklatura itself – a Moscow bureaucrat had to envisage the possibility of finding himself shifted to Central Asia. His nemesis came when he insisted on dividing the

CPSU into two separate sections, one to handle the administration of agriculture, the other of industry, a move which resulted only in indescribable confusion and was detrimental to agricultural production. In October 1964 Khrushchev was dismissed by the Central Committee and 'unpersonned' so far as the Soviet media were concerned, though he suffered no bodily harm.

His successors Leonid Brezhnev and Alexi Kosygin were two grey men (who both nevertheless remained in office for the remainder of their careers). Khrushchev's more provocative reforms were put into reverse, the titles of General Secretary and Politburo restored, criticism of Stalin abated and a crackdown commenced against cultural dissidents, though there was of course no return to the full rigour of the Stalinist system. Brezhnev and Kosygin in the event were initially quite successful in stabilising Soviet society and balancing the general public interest against that of the nomenklatura. Party members in responsible positions were assured of job security so long as they behaved themselves politically and displayed minimal levels of honesty and competence. The military were satisfied by vast expansions and upgradings of arms programmes which were in the end to give the USSR superpower parity with the USA. On the other hand, the agrarian crisis was contained, industrial growth sustained and consumer standards improved modestly but steadily. Khrushchev's flamboyant promises were discreetly buried.

At the time of Khrushchev's overthrow many expected that the new regime would initiate some form of reconciliation with Beijing. Indeed for a time, as Chinese propaganda expressed satisfaction with the downfall of the renegade Khrushchev, both sides considerably toned down their polemic. It became clear soon enough, however, that in this respect the deposed leader had not been acting on his own impulses but had represented the real preferences and judgements of the leadership collective. The dispute was less about ideology and internationalism than about the antagonistic interests of two state leaderships and very soon the mutual anathemas, especially once the Cultural Revolution had begun, were even more embittered than before and in addition accompanied with physical violence. Communist opinion in the USSR itself, in the bloc and in all of the parties which followed Moscow had to be provided with an interpretation appropriate to the situation of a divided communist movement in an era of peaceful but competitive coexistence and a still formidable imperialist global power. It was the Soviet leadership which set the basic framework of such an interpretation which, it has to be stressed, was accepted by even the most maverick of the parties within its orbit, who confined their maverick outlook to analysis of realities and policy perspectives within their own borders.

No more did the history of the CPSU itself provide the model and the template for the interpretation of universal reality as the *Short Course* had done. That was superannuated shortly after the 20th Congress, even before Stalin's corpse had been removed from Lenin's mausoleum and Stalingrad renamed. A new, updated CPSU history was produced – tellingly, it was read by hardly any communist outside the bloc.[3] There were, however, plenty of other texts available to convey the message, which in its essentials did not differ from the one that Khrushchev had propounded. The change at the top had been one of personnel and internal policies, not of world outlook.

'Declining capitalism, advancing socialism' may be said to summarise the dominant theme. Capitalism was judged to be in a state of general crisis, which, while it might not yet be terminal, was certainly irreversible.[4] It was doomed to perish through its own unresolvable internal contradictions and its inability to satisfy the needs and aspirations of the populations subjected to it. The international proletariat was its grave-digger and the latter's instrument the parties which understood 'the historic mission of the working class' at the highest and most general level, namely the communist movement. The classic proletariat, however, did not stand alone, for 'The Working Class is the Liberator of the Working People'.[5] According to the typology which was developed in this decade there existed three bastions of anti-imperialism and progressive advance. The first was the socialist states themselves, where the working class had been politically victorious – with China and Albania reluctantly continuing to be accorded that status even though their politics were regarded as totally deviationist and obnoxious. In principle it was held not to be impossible that their ruling parties would recover their souls and return to the fold. The second was the working-class movement in the imperialist countries, although its dominant parties, the various forms of social democracy, had chosen to side with imperialism, their leaderships having been bribed subtly or not so subtly. That too, however, might change in the future and it was the responsibility of the communist parties in the imperialist states to make it change. The third was the national liberation movements of the Third World (though Marxist–Leninists avoided using that term) which undermined and sapped imperialism, and if they followed through the logic of their struggle would remove their countries altogether from imperialism's orbit, for 'The World Socialist System is a Bulwark of the Peoples in the Struggle Against Colonialism'[6] and 'The Working Class is the Irreconcilable Enemy of National Oppression'.[7]

It can be seen from this summary that no long-term historic compromise was envisaged on a world scale, 'peaceful coexistence of states with different social systems', to quote the complete formula, envisaged a fight to the death in historic perspective, and this was held to be quite independent of the will of states or governments on either side of the divide but to be structurally intrinsic to capitalism and its development through imperialism to the inevitable transition to socialism, which would necessarily occur piecemeal, on a country-by-country basis. Imperialism would, of course, not vacate the stage peacefully simply because its historical time was up, but would fight desperately to survive. Hence, being inherently aggressive, it would be the source of wars both threatened and actual, and most danger-ously of all, would be liable to tip the world into nuclear armageddon, the supreme danger. This, however, was preventable by a combina-tion of resolute firmness and deterrent power, diplomatic negotiation and agreement, with pressure on imperialist governments by their own masses. This would be the more effective the more there was co-operation between the socialist states, the Western labour move-ments and the national liberation forces. Thus the theoretical circle was neatly closed.

So far as actual dealings with the national liberation movement were concerned, the record during these years turned out to be a mixed one, producing both successes and defeats. The setback for Soviet diplomacy suffered in the Congo[8] in 1961 was not recouped; the US installed its own power unbreakably there through its local puppet, President Mobutu. All that could be done was to name the university set up in Moscow especially for Third World students the Patrice Lumumba University after the murdered Congolese prime minister. Two years later a second such major defeat was sustained when the Iraqi nationalist military government, with which the local CP had close relations, was overthrown by rival anti-communist factions and the communist party bloodily suppressed. Less murder-ously, in 1965 the Algerian government, which had emerged from the anti-colonial conflict with France, was displaced by a military coup. The regime had been led by Achmed Ben Bella, who was left-wing and Soviet-orientated, though anti-communist. His successor was a good deal more neutralist.

On the other hand, links with Nasser's nationalist Egyptian regime were drawn tighter; it became largely dependent on the USSR for military supplies, and the Soviet navy received facilities in its ports.

Although the projected Egyptian–Syrian union proved abortive, relations with Syria were also good. Anti-feudal revolution in North Yemen installed a Nasserite and hence pro-Soviet government, though that was fragile and challenged by civil war. In south-east Asia, US efforts to subdue the guerrillas in South Vietnam, supported as they were by a loyal pro-Soviet regime in the north, were proving manifest failures and a growing problem and embarrassment to the US itself. Revolution in Latin America had been comprehensively stalled, but the Cuban regime itself was well entrenched and disseminated Moscow's ideological message move attractively than the USSR could do itself. In tropical Africa, there were some consolation prizes for the Congolese disappointment. A military coup in the smaller former French Congo installed a regime which purported to be Marxist–Leninist and Soviet rather than Chinese inclined. The regimes in Ghana, formerly the British Gold Coast, the former French colonies of Guinea and Mali, ex-British Tanganyika (from 1964 Tanzania), though basically neutralist and nationalist, were well-disposed; while the Somalian regime had become a close ally.

By the end of 1967 the CPSU leadership was in a position to congratulate itself on having successfully coped with destalinisation and its aftermath, to have restored stability in Soviet political affairs and to enjoy a satisfactory level of popular acquiescence, if not acceptance. It had also fought off the Maoist challenge to the extent that it had succeeded in retaining in its orbit the majority of foreign communist parties, although that was at the expense of a significant degree of loosening in the detail of its former control over them. Relations with the Chinese, at state as well as party level, had admittedly suffered catastrophic breakdown, but China and its party had descended into such turmoil that Maoism's hold might well turn out to be a temporary one.

A question which inevitably presents itself concerns the extent to which the Soviet and the bloc nomenklatura took seriously the Marxist–Leninist ideology to which they were formally committed. Were they true believers who directed their policies and actions in line with the conclusions they derived from applying ideological principles to the internal and the international situations? Or were they, on the other hand, cynical power-manipulators, Machiavellians who consciously used the Marxist–Leninist categories in which they explained and justified themselves as a cover and distraction to deceive the gullible and divert attention from their real motives?

As might be anticipated, neither of those extreme positions will stand up to concrete analysis – the truth as usual is a mixed one. On the one hand, the constraints of exercising power are notoriously incompatible with the purity of a fixed belief system. The Bolshevik state from the very beginning was compelled to tailor its principles to the realities imposed upon it by the reqirements of government and diplomacy – and often enough at the price of alienating its more rigorous political elements and leaders. The signature of the extremely punitive Brest-Litovsk treaty with Imperial Germany in 1918 produced a deep split at the top of the party and was only accepted in the end at Lenin's unyielding insistence. Later on, the New Economic Policy involved dramatic concessions to market forces in Soviet Russia.[9] Even more specifically the Bolsheviks from 1922 entered into close relations with the Weimar government and its military high command, a regime and an institution which were its mortal ideological foes. Turkish communists were sacrificed to the need for good relations with Ataturk's nationalist regime. As Adam Westoby argues, the desire to encourage anti-imperialist nationalism and regimes based upon it (which generally took exception to local communist rivals) soon enough ran into conflict with the wish to develop strong communist movements throughout the colonial and semi-colonial world. An in-built contradiction existed between the purposes of the Comintern and those of the early Soviet state and were only resolved by the eventual total subordination of the former to the latter. This did not mean that Lenin and his colleagues were any the less committed to global revolution as an ultimate goal.[10]

Although the Stalin era witnessed the complete subordination of principle to expediency it is not to be doubted that Stalin was driven by an ideological vision which derived, in hideously distorted configuration, from his original Bolshevik outlook. Although Marxism–Leninism, already a dogmatically ideological formula, unscientific in essence, was turned under his direction into a universe of lies, it was nevertheless intended to be absorbed by its acolytes as a world outlook – one which embraced global revolution as a distant prospect but meantime put the Soviet Union and the system Stalin designed at its centre.

His successors, too, were obliged to reconcile their own immediate interests and those of their regime, including all its accumulated bureaucratic interests and inertias, with the long-term ends which they were supposed ultimately to serve. In achieving this, the concept of 'peaceful coexistence of states with different social systems' served as the philosopher's stone which turned the lead of everyday bureaucratic routine in economic, social, military and diplomatic affairs into the gold of socialist principle – for by developing the economic and military strength of the Soviet Union and the international standing of the Soviet bloc the conditions were being created which undermined imperialism and advanced the ultimate realisation of a socialist world: nationalism thus complemented internationalism. 'Experience has shown that the policy of peaceful co-existence promotes the creation in capitalist countries of conditions . . . for all democratic forces to unite around the working class into a political alliance capable of striking a telling blow at reaction.'[11] None of this was necessarily incompatible with the reality of bitter intrigue at the party centre or that Soviet planning, management and society at large was riddled with inefficiency, bureaucratic rigidity, careerism and straight corruption and that urban life was only rendered tolerable by means of a proliferating grey economy, especially in services. Cynicism abounded, emerging in the form which multiplied when more orthodox avenues of dissatisfaction were closed off, the verbally circulated joke. Among these, one of the most telling, with its reference both to production standards and continuing consumer shortage, was – 'you pretend to pay us and we pretend to work'. Members of the nomenklatura, especially at its higher levels, had access to privileges in accommodation, health care and consumption goods and services denied to humbler citizens. In the military the gap in status between the officer corps and the rank and file was even more extreme than that found in the Western forces. Any objections voiced to these civil or military distinctions were dismissed by official discourse as petty-bourgeois moralising.

Nonetheless the scope of social inequality was limited by the character of Soviet society. The nomenklatura, though it could enjoy individual affluence denied to the working class (and other 'toiling masses') whose vanguard it purported to be, could nevertheless not privately accumulate property beyond a restricted range of personal possessions. Rather its members had access to the collectively owned material advantages of the elite, which, though important, were comparatively modest by Western standards. Nomenklatura members were not personally rich individuals and in that respect the Eastern social pyramid was indeed much flatter than the Western one. It could be suggested that the opposite was true in the case of the political pyramid, and certainly the ruling castes of the bloc collectively possessed power that their Western counterparts could only dream of. At the same time it was an unusually open hierarchy in which in principle virtually anybody could enter and secure preferment provided they were willing to subordinate themselves to the requirements of the ideology, recite its formulae, abandon independent judgement and zealously execute the commands of the party. In ascending the ladders it was an advantage (though by no means decisive) to come from a nomenklatura background – or a solid proletarian one: possibly the last surviving echo in reality of the official proletarian dictatorship.

The real proletariat in the USSR enjoyed a general standard of living well below that of the working classes in the Western industrialised countries,[12] if far in advance of that of the average Third World citizen. There were, however, certain compensating advantages, of which the principal one was employment security. How really beneficial this was can be argued, for it deprived management of any sanction in enforcing diligence or efficiency and thus probably had adverse effects upon the level of economic performance overall once the sanction of Stalinist terror was lifted. A range of welfare benefits, albeit of a rather basic sort, was also typical of the Soviet Union (and the bloc states). They included cheap housing – though mostly of very inferior quality – free medical services, free education at all levels, cheap urban transport, and extensive crèche facilities for working mothers. In formal terms absolute gender equality prevailed, although in reality very few women ascended to top positions in state or party. Women were encouraged to take on factory or tertiary sector employment, and the crèche and kindergarten facilities were designed to facilitate this. However, since the socialist male tended to remain an unreconstructed male chauvinist and feminism in the western sense was condemned as a bourgeois deviation, what it meant in actuality was that the working socialist woman was commonly carrying two full-time jobs – her paid employment and all the household's domestic labour.

However, in the last analysis, all the countless contradictions that could be identified between the concept of Marxism–Leninism as expounded in a text like the *Fundamentals* and the realities existing in the states which officially adhered to these principles did not necessarily mean that the doctrine was not taken seriously, or that it did not provide the conceptual framework for the political elites who acted in its name. Marxism–Leninism was the world-view into which into which they had been educated, trained, indoctrinated. In a banal sense it had worked for them, since it had after all been the instrument of their personal advancement; but it was of course a doctrine which repudiated individualistic success and demanded that its adherents always have the public good as their foremost concern. Conscious disjunction between an ostensible belief system and real modes of behaviour or aspiration can hardly be sustained over a long period in a single individual, certainly not in vast collectives.[13] We can safely conclude that the Soviet leaders really did believe what they purported to believe and regarded what they were doing as a matter of central historic importance and something which would pave the way for humanity's advance towards a future in every respect superior to the present – which is not to say that it might not have been better for their country had they simply been power-hungry opportunists.

The Eastern Bloc Parties

Many of the points made above applied equally during the early and mid-sixties to the subordinate regimes of the Eastern bloc. Each possessed its local nomenklatura, each an economy of centralised planning and distribution, with guaranteed employment and spartan but comprehensive welfare systems. From these latter derived such public legitimacy as they enjoyed, for while the achievements of the CPSU undoubtedly made it respected, if also feared by Soviet citizens, the satellite parties continued to govern courtesy only of their security apparatuses and Soviet strength in the background. They represented and enforced the denial of national self-determination and the associated subordination to a foreign power.[14] Not one of them could have won an open election if it had taken place, whereas the CPSU might just possibly have done so. As with the USSR, what in the West would have been termed civil society was hollowed out; all public collectives, even those which were not formally part of the party's structure, functioned under its close supervision and direction. Even informal gatherings were subject to the invigilation of the security services' pervasive spy system and were disallowed if they presumed to discuss matters deemed to be of public import – which could include literature and philosophy as well as strictly political concerns.

In spite of that homogeneity it was also the case that during those years a greater degree of differentiation began to emerge in the East European states than had been apparent at any time since their incorporation into the Soviet bloc. The most notable case at the time was that of Hungary, where what was sometimes referred to as 'consumer communism' had been instituted under Kadar's guidance. Drastic police repression continued for several years following the overthrow of the 1956 revolution, but it was accompanied by serious attempts to supersede the miseries of barrack socialism at the material level. Public mobilisation was de-emphasised in favour of private satisfactions, a shift summed up in Kadar's slogan of 1961, 'whoever is not against us is for us' – passive acceptance was pronounced to be acceptable. The mechanism employed to bring about material improvement, officially proclaimed by Kadar at the end of 1966 under the term New Economic Mechanism, was a controlled use of economic decentralisation and injection of market principles. In the immediate term these policies proved successful – production picked up, consumer goods became more plentiful and variable than anywhere else in Eastern Europe and public dissatisfaction died away. In these circumstances the regime was even able to permit a greater degree of cultural relaxation (though emphatically not in the political sphere) than was to be found elsewhere in Eastern Europe or would have appeared imaginable in the immediate aftermath of 1956.

Modest economic success appeared also to characterise most of the other People's Democracies, though they developed along disparate lines. The closure of the East German border with the Berlin Wall in 1961 appeared at the time an act of desperation and marked a terrible propaganda blow for the GDR and its regime. Nonetheless the decision did achieve its objective: the haemorrhage of skilled personnel to the West was stopped and the citizenry, however unwillingly, came to terms with the permanence of the state and applied their endeavours to production and construction. Economic growth resumed and in the course of the sixties the GDR became the leading per capita industrial producer of the bloc, with the emphasis on heavy industry rather than the greater consumer orientation of Hungary, though consumer standards did improve in the process.[15] In theory the ruling party, the Socialist Unity Party (SED) was the product of an amalgamation of the revived post-1945 communist and socialist parties in the Eastern Zone, in reality, needless to say, the union was merely the complete absorption of what was left of the socialists by the Moscow exiles of the KPD. Its leader Walther Ulbricht was a Stalinist of the deepest dye (doubtless the principal reason for his survival in the Great Purges) and the regime he directed, though eschewing terror,[16] remained in all other respects incorrigibly Stalinist (or, possibly better, neo-Stalinist). Censorship was total and the penetration of the secret police exceptional even by Eastern European standards. Official propaganda reminded the country's citizens unremittingly of the crimes of 'Hitler-fascism' in which the nation had been involved and schoolchildren were taken on compulsory visits to former concentration camps where they were stood in line to be lectured at great length on the monstrous significance of these sites. The intentions were good, certainly when compared to the official amnesia across the border, but the effects were counter-productive – participants recall overwhelming boredom and even inclination to disbelieve the official account.

A paradox is evident in the fact that Hungary, which suffered in 1956 the full weight of Soviet military intervention with widespread destruction, numerous casualties and subsequent executions, developed within a decade into the most relaxed of the bloc regimes; while Poland, which through adroit manoeuvre on the part of its ruling party, had avoided attack while saving its reform programme, proceeded in the opposite direction. Although it is true that political discourse did remain unusually free in Poland, in every other respect the hopes of the 'Polish October' turned to dust. Poland's intrinsic economic problems were admittedly unusually intractable. The root of the problem lay in the balance between town and countryside. The attempted collectivisation undertaken in Stalinist times was abandoned and reversed, but Polish small-scale private agriculture, in contrast to Hungary, was not particularly efficient, nor was the distribution mechanism. To conciliate the urban population and especially the industrial workforce, agricultural prices were maintained at an artificially low level, but this in turn removed incentives to agricultural investment and improvement. The economy was thereby locked into a vicious cycle of deterioration to which the government responded with increasing reliance on imports funded by external debt.

Despite these acknowledged serious difficulties there is no reason to think that the problems of the Polish economy were insoluble if national effort and enthusiasm had been mobilised around an effective programme designed to overcome them. The leadership of the PUWP (effectively the Polish CP) was, however, unable to measure up to the challenge. Gomulka had taken over amid enormous popular acclaim, but in office he showed himself to be more concerned with establishing and enhancing his own position than with addressing the urgent problems confronting his nation. Personality deficiencies were undoubtedly part of the explanation. Because of the way he had suffered at the Stalinists' hands, Gomulka had risen to become a popular icon both in the party and among the general public, but he was in fact a vain and rather petty-minded individual as well as lacking in administrative capacity, public charisma or the skills of personal diplomacy. Under his leadership the impetus for change in late 1956 was squandered and the crisis of Polish economic and social relations allowed to fester while top-level intrigue occupied the attention and the energies of the party leadership. Up to the late sixties however, such realities remained concealed from the world at large.

Interesting comparisons can be made with the leadership of the Romanian CP, which in the mid-sixties became concentrated in the hands of a particular individual, Nicolae Ceauçescu, who developed around himself a personality cult worthy of Stalin. Possibly even more than the GDR, Romania was regarded as the most unyieldingly neo-Stalinist of all the bloc countries. To a greater extent than any its leadership chose to play the nationalist card, and although in this case that did not result in rupture with the USSR, it might well have done so. It has already been noted how independence was asserted in foreign policy by the maintenance of friendly relations with China and abstention from the Warsaw Pact. A further symptom was Ceauçescu's insistence on the repayment of foreign loans accumulated before his ascendancy, so that Romania's international debt was cleared and the regime, unlike its Polish counterpart, was obligated to no lender.[17] It was done, however, at the price of living standards, domestic consumption being squeezed to meet the repayments, while the regime used scarce resources trying to inflate its national status by indulging in grandiose building projects. Nationalist obsession had other domestic consequences. Ethnic Romanians, marked out by their Latin language, comprised only about 75 per cent of the country's citizens. Although Stalin had seized and his successors had retained the provinces occupied by the pre-war Russian minority, there remained very large Hungarian one, which made up around half the population of the Transylvanian region.[18] Beginning slowly, but with accelerating pace, it was the regime's policy to Romanianise its national minorities and pursue a policy of ultimate national homogeneity. That meant discrimination against ethnic language and lifestyles, to an extent sufficient to provoke protest with irredentist implications on the part of the Hungarian government, and even a shadowy threat of national conflict between the two socialist neighbours.

The two remaining bloc states of Czechoslovakia and Bulgaria were the ones which pursued courses of the most apparently even tenor during those years. Both remained devotedly loyal satellites and both maintained regimes of neo-Stalinist rigidity, though less intensively and without the personality cult which characterised Romanian communism. They differed substantially in their economic levels, Czechoslovakia being the most advanced state of the bloc after the GDR and Bulgaria the most backward. Czech consumption levels (Slovak ones less so), though much inferior to those of the West, were comparatively high by bloc standards.[19] In the latter country a quiet rehabilitation had taken place of surviving victims from the purge of the early fifties, this being particularly pertinent to Czechoslovakia, which had suffered much the worst one, no doubt on account of its partially westernised culture. There was, however, no question of their persecutors suffering any punishment, or of official apology and compensation. A further common feature of those two countries was that both were led by characterless grey men, individuals who had risen without trace through the ranks of their respective parties; Antonin Novotny in the Czechoslovak case and Todor Zhivkov in the Bulgarian.

The Legal Western Parties

As they surveyed the fortunes of communism on a world scale during those days of relative hope, the members of the Western communist parties which functioned openly but without power or much prospect of getting it, could regret the split and irreparable political division which had sundered the world movement; they might well feel concern that the rising surge of political radicalism in the Western world appeared to be bypassing its CPs and flowing into other channels, but they could convince themselves with a little imagination that the USSR and the bloc of states which adhered to it were, under the sign of peaceful coexistence, embarked upon the right road towards expanding collective wealth, rising cultural standards and the ultimate goal of the society of material abundance and dynamic social harmony. How long such Western communists would have expected the bloc states to need to reach that happy destination would have depended on how much face value they accorded to the official pronouncements emanating from these sources. If the Soviet bloc of the sixties was not the heroic inspiration that the workers' state had been in the thirties, it could at least be regarded as validating the historic scenario of the past and the future that remained central to the communist consciousness, humanity's march from 'primitive communism' to advanced communism through the wilderness of class society.

On the international scene, though, there was a more immediate source of concern and inspiration. The escalating war in Vietnam had all the elements of a David and Goliath contest with the USA in the unmistakable role of villain. The record of the Vietnamese guerrillas and their performance against the mightiest military power on earth using all its resources short of nuclear ones appeared to vindicate the ideology and the social order under which they fought. In contrast to the Korean War, when communists had been isolated in their condemnation of the West, opposition to US intervention in Vietnam was highly popular, and in campaigning against it the Western CPs were very much swimming with the stream.[20] Where they were strong they organised large demonstrations and public protests; where they were weak they participated in those mobilised by other radical elements. In doing so they aimed to declare their indignation against US policy and to assist the Vietnamese to the best of their abilities, but also no doubt to attract fresh support to their parties from this particular 'experience of struggle' and the lessons to be drawn from it. Another favoured means of declaring support for the Vietnamese resistance was the organisation of collections for medical aid.

Of necessity, however, these Western parties could not confine themselves only to carrying out the routine electoral and trade union tasks and functions which they had been largely confined since becoming an institutionalised if isolated element in their respective societies since the Second World War. Nor could they survive indefinitely on a diet of cheering on presumed Soviet bloc successes and colonial revolutions. The nature of their origins and their own revolutionary ideology and traditions could not be simply discarded;[21] to retain any sort of distinction or credibility it was necessary to postulate a possible revolutionary path from the reality of the present consolidated and flourishing capitalist societies to a putative socialist transformation.

The old notions of a sudden revolutionary overturn no longer possessed any credibility – at least until the student radicals briefly revived them – and so the party leaderships of the Western CPs had either explicitly or by implication committed themselves to achieving socialist revolution – for they continued to think in such terms – by utilising the constitutional electoral machinery that had become embedded in their countries' political traditions, in effect to bring about the revolution by majority consent. The pioneers in this respect were probably the British, appropriately enough given that state's historically long experience of constitutionalism, although the tiny size and modest influence of the CPGB ensured that its programme was never likely to be anything other than theoretical. This programme, *The British Road to Socialism*, was published (with Stalin's blessing) in 1952 and replaced the one adopted in 1935 with a title more appropriate to the movement's early days, *For Soviet Britain*. The new perspective argued that because the balance of international forces had changed since 1945 the British revolution could be secured by exploiting a parliamentary majority committed to it, provided that it was underpinned at the same time by an extra-parliamentary mass movement.

It was conceded that, although the working class and its party or parties would necessarily lead that revolution, other social forces would be required to be mobilised in support. Britain was the only country in the world where the working class on the party's definition – manually employed wage-earners and their dependants – represented the majority of the population. If in these circumstances even, other classes would have to be mobilised in support, how much more fully would the same requirement apply in countries where the working class was proportionately smaller?[22] Communist parties in other West European states, including those still underground, therefore adopted the same general principles. The initial strategic aim was the construction of a class alliance under communist hegemony which would have as its immediate objective not a full-blown socialist revolution (for the non-working-class components of the alliance would never adhere to such a programme) but a state of 'advanced democracy' which would prove so advantageous that the logic and attractiveness of advancing to a fully socialist order would become evident and irresistible to the masses.

In most West European states, where communist parties were small and fairly marginal, these theoretical schemes had very limited practical implications. In two, however, communism constituted a major political force, namely France and Italy. At the same time the two parties were as different as mass legal communist parties could be. The PCF and the associated organisations which it controlled, much as they endeavoured to propagandise, recruit, make themselves into poles of attraction, and call for 'common action by all the strata stricken or threatened by the monopolies',[23] had the reputation of forming a closed hermetic society, on the lines of a sectarian church, which sustained itself by its exclusive rituals, relentlessly excluded heretics and dissidents, whose principles were non-negotiable and which was prepared to relate to the wider society only on its own terms.[24] Not surprisingly, the party was also celebrated for its residual Stalinism and Soviet loyalty. The PCI, by contrast, considerably larger in membership and with a much greater national political leverage (though systematically excluded from government coalitions), was distinguished for its openness to the outside society (it was commonplace, for example, for Italian communists to be married and buried in church),[25] as well as for its immensely deeper theoretical sophistication.

The Italians drew upon the legacy of their early leader Antonio Gramsci, whose independence of mind would certainly have resulted in his denunciation and excommunication had he not been removed from the political scene during the later twenties and the thirties by incarceration in the fascist regime's prisons, followed almost immediately by his death. Even so, to protect his reputation his prison writings had to be suppressed during Stalin's lifetime. Gramsci had been involved in the failed revolution in Italy during the years 1919–21 and had spent his time in prison reflecting and writing on the conditions which led to the failure and the success of the fascist takeover in 1922. In doing so he evolved the concept of 'hegemony' (*egemonia*), the ideological ascendancy of a social bloc (rather than a single class, though structured around a dominant one) over subordinate classes, not by brute force and violence or even simple fraud but through its 'organic intellectuals', successfully making its ideas and the perpetuation of its dominance the 'common sense' of the entire society, including its lower orders. He argued (though his arguments, being subjected to the supervision of the prison censor, were coded) that while the Bolsheviks in the more volatile and chaotic conditions of Tsarist Russia had been able to win by a speedy 'war of manoeuvre', in the more stable and integrated societies of western Europe a 'war of position' was required in which the exploited classes had to construct their own 'hegemonic bloc' and succeed first of all in transforming social common sense in a revolutionary direction.

Although the *Prison Notebooks* were not written with the conditions of post-war European democracy in mind, they fitted them admirably for a communist party seeking new directions. The CPI's mass presence, its relationship to Gramsci and its relative independence of Soviet ideological guidance fitted it no less appropriately to exploit and develop his ideas. A further factor pushing it in the same direction was its collective memory of the sectarian errors of the early twenties which had helped to open the road to fascism's triumph. At the first hint of crisis which might stimulate a fascist resurgence,[26] the PCI's instinctive reaction was to place its own programme on the back burner and redouble efforts to close ranks with all other democrats – to recapitulate the strategy of the thirties Popular Front. The programme itself, however, was termed 'The Italian Road' and was elaborated most extensively by Palmiro Togliatti, the CPI leader in the post-war years. At its centre was the concept of structural reform which would 'offer a solution to the country's problems and consolidate a broad alliance, including the petty bourgeoisie and part of the bourgeoisie, around the working class . . . intended to strengthen the working class and its system of alliances and weaken its enemies'.[27] Each set of structural reforms would consolidate working-class (and communist) hegemony ideologically and politically, while drawing the allied classes and strata into voluntary and democratic advance on to new terrain as the logic of structural reform unfolded – it was intended to be a dynamic process.

This notion, while laying down a broad strategic direction overwhelmingly accepted in the PCI's ranks, was nevertheless capable of
radically divergent interpretations, especially in a country as socially
and politically fragmented as Italy. The route through which the
Italian communists sought the unity that was the precondition of
the Italian Road was conceived of as a unity achieved at the level of
the political representatives of the classes with whom co-operation
was pursued, in other words through the established political parties.
The dominant party in Italy being Christian Democracy, not possessing an overall electoral majority but central to all parliamentary
combinations, it was upon the DC that the effort to achieve unity
and structural reform was focused – paradoxically, for the principal
rationale of the Christian Democrats was anti-communism. The PCI,
however, could not ignore it, for it held under its influence large
swathes of the subordinate petty bourgeoisie, particularly in the rural
areas and the south. The communists hoped to resolve the contradiction either by detaching the Christian Democrats' left wing (for it
was an extremely fissiparous formation) or by encouraging left-wing
tendencies within it. Their parliamentary, local government and general political tactics were ordered towards this end.

There was, however, another way of interpreting the Italian Road,
and one which implied a very different political strategy. This alternative defined the left wing of the party in the sixties and postulated
that the PCI, instead of trying to achieve consensus at the party level,
should instead bypass the other parties representing subordinated class
interests and appeal over their heads directly to the members of these
classes, presenting *itself* not only electorally but organisationally as their
best representative and pursuing a much more militant and confronta-
tional line against the monopolies to win material concessions and
social reforms in the interests of both the workers and the other
exploited groups whose interests were being betrayed by their political spokespeople. This line is exemplified in the following statement:
'A class-based union must realise and make known that its demands
undermine, disturb and compromise the capitalist social equilibrium;
they act, that is, in a tendentially anti-capitalist direction.'[28] Such was
the left-wing version of the *via italiana* and was associated particularly
with the name of Pietro Ingrao. Although not without considerable
support, it remained a minority tendency and was decisively defeated
at a succession of party congresses. The initiative remained firmly
with Togliatti and his successors, who spoke for the central bulk of
the party's members in rejection of both the Ingrao left and a right-
wing tendency, also strong, which favoured an even more conciliatory

attitude towards rival political forces and Italian capital.[29] It is indicative of the character of the PCI, however, that these tendencies, despite their fierce and open controversies, were able to co-operate relatively amicably inside the same organisation. That would have been unthinkable in the PCF.

1968

The basic strategic conceptions of the Western communists were to be put to the test more than once during the course of the seventies, but the most dramatic of these episodes was the one which occurred earlier and is inseparably associated with the year 1968, although in fact the crisis ran on into 1969. All of the Western parties were affected in some degree, but the smaller ones were largely confined to the sidelines.[30] It was the two mass parties of France and Italy, especially the former, which found themselves in the position of having to take decisions of the most profound political consequence.

As much as any other observers the communists were taken by surprise by the eruption of student radicalism and activism which reached a climax in 1968, and even more so by the upsurge in working-class militancy which accompanied it. Both of the parties had been inclined to discount the significance of a rising student protest which took place outside the control of their own organisations[31] and certainly they were wholly unwilling to accord it any revolutionary vanguard role. The latter, in the CPs' conceptions, was exclusively reserved to the working class and its Marxist party – i.e. themselves. Their publications did not fail to point out that in the main the students' background was petty bourgeois, only about 10 per cent of their number being able to boast working-class origins. In consequence of these attitudes support drained away from the CP student organisations to their less cautious and more rhetorically heated rivals.

The explosion of 1968 therefore caught both parties largely unawares. The student riots in Paris during May, detonated by relatively minor grievances, were largely spontaneous and largely outside the control of any organisation, even those of the extreme left groups which resonated much more than the PCF did with the then current student attitudes of utopian ardour. Certainly the communist student union was marginalised and unable to exert any influence upon developments. The balance of forces changed dramatically, however, when industrial workers, who had their own reasons for grievance against the Gaullist authorities, began to express sympathy for the

demonstrating students in the repression to which they were subjected by the Parisian riot police, the infamous CRS.

Through the trade union federation which it controlled, the
CGT, the PCF was the major power in French trade unionism. Partly
because of the restiveness and indignation of the CGT members at
the unfolding events and partly because it feared losing the initiative
to the rival socialist and Catholic federations, the party mobilised its
industrial forces for solidarity strikes which very quickly escalated
on 13 May into a general strike gripping the entire country. The
Gaullist regime of the Fifth Republic was paralysed and tottered.[32]
The General himself disappeared from the scene. The question of
political power was concretely posed.

The PCF was derided at the time by left-wing critics – Trotskyists,
Maoists, anarchists and others – and criticised no less in similar subsequent analyses for not seizing the power that was apparently falling
into its lap and thereby missing an irrecoverable opportunity. The
party, however, for better or worse, was wholly consistent in its
strategy and never had the slightest intention of attempting any such
seizure in the classic French manner of 1793, 1848 or 1871, even if
conditions had appeared more favourable still than they actually did.[33]
'For a democracy that will pave the way to socialism!', 'For an authentic modern democracy, consistent with the interests of the French
people!' and 'For a people's government of democratic union!' were
among its slogans. The PCF was committed to the unity of the left
which it believed to be the essential foundation for the establishment
of an 'advanced democracy' and was determined that any successor
regime should include as partners the French Socialist Party and
smaller (constitutional) left-wing formations.[34] However, at the same
time it had to be careful, as the Fifth Republic appeared to crumble,
not to be outmanoeuvered and to avert the formation of a successor
which would exclude and isolate the communists.[35] Accordingly, it
entered negotiations and declared itself ready to take its rightful place
in the anticipated new government, but gave no hostages to fortune.

All such calculations were rendered nugatory when de Gaulle
reappeared in the shape of a broadcast from a military base (where
anyone familiar with his personality might well have guessed he
would have resorted). Announcing material concessions to strikers
and students plus a general election and referendum, he implicitly
threatened civil war if his opponents, pre-eminently the PCF, failed
to play the political game on his terms. The Communist Party, like
the rest of the parliamentary opposition, had no hesitation in conceding and accepting the electoral challenge; in which they were duly

thrashed, as the right wing and all opposition to the left recovered its nerve and mounted monster demonstrations in support of de Gaulle, while the left's morale, in spite of material gains that would have seemed remarkable in other circumstances, deflated dramatically at the reversal of its political hopes and expectations.

The PCF leadership, however, although some of its own intellectual luminaries[36] as well as the leftists criticised its alleged timidity, had no regrets nor any doubts that its strategy and tactics had been the correct ones. The essence of its position was that, superficial appearances to the contrary notwithstanding, the situation in France had been far from ripe for an attempted seizure of power, a tactic which was in any case no longer viable in bourgeois democracies. The French working class, it was claimed, had no such objective in mind. The advance to socialism in France, including the initial stages of advanced democracy, was only possible in the context of electoral majorities and a firm alliance of anti-monopoly forces, and must in addition be protected by legal continuity. Any other course would be adventurist and risk provoking civil war, in which the balance of forces would be overwhelmingly adverse. No doubt the PCF leaders had in mind the horrors that followed the attempted putsch in Indonesia only three years previously. According to Ronald Tiersky:

> In the 'peaceful transition to socialism' doctrine, the key moment in strategy is no longer a general strike or widespread disorder, such as the events of May 1968, rather the 'revolutionary situation' is to be created at the time of general elections: by voting the Left into power the people initiate a process with a potentially revolutionary conclusion.[37]

It might still be argued that from the left's point of view a bold gamble on the seizure of power in Paris (which might well have been possible) could have decisively tilted the balance of forces in its favour and would, in any case, have been preferable to tamely allowing Gaullism to recover its authority and re-consolidate its grass-roots support. In view of the odds against success and the horrendous consequences if the gamble had failed, it may well be concluded that the PCF's course of action was the most sensible one in the circumstances;[38] though a more pertinent criticism is that it failed to take advantage of all the opportunities which were available for extending its influence among students and young people generally by showing a better appreciation of their grievances and outlook.

The CPI was not put in a position of having to take the same life-and-death decisions as its brother party, since the Italian state never came close to collapse, but it was placed in invidious dilemmas and was profoundly affected, to an even greater extent than the PCF, by the quasi-revolutionary events of the two years. Its sophisticated and tightly organised scheme of political, ostensibly revolutionary, development left no room for uncontrollable outbursts of elemental popular feeling, whether by workers, peasants, or students, which tended to destabilise its careful and meticulous strategy of establishing alliances on the basis of programmes which would not frighten away its potential partners.

Conditions in Italian universities in terms of overcrowding, poor instruction and authoritarian management were even worse than in their French counterparts, and the students of the time had also been radicalised by the Vietnam War. The spontaneous protests which developed outside the orbits of the official political student organisations (though often guided by veterans of these parties' youth movements) were at first viewed as unsympathetically by the PCI leadership as the PCF did those in France, but in April 1968, the party, alarmed at the loss of influence it was suffering in the academic milieu, tried to mend its fences with statements of a sympathetic tenor. By then, however, the damage had largely been done and the official PCI was largely sidelined in the student actions which continued throughout the year and into the next.

Though formidable enough, these protests never acquired the dimensions reached in Paris in May 1968, but the industrial action which occurred simultaneously, though never escalating into the kind of general strike which threatened the government's overthrow, was much more protracted and in some senses a great deal more traumatic. It is hardly going too far to suggest that its long-term consequences still haunt Italian politics. The autumn of 1969 came to be termed the 'hot autumn' in consequence of the frequency and bitterness of the strikes. Five and a half million workers, over a quarter of the labour force, participated at one point or another. They broke out over traditional issues of wages, conditions and control of the labour process and on 19 November a general strike calling for reform in the pensions system involved twenty million. By and large these actions were successful and extracted eventually from the government a highly favourable industrial relations act.[39] On the face of things the 'hot autumn' represented a major achievement for militant and mobilised labour, but other aspects were less encouraging. Profitability in Italian industry was compromised, provoking recession in due course. More seriously, from the PCI's viewpoint, their effect in the political sphere (together with the recession they generated) was to provoke a recoil to the right on the part of the non-communist parties, visible among the Christian Democrats and the Socialists and soon reflected in the polls. Most seriously of all, more extreme reactions also emerged – electoral and numerical strengthening of the fascist MSI, episodes of fascist terrorism – sixteen people were killed by a bomb in Milan in 1969 – an and even hints of a military coup.

The PCI leadership was gravely alarmed, as indeed it had reason to be. On the one hand it perceived syndicalist overtones in the way the industrial actions went ahead: the unions, pushed by their rank and file, gave the impression of superseding the party as the principal representative of working-class interests. They were achieving for their members through industrial action what the PCI in the political sphere was unable to deliver. If this was worrying, the political backlash which was being provoked was infinitely more so. The alienation of the petty bourgeoisie by aggressive working-class militancy sent every alarm bell ringing in the PCI Politburo. The leadership, schooled by Gramsci and Togliatti, was haunted by the memory of 1922 and the way in which Mussolini had been able to rally the middle classes around his fascist movement because the working-class organisations of the time had intransigently refused to give any consideration to the interests of other classes.

The party's response, under its new leader Enrico Berlinguer, was to apply the brakes so far as it was able, and while student and worker militancy abated – helped by the recession which the successful strike action had generated – to itself make a turn towards the right, take a yet more conciliatory attitude to the forces and parties it was trying to win over and evolve political reformulations which were the beginning of the notion of 'historic compromise' elaborated later in the seventies. In doing so, however, it suffered more severely than the PCF and brought into being not a minuscule grouplet but a significant (if much smaller) political force to its left. This was the Manifesto Group, named for its journal *Il Manifesto*, around which part of the left of the party coalesced. It was not in any sense Stalinist, or even Leninist, but, with an explicitly positive evaluation of the Chinese regime, advocated a 'direct struggle for socialism' through a 'new kind of struggle which would express immediately some of the contents of a socialist society':

> As far as class alliances were concerned, the Manifesto's most notable innovation with respect to the position of the PCI was their attitude to the intermediate strata . . . the state bureaucracy, workers in the scholastic and cultural spheres, the professions, the sphere of circulation, etc . . . . The object of the left's action towards the vast majority had to be their neutralisation rather than an alliance, because these

strata were beneficiaries of the capitalist system, privileged in many
ways, in fact largely parasitic . . . the workers' struggle had to reduce
their privileges in order to force them to make a clear choice of sides.
This also was analogous to the policy followed by the PSI in 1920–2,
which Togliatti had criticised because it had driven the intermediate
strata into the Fascist camp.[40]

In the upshot, although the dominant element within the PCI leadership, reluctant to lose the talents incorporated in the *Manifesto* group,
tried to reach an accommodation, they were expelled in 1969. It is
possible and even likely that the expulsion occurred on the insistence
of the CPSU, which threatened otherwise to instigate a breakaway
communist party, and that in France Moscow also demanded the
expulsion of Roger Garaudy, a leading intellectual and most vocal
critic of its 1968 policies both in respect to the May events and the
invasion of Czechoslovakia.[41]

Prague Spring and Winter

The CPSU in general endorsed the line adopted by the PCF and the
PCI during the student and industrial turbulence, although not without hints that both of them, and especially the PCI, might be too ready
to compromise that fundamental principle of Marxism–Leninism,
the leading role of the communist party. It was accusation of a similar
sort, this time delivered at full volume, which furnished the pretext
for the next major crisis of the year – the invasion of Czechoslovakia
by the combined forces of the Warsaw Pact (excepting Romania) in
August.

Since the trauma of the 1952 purge trial Czechoslovakia had been
one of the two bloc states – the other being Bulgaria – which had
given the Soviet authorities least cause for concern. It was run by
irreproachable Stalinists, who, when destalinisation became the order
of the day loyally purported to implement it, since that was what was
required, but did so sluggishly and half-heartedly. The Czechoslovak
'people's democracy', like the USSR, ceased to be a regime based upon
perpetual threat of terror, but the reforms did not go much further
than that. A few of the most guilty individuals were dismissed from
their official duties and political prisoners surviving from the purge
era were gradually released, though without any acknowledgment of
the injustice they had suffered. There was no political liberalisation,
nor any cultural one. The token non-communist parties incorporated in the ruling 'National Front' remained purely symbolic and the

internal regime of the CPCz itself remained as rigid as ever, though even its monolithicism could not entirely obliterate national tensions between the Czech and Slovak halves of the Republic.

Economic difficulties precipitated the dramatic political trans-formations which occurred towards the end of the decade. It became clear that the centralised command economy was running out of steam, and was incapable of coping with rising consumer demand generated in part by public knowledge of the expanding consumer societies in neighbouring West Germany and Austria or even in the consumer-orientated bloc state of next-door Hungary. Hungary had employed market mechanisms to produce its relative economic miracle and economic reformers proposed to do the same in Czechoslovakia. The suggestions won much acclaim from the public at large, though less from the industrial workforce, who saw in them potential threats to their working conditions and job security. The significance of these developments was such that the neo-Stalinist regime's structures could not contain them and resulted in an internal revolution at the top of the party. The discredited General Secretary, Antonin Novotny, was sacked in January 1968 and replaced by Alexander Dubcek, the then head of the Slovak section of the party, who took over specifically on a reforming agenda.[42]

Up to this point nothing had happened that was especially contro-versial from the Soviet point of view – bloc leaders, including those in the USSR, who had failed to measure up to their responsibilities in economic management had in the past been given their cards. What followed was a different matter altogether. The reorganisation at the top broke the dam restraining public discontent and expectation, which then turned into an unstoppable cascade. National sentiment and bitter resentment at all the inflictions laid upon the country since 1938 was the motive force and inspired public determination to estab-lish a social and political order in which justice, equality and cultural freedom would prevail. The industrial workforce, initially suspicious of the novel conditions, now embraced the reform process as the reality of national liberation. Centrally important was the fact that the CPCz, implementing the reforms, was popular and respected for the first time since it seized power in 1948. Any question of revers-ing the essentials of the socialist order was not even posed. Dubcek referred to 'socialism with a human face'.

The reform programme acquired its own momentum. Novotny had been allowed at first to retain his other post as state President; soon he was disgraced, removed from all responsibilities and threatened with investigation into corrupt and illegal activities during his period in office. This was symbolic. Stalinist irreconcilables began to be cleared out of the leading ranks of the party and from public office. Steps were taken to open the books on the era of repression and to compensate the victims. Above all, an explosion of cultural, journalistic and academic creativity was let loose as the Czechoslovak intelligentsia hastened to tell the truth about their country's situation and experience, whether in investigative or imaginative terms. An atmosphere of exhilarated liberation was manifest, above all in the capital, Prague. In April the party published its Action Programme, which declared:

> 'We wish to develop in our country a progressive Socialist society free of all class antagonism . . . .
>
> We wish to advance towards the construction of a new model of a Socialist society, profoundly democratic and suited to the Czech situation . . . . Our personal experience as well as scientific Marxism have led us to the unanimous conclusion that these objectives can never be achieved on the old lines and by using rude means which have outlived their usefulness and continuously hold us back.
>
> We can no longer force life into moulds . . . we seek support from the creative ideas of Marxism and from international recognition . . . we are convinced that these measures will help us to free ourselves from the burden which has given our opponents the advantage for so many years, and by means of which they have blunted and prevented the effectiveness of Socialist ideas and negated the attraction of the Socialist example.[43]

The CPSU leadership appears to have been happy enough at the time with Dubcek's election, though very soon afterwards it was warning him in a comradely manner about the danger of 'revisionist' tendencies developing within the CPCz. The mood changed abruptly once the scope and intentions of the reform programme became clear.

Nor was it only in Moscow that suspicion and anger were being voiced. The lesser bloc leaders, only too conscious of what the Czechoslovak example might have in store for them if it infected their own regimes, denounced the direction of developments with greater or lesser degrees of vehemence. The most strident was Walther Ulbricht of the GDR, the East European ruler least inclined to liberalisation in any shape.

The gist of the various accusations directed against Prague was that the CPCz, by effectively abolishing censorship, was allowing anti-socialist tendencies to proliferate and rampage. This could only indicate that it was in the process of abandoning its leading role and might soon be expected, in spite of denials, to allow a genuine multi-party system to develop. More sinister still, the loosening or even extinction of controls was permitting the espionage and subversion agencies of the USA and West Germany to penetrate Czechoslovakia with ease and to work unrestrained to undermine its socialist system and detach it from the socialist bloc.

Whether the Kremlin, East Berlin, Warsaw, Budapest or Sofia really believed any of this is difficult to be sure. What is clear is that they feared the example the Czechoslovaks were setting might spread beyond the country's borders, and that a forcible popular reformation of the systems of government and party management would sweep away the apparatus of bureaucratic regimentation in the lands of barrack socialism – along with the party bureaucrats who managed it. At best they would be liable to go the way of Novotny and might well experience something much worse. In the depths of their souls, for all their carefully cultivated stances of historic optimism and Marxist–Leninist invincibility, they were profound pessimists. They were aware at this level of how lacking in genuine popularity their regimes really were and how attractive the Czechoslovak renewal looked. These leaders very likely did really think that the ultimate end-point of the Czechoslovak developments would be a reversion to capitalism, for again at some deep level they probably were convinced that while the majority of a nation might at some point opt for socialism, they would not continue to sustain their choice it unless compelled to do so – for socialism, despite (or because of) its collective advantages, necessarily imposed individual sacrifice and discipline which only a minority were capable of accepting voluntarily.[44] Not for nothing was the Berlin Wall a prime symbol of 'actually existing socialism'.

Such considerations did not of course feature in the official statements when in August, following discussions which seemed to have resolved the disagreements but were almost certainly intended as a smokescreen while military preparations were finalised, the armies of the Warsaw Pact states suddenly invaded Czechoslovakia, arrested all top members of the CPCz and government who could be rounded up[45] and spirited them away to Moscow. Instead, the perils of supposed counter-revolution in Czechoslovakia were cited, along with those of nefarious secret intervention by West Germany and the United States. At first it was pretended that the intervention had been invited by leading members of the Prague government itself, but when none, even among the surviving neo-Stalinists, could be found to substantiate this the line had to be changed. The intention had been, under a flimsy and unconvincing cover of legality, to establish a new government subservient to the USSR, but when this proved impossible the Dubcek leadership itself was pressured and intimidated in Moscow until it agreed to do what was wanted, then returned to Prague in an atmosphere of total demoralisation to implement the counter-reforms under the supervision of Soviet troops:

> Should the recent developments [i.e. resistance to dismantling the Prague Spring] .... continue to impede the way out of the present situation, the leadership of the Party, the government, the state and the National Assembly will come before the Party and the people with inevitable measures. It may well be that these measures will appear undemocratic .... I think that this is sufficiently clear. Naturally there would be other politicians seeing to that. You may think this is a harsh way of putting things, but we are convinced that it is the truth.[46]

Once 'normality' had been restored all the erstwhile proponents of the Prague Spring were removed from their offices and expelled from the CPCz, to be replaced by more compliant apparatchiks, who proceeded to carry through an intensive, though bloodless, purge of the party, the media and academia.

The Soviet leaders were left with no alternative but to acknowledge that they had invaded Czechoslovakia (they termed it 'intervention') against the will of its communist party and popular masses. Their justification was formalised in the infamous 'Brezhnev Doctrine' enunciated by the General Secretary in November. According to this the respect for national rights and the sovereign independence of national CPs which Moscow had constantly affirmed since the fifties were not to be understood in an abstract sense but in relation to the global class struggle. Therefore the socialist community was entitled to take action if one of its members, by opening the door to counter-revolution, endangered the collective safety of them all. 'Naturally the Communists of the fraternal countries could not allow the socialist states to be inactive in the name of an abstractly understood sovereignty, when they saw the country stood in peril of an antisocialist degeneration.'[47] Brezhnev did not hesitate to rub in the lesson in his speech at the CPSU's 24th Congress in 1971, in front of Czechoslovak fraternal delegates:

> The Czechoslovak events were a fresh reminder that in the countries which have taken the path of socialist construction the internal socialist forces ... may, in certain conditions, become active and even mount direct counter-revolutionary action in the hope of support ... from imperialism ....

> The danger of Right-wing revisionism, which seeks on the pretext of 'improving' socialism, to destroy the revolutionary essence of Marxism–Leninism . . . has been fully brought out in this connection.
>
> It was an attempt to strike in this way at the positions of socialism in Europe as a whole and to create favourable conditions for a subsequent onslaught against the socialist world by the most aggressive forces of imperialism.

He went on to repeat the lie that Moscow had received appeals for intervention from 'Party and state leaders, Communists and working people', and therefore 'We and the fraternal socialist countries then jointly took a decision to render internationalist assistance to Czechoslovakia in defence of socialism.'[48] Moreover, in the enunciation of the 'Doctrine' no distinction in principle was made between Europe and any other part of the world. The Chinese leaders, who abhorring all that the Czechoslovaks were doing, had condemned the invasion for purely opportunist reasons, interpreted the Doctrine as an implied threat to themselves.

The impact of these events upon the communist movement internationally was unprecedented and far-reaching – though paradoxically, when viewed in perspective, not as profound or cataclysmic as might have been expected. For the first time ever the behaviour of a Soviet government was condemned by a large number of other communist parties that were in basic loyalty to the CPSU but had approved in greater or lesser measure during 1968 the changes occurring in Czechoslovakia. The severity of these condemnations varied, with that of the CPI being the most forceful, as might be expected,[49] and that of the PCF among the most restrained. (The PCF leaders, prior to the invasion, had refused a proposal from the Italians to issue a joint declaration of solidarity with the CPCz and later pretended that the submission made by the Czechoslovak leaders in Moscow was a voluntary one.) The dissident parties did not thereby repudiate their stances in 1956, but argued that the two situations were wholly dissimilar – in Hungary there had indeed been a manifest danger of counter-revolution (so they claimed) while in Czechoslovakia perfect calm had prevailed and the communist party had remained in unchallenged control. The unstated presupposition of the critical CPs was, however, really no different from that of the bloc. The former, too, recognised, though they never admitted it, how unpopular 'actually existing socialism' really was, and they saw emerging in the Prague Spring the hitherto unknown example of a ruling communist party which would actually command popular enthusiasm – with consequent major implications for their own public standing and credibility.

All the Soviet-aligned parties which condemned the invasion were in Europe (though not all European ones did so). Those elsewhere either swallowed the stories of imminent counter-revolution or were too closely bound to the CPSU by material ties to dissent. The latter were exemplified by the CPs of Vietnam and Cuba, both of which might have been expected to be especially sympathetic to the situation of a small country under attack from a superpower. Both, however, were far too reliant on Soviet support and supplies to do anything other than pronounce their approval – though Castro's was very qualified.[50] Nor did any of the objectors take their criticism to the stage of breaking relations with the CPSU or re-evaluating their basically positive assessment of the Soviet bloc and the historic direction in which it was headed. The essence of their posture was that it was sometimes both necessary and salutary to point out the errors of a close friend. Before very long the episode was bracketed off, so to speak, and normal fraternal relations resumed. Most of the dissident parties continued to participate in the work of and contribute articles to the Prague-based *Problems of Peace and Socialism*, which never printed anything other than approval for the invasion. In the May 1973 issue for example, Vasil Bilak, one of the leading Czech Stalinists, was referring to the 'attempt of domestic reactionaries and international imperialism at a counter-revolutionary coup' (p. 4). The Italians, however, appear to have stopped writing for it.

The long-run implications did not disappear, however, any more for international communism than for the Czechoslovaks themselves. The measure of goodwill which the USSR had gradually re-established in Eastern and Western Europe since 1956 was recklessly squandered and the poison penetrated much deeper still. In the words of Julius Braunthal,

> The frustration by the Soviet Union of the Czechoslovak experiment of creating a 'new model of Socialism' was the heaviest blow which Socialism had ever suffered – a blow of even more importance than that which had struck it through Fascism. For while Fascism had been able physically to suppress the Socialist parties, it had not been able to kill their spirit; this continued to live on in the masses . . . .

> Moscow's struggle against 'revisionism' is, on the other hand, a crusade against the very spirit of Socialism . . . the reimposition of a system which suppressed the elementary rights of freedom . . . shattered faith in a gradual transformation of that Russian autocracy which had made the Soviet Union into one of the great reactionary forces of the present age.[51]

Neither the critique of the dissident CPs, nor the Czechoslovaks' anger and despair, was directed against the society of planned economy and public ownership or against Leninism as such. One popular theme of the protesting mural art in in Prague was a representation of Lenin in tears. Neither socialism nor communism was immediately discredited, even in Czechoslovakia. It took another two decades of continuous repression to achieve that.

Polish Atavisms

Although events in Czechoslovakia monopolised all the headlines relating to the Soviet bloc in 1968, developments in Poland during that year were taking a course which, though incomparably less publicised, were if anything even more sinister and equally significant as a sign of internal rot in the ruling parties which had only been superficially destalinised.

The promise of the Polish October of 1956 was not fulfilled. Under Gomulka's stewardship the regime lapsed back into classically rigid patterns of administration, albeit with what was for the bloc an unusual degree of cultural openness – though even that had its limits. Most seriously, in terms of public satisfaction, the economy remained intractable and mired in the insoluble contradiction between low-productivity agriculture and urban consumer demands. Gomulka's own vain and irascible personality did not assist in providing effective and co-ordinated leadership from the top. As during the course of the decade the problems intensified rather than being resolved, the same kind of public dissatisfaction as had propelled the changes in Czechoslovakia was manifested, and duly reflected in the organs of the ruling party.

The outcome, however, was dramatically different. Pressured from all sides and finding his own position under threat, Gomulka leaned for support increasingly upon his internal affairs minister General Mieczyslaw Moczar, a veteran of the underground wartime campaign and subsequently of the Stalinist security apparatus. Moczar possessed a considerable following among the veterans, and he utilised this to launch a political campaign against the dissident intelligentsia. He found his pretext in student riots, which were severely repressed, and their instigators stigmatised as 'fascists, counter-revolutionaries or any kind of bourgeoisie'.[52] The General, with Gomulka's blessing, then turned to inciting the traditional anti-semitism endemic in Polish popular culture, though for appearance sake the term 'Zionist' was used in place of 'Jew', a code that all listeners readily understood. The purpose behind the campaign was also traditional – to divert on to scapegoats, disloyal anti-national elements, responsibility for economic and other failures.[53] Edward Ochab was moved to write to Gomulka (though not to declare openly): 'As a Pole and a communist it is with the greatest outrage that I protest against the anti-Semitic campaign being organised in Poland by various dark forces.'[54]

The campaign poisoned public life in Poland. It resulted in sweeping dismissals of Jews from positions of public responsibility, including the highest, and eventually provoked the emigration of around 30 000 of the 35 000 Jews living in the country. It saved Gomulka only temporarily, however. In 1970 attempts to break the economic log-jam by raising food prices brought on large-scale riots in the coastal cities and among the industrial workforce. Gomulka, having used the military to quell them, could not hold out against public outrage and was thrown from power and into disgrace at the beginning of 1971. His successor, Edward Gierek, was a particularly unfortunate choice, an unimaginative bureaucrat who had been deeply involved in the anti-semitic excesses. The economic policies he instituted drove the country into an even deeper mess and General Moczar remained at the centre of affairs until 1981.

'Socialist Internationalism'

The phrase 'socialist internationalism' was never far from the mouths (or the pens) of Soviet spokespersons during those years or for more than another decade thereafter. What they meant by it was the subordination of lesser communist regimes and parties to the perspectives and policies of the USSR when it came to the crunch (rather than in detail, as in the time of Stalin). That was the reality behind formal declarations of equality and sovereignty – the CPSU claimed for itself the right to determine what was in the best interests of the international movement. Moscow demonstrated, moreover, in 1968 its continuing determination and power to enforce its authority in its own designated sphere. Yet it was clear to any observer at the end of the sixties that the communist movement had ceased to be an international unity and was becoming steadily less so. At the last international conference of the parties, convened in Moscow in 1969 but without such important participants among others as the Chinese, Vietnamese and Yugoslavs (the Cubans sent only an observer), the final document dropped the loaded term 'proletarian internationalism' and replaced it with 'voluntary co-operation and solidarity'. It went on to refer to 'principles of sovereign independence for each party, non-interference in internal affairs and respect for free choice of different roads in the struggle for social change'. Though all this was of course in blatant contradiction to the state of affairs prevailing in Eastern Europe, it was a sign of the times that the CPSU accepted such notions, even if only on paper.

The breach with China and the bitter hostility which pervaded relations between the two powers was the most evident symptom, but within the Soviet bloc itself, despite Czechoslovakia, the individual party-states were unmistakably moving along different paths to divergent national agendas. Poland, the GDR, Hungary and Romania, though united by a common socio-political order, presented strikingly different features in their internal regimes and their political stances. Among the parties outside the bloc diversity was even more marked, both in the degree of criticism of Soviet policy which they permitted themselves and in the programmes they developed for achieving the socialist revolution – within national bounds – which they nevertheless did continue to adhere to as a common if abstract objective; likewise they were united in the conviction of slow but irresistible world advance towards socialism for which the USSR remained the working model, though not to be slavishly imitated.

Though much less clearly visible and obscured by the continuing lustre of Soviet space triumphs, the first signs were beginning to appear of endemic and irresolvable contradictions in the system of centralised economic management to which the regimes and the movement were committed by their nature. After decades of unquestionable if violently spasmodic growth, which Khrushchev could take as a fixed datum for his projections, long-term erosion started to set in. There was no immediate absolute decline, but in the USSR the rate of growth was tending to tail off, agricultural problems remained unresolved and statistical indicators of social welfare showed stagnation or retreat.[55] No crisis was yet apparent or even on the horizon in the Soviet Union itself, but in the Eastern European bloc countries it had arrived, albeit patchily, and had been responsible for the political convulsions which had seized some of them. It was a trend destined to grow stronger as the years passed.

6

Indian Summer, 1970–1981

If by the end of the sixties world communism appeared to be severely discredited and on the defensive both politically and ideologically, the following decade witnessed an impressive recovery, principally, though by no means exclusively, on account of successes in the Third World. Remarkably enough, this occurred with hardly any change of personnel at the top of the Soviet leadership, which by the end of the decade could only be described as a gerontocracy. Most notably the General Secretary, Brezhnev, despite failing health and being technically dead for a few moments during an illness in the middle of the period, continued in office, acquiring the additional responsibility of Soviet President.

To be sure, the early years of the seventies did not seem particularly promising either. In 1970 the Chilean communists, following electoral victory for Salvador Allende, a socialist whom they supported as presidential candidate, became part of a government of Popular Unity. At the time it looked like a very significant breakthrough. The CP, in this position, conscientiously followed strategies similar to those the West European communists had committed themselves to or were in the process of doing so. They did not try to take advantage of their governmental positions or their party organisation to attain dominance over their political partners, or mobilise militias. They stuck rigidly to constitutional principles,[1] tried only by persuasion to broaden the government's base of support and they did not attempt to subvert the military. It was all in vain. The freely elected

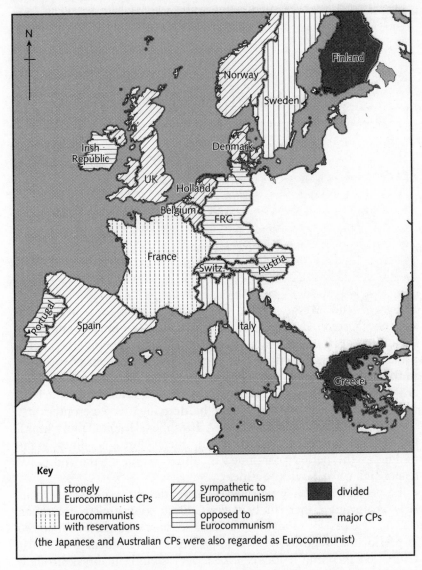

Figure 7 The Eurocommunist divide, *c.*1976

regime, which polls suggested was growing in popularity, was destabilised economically by covert US intervention and overthrown in September 1973 by a right-wing military coup which engaged in an orgy of terror and suppression. It looked like a bad omen for the electoral road to socialism.

Matters went no better in the very different circumstances of the Sudan, one of the few African states with a strong and influential com-

munist party. This party *had* subverted the military, and very successfully, for it was at the centre of a series of coups which steadily
moved the regime to the left. In 1971, however, internal divisions led
to a further but this time unsuccessful coup attempt, which resulted
in the execution of the communist leaders and the destruction of
the party.

There were some diplomatic successes to counterbalance these
defeats, mostly in the shape of favourable alignments by Third World
regimes, but these were overshadowed by another diplomatic development of nightmare proportions, namely rapprochement between
the USA and China, which had the potential of creating an overwhelmingly powerful hostile coalition against the Soviet bloc. With
this departure, with which Mao repudiated the central theme of his
propaganda and rhetoric over the previous decade, Beijing abandoned all its pretensions as an international revolutionary centre and
nakedly exhibited its great-power interests.[2] It was for all that no less
formidable on the international diplomatic stage, especially as it had
by then manufactured its own nuclear weaponry.

1974

Dramatic turnaround commenced in 1974 when a number of very
reactionary Western-aligned regimes fell with a resounding crash and
in doing so created considerable openings for communist party or
else Soviet diplomatic resurgence. The first to go was in the most
unexpected quarter – western Europe. In Portugal a regime of fascist
inspiration had existed since the twenties (it had, in the post-war era,
erected a democratic façade so as to qualify for international respectability and membership of NATO). The final years of its dictator,
Salazar, were dominated by vain efforts to suppress insurrection in
Portugal's extensive colonial empire, the last one remaining from the
era of classic imperialism. His successor did not rule for very long
before being overthrown in a relatively peaceful revolution led by
junior army officers exasperated by the country's political backwardness and the unwinnable colonial war.

Two factors converged so as to make it appear for a time possible
or even likely that the Portuguese communists would succeed in coming to power and setting up a People's Democracy on the Atlantic
seaboard. The first was the existence of an exceptionally strong underground CP, small but determined, under an able if Stalinist-minded
leader, which had gained great credibility in the struggle against the
dictatorship, especially in the south of the country among industrial

workers and the landless peasantry working the great estates. It now emerged as by far the best organised and grew rapidly to become the largest single political force in the country. The second was the rapid radicalisation of the armed forces themselves, who soon drove out the original conservative front-man of the revolution and whose ascendant leaders established close links with the PCP and relied upon its political advice.

The PCP was a very different entity from the other West European CPs, whether in France or Italy – or for that matter neighbouring Spain, despite the similarity of the circumstances the two parties confronted. The Portuguese communists were undeviating Soviet loyalists and were sometimes, with the prestige of their illegality, used by the CPSU in the late sixties to answer criticisms emanating from the other Western parties. Their internal perspectives reflected this orientation: they preferred to rely upon their own strength in establishing a vanguard role rather than going to elaborate lengths to establish links with other potential opposition ('anti-monopoly') forces to their right. During the course of 1974 the test of practice appeared to bear out the soundness of the PCP's strategy, for politically it appeared to be unstoppable and dominated all the revolutionary committees as a regime of public ownership and quasi-soviet government was introduced.

A second political upheaval in Europe later in the year, though it did not pay quite such exceptional dividends for the local communists, altered the political balance greatly in their favour. Like their Portuguese counterparts the Greek communists, though they commanded considerable popular sympathy, were underground and had been since their defeat in the civil war of the forties, driven even deeper after the colonels' coup of 1967. Unlike the PCP, which had maintained its unity and cohesion in the underground, the KKE had split between a hardline neo-Stalinist majority and a reforming Western-CP orientated group. These were known respectively as the communist parties of the Exterior and Interior. Their subsequent political evolution was extremely complex and incoherent, with further splits and recombinations,[3] which certainly reduced their effectiveness. The contrast with Portugal is striking.

On mainly Greek-speaking Cyprus the local communists, known as AKEL, dominated the labour movement and were of considerable political importance under the island's President, Archbishop Makarios, whom they served loyally and constitutionally. The political set-up on Cyprus was a source of offence to the Greek junta, who also coveted union between the island and their mainland regime. In the summer of 1974 they instigated an anti-Makarios coup by their adherents, under the slogans of right-wing Greek nationalism. The threat which this implied to Cyprus's Turkish-speaking minority provoked a Turkish invasion and seizure of the northern third of the island. Discredited, the junta collapsed, as did the Cyprus coup, and Greek democracy re-emerged. The left, however, was overwhelmingly dominated by the socialist party PASOK, created by the charismatic politician Andreas Papandreou. Nevertheless the communists, now legal, albeit much weakened, were able to establish a political niche for themselves, with parliamentary representation, and PASOK's brand of socialism was renowned as being unusually left-wing, thus holding out hopes for future collaboration. In global terms the events in Greece certainly represented a set-back for the ambitions of the USA, whose clients the colonels had been, and an advance, if modest, for communism internationally.

The US lost something much more materially important in 1974 as well as a key international position, thanks to the volcanic revolution which overturned the Ethiopian monarchy along with the country's social and political structures. This African kingdom, best described as feudal in its social framework, dominated by a tribal aristocracy and the Coptic Christian church, was wholly within the US political sphere and hosted listening-stations for intercepting Middle East and African radio traffic. The revolution began with a coup against the decrepit emperor, Haile Selassie, by the military, the most modernised element in Ethiopian society, and proceeded with ever-deepening ferocity to internal disintegration of the country and the extermination of the aristocracy in a fashion reminiscent of the French Revolution.

The political convolutions of the revolution, as well as being spectacularly bloody, were indescribably complex. No communist party attached to the world movement existed there. The military chief who emerged through the exterminatory political process to head the central government, Mengistu Haile Mariam, however, adopted Marxist–Leninist pretensions and closely aligned the country (or what he controlled of it) with the Soviet bloc. He proceeded to receive material and military assistance from the USSR and its allies; both direct naval support from Soviet warships in the Red Sea and a substantial complement of Cuban military advisers. At a stroke a highly important African state was added, not to the Soviet bloc proper, but to the outer ring of 'states of a socialist orientation'. The prize was gained at a price, however, for in allying closely with revolutionary Ethiopia the USSR forfeited its relations with the Somalian regime, Ethiopia's long-standing enemy and claimant to some of its territory. The Somalian rulers now passed into the American camp. In addition, in a move of singular cynicism on Moscow's part, it now turned from supporting to attacking the guerrilla movement which had been fighting to establish independence form Ethiopia in the Eritrean coastal strip.

In the course of the year an ambiguous development from the Soviet point of view, though more clearly positive from the perspective of the non-ruling parties, was the political convulsion gripping the principal enemy, the United States itself, with the discredit and fall of its President Richard Nixon, a long and implacable enemy of communism and the USSR as well as architect of the emerging Sino-US alliance. Brezhnev had established reasonable relations with Nixon and instability in the USA was not necessarily to Soviet advantage, for it added uncertainty to the relationship, but the US governmental deadlock in the later part of 1974 retarded the state's ability to function as a superpower and leader of the Western coalition.

Year of Victories

The year 1975 marked a climax of post-war success both for the communist movement at large and specifically for the USSR in its international role – although within that pattern there was also one significant and major disappointment. In the Iberian Peninsula the last surviving fascistoid regime in Europe finally expired in Spain along with its founder, General Franco. In conditions of restored democracy the Spanish Communist Party re-emerged, strongly supported among industrial workers and tempered by its long sojourn underground. Like its Portuguese counterpart it was expected to play a major role in democratic Spain, though in fact it did not. The greater setback (albeit a relative one) occurred, however, across the border in Portugal.

The PCP, as noted previously, had defied the recent trend prevalent in West European communism to seek political alliances across a broad social spectrum, combined with discreet distancing of those parties from Kremlin policies or complete identification with the Soviet model. In the circumstances of the Portuguese revolution its approach did not appear initially to be any disadvantage: the party grew rapidly, expanded its mass base, exercised control in the grassroots revolutionary committees and enjoyed much influence at the centre of affairs. Naturally it also evoked a great deal of hostility, which existed everywhere but was concentrated geographically in the northern part of the country, where social relations were less polarised than in the south and a middle class of independent peasants and urban petty bourgeoisie was of proportionately greater social weight.

Indigenous anti-communists as well as Western chancelleries viewed the situation with the utmost alarm, but were deprived of the usual weapon of last resort in such circumstances, military intervention, because the army itself was radicalised and its leaders on excellent terms with the PCP. From the party's viewpoint the circumstances appeared almost too promising to be true – as indeed was the case. Scorning class alliances, the PCP relied upon the mobilisation of its mass base among industrial and agricultural workers and its influence with the military leaders. These proved to be insufficient. Since the general atmosphere was so left-wing that no openly right-wing force possessed very much credibility, a Socialist Party to rival the communists was put together more or less from nothing with the organisational and material assistance of the West European socialist parties. An intense propaganda offensive was launched, again with the generous encouragement and support of the Socialist International.[4] Elections to a Constituent Assembly in April 1975 confirmed that the PCP was far from commanding majority adherence among the electorate, and with this demonstration it became possible for the anti-communists at home and abroad to win over a crucial element of the military leaders and so remove the PCP's protectors from power. A bungled coup attempt by leftist officers in November accelerated its defeat and it was driven out of government in 1976. For all that, the situation remained an incomparable improvement over what existed prior to April 1974. In place of a hunted underground organisation Portugal now had a mass CP with great influence in labour organisations, though not in central government.

The Portuguese revolution did not affect only mainland Portugal, but its extensive overseas empire as well. The irrepressible colonial wars in the African colonies had been among the principal circumstances which had provoked the revolution and there was no question but that the empire would be dismantled in its wake. In the southern African colonies of Angola and Mozambique and West African Guinea-Bissau, the successor regimes, emerging from the guerrilla struggle, to which power was transferred, were all 'of a socialist orientation' – i.e. left-wing and well disposed towards the Soviet bloc.[5] The Marxist MPLA in Angola was challenged by enemies who had the backing of the US and South African governments and were supported by the latter by means of a full-scale invasion. It is unlikely that the MPLA on its own would have been able to cope with such an emergency, but was saved by a Cuban expeditionary force which crossed the Atlantic and in 1976 defeated the invaders and enabled the MPLA to establish its authority over most of the country. At the time it represented a great victory for the bloc, although in subsequent years both Angola and Mozambique were to be worn down to destruction by South African-backed guerrillas.

Important though these successes were, they were entirely over-shadowed by the sensational military defeats inflicted on the USA in south-east Asia. Technically the US, unlike its colonial French predecessors, did not suffer the actual collapse for it had withdrawn its own troops in 1973 under the impact of unsustainable losses and escalating domestic opposition and handed over the maintainance of its tottering position to local surrogates – the regimes it had installed in South Vietnam and Cambodia. Both of them fell in April 1975; Cambodia first to the peasant guerrillas of the Khmer Rouge. In due course the aftermath was to turn into what was proportionately the most grisly episode in communist history, but when the citizens of Phnom Penh welcomed the Khmer Rouge units as liberators into the city there was no way of anticipating, abroad any more than in Cambodia, the manner in which the Pol Pot regime was about to conduct itself.

The fall of Saigon at the end of the month represented the most profound political overturn since the Chinese Revolution, and its meaning was underlined by newsreel footage of US embassy staff flee-ing ignominiously by helicopter from the roof of their premises. Com-munists around the world (along with other well-wishers) rejoiced, convinced that historic justice had been attained, right had triumphed over wrong and that the irresistibility of the long-term global revolu-tion had been affirmed. The Chinese leadership joined in the con-gratulations – they could scarcely do otherwise – though they must have had mixed feelings in the light of their new relations with the USA and the definite orientation of the Vietnamese regime towards the USSR.

The US position in former French Indo-China had evaporated (Laos soon became effectively a Vietnamese protectorate), but the damage to its prestige and the credibility of its anti-communist project was much more important. On another front, too, 1975 brought a con-solidation of Soviet strength, with Western recognition of and appar-ent long-term legitimacy for the political order which it had imposed upon Eastern Europe. Since the West German social democrats had been elected to office at the end of the sixties their government had been engaged in a far-reaching attempt to reach accommodation with the East European states in general and its communist neighbour in particular. Under the term Ostpolitik it involved the renunciation of West German claims upon the eastern territories that had been acquired by Poland at the end of the war, mutual recognition of the two German states and the establishment of diplomatic relations with the countries of the Warsaw Pact.[6]

During the early seventies the process of détente was broadened and in 1975 reached its culmination with the Helsinki Conference, the Final Declaration of which, though it did not accord formal ratification to previously disputed east European borders, implicitly recognised the political outcome of the Second World War and the Yalta agreement; the West thereby abandoning its ostensible hopes, abstract though they had become, of pushing communist hegemony back to the Soviet border. The Declaration also contained phrases on respect for human rights which Moscow never took seriously, but could be and were employed at a later date when relations had again deteriorated, as a propaganda weapon against the Soviet government. In the immediate term, however, Helsinki represented a big diplomatic triumph for Moscow.

The mid-seventies therefore appeared on the face of things to bring unexampled, even though not quite unqualified success to the communist movement which the Soviet regime purported to lead – even if its important Western brother parties were growing increasingly sensitive about the justification for that leadership or whether it ought to exist. On a longer perspective, communist theorists believed they could detect the long-awaited signs of debility in the capitalist system. The US economy itself was labouring under the accumulated strains of its global role and the heritage of the Vietnam War, with mounting debt and inflation. The capitalist world economy itself was in turmoil in consequence of the Arab–Israeli war of 1973 and the long-term oil price rise which had resulted from it. The major capitalist economies were experiencing unprecedented levels of inflation and their political systems were showing the strain. Though not obviously related, President Nixon's debacle, the escalation of armed conflict in Northern Ireland, the industrial insurgency which drove the Heath government from office, the fall of the Iberian and Greek regimes, and lesser political crises in Western Europe, could be viewed as part of a consistent pattern. If the long post-war boom was coming to an end with consequent mass discontent, genuine socialist solutions could be expected to reach the top of the agenda and the parties which embodied them to occupy an increasingly central role. They perceived a crisis and hoped that it could become the starting-point for structural transformations in their societies. The mass parties of France, Spain and Italy found their discussions of the route to power taking on more concrete dimensions (with the failures in Chile and Portugal contrasting warnings of what to avoid) and finding a viable strategy for advancing along the road to power became an increasingly urgent priority.

Eurocommunism

Principles

At its congress in 1976 the PCF, following the Italian, Spanish and several smaller CPs, resolved to delete from its phraseology the phrase 'dictatorship of the proletariat' – a decision that was rightly seen as momentous and highly significant, for it was a term that had been central to Leninist perspectives ever since the October Revolution. The concept originated with Marx himself and indeed, as communists never tired of pointing out, did not have the connotations which the word 'dictatorship' acquired in the twentieth century. It derived, in Marx's formulation, from the ancient Roman practice of suspending the normal constitution and conferring temporary absolute powers upon a single individual in order to deal with a pressing emergency. (Literally, 'dictator' has the meaning of 'commander', which was also the original sense of 'emperor'.) Marx intended it to denote certainly a regime of exceptional government in which the ground rules of bourgeois legality would be suppressed, but assuredly not one of arbitrary authoritarianism. His concrete example was the short-lived Paris Commune of 1871, whose political arrangements had been ultra-democratic.

Marx envisaged the 'dictatorship of the proletariat' as a form of democratic state controlled by representatives of the working class, bridging the interval between the overthrow of bourgeois rule and the establishment of the society of abundance which would have no need for a state of any sort, and 'rule over men' would be replaced by the 'administration of things'. (We leave aside here the real practicality of such a conception.) In the days of the Second International it remained a purely theoretical construct, deferred to on account of its origins but having no relevance to the activity or programmes of the socialist parties. Lenin took over the idea from Marx and he took it seriously, but he also greatly amplified it in one of his central writings, *The State and Revolution*. The circumstances of the composition of this work are significant, for Lenin wrote it when in hiding from the Provisional Government of Russia at a time when the Bolsheviks were being suppressed, and it must have appeared very unlikely that they would ever come to power. It has therefore to be regarded as a form of political testament, a summing-up of his conclusions on the reality of political relations in class societies and the essential nature of a workers' regime.

Lenin did not literally contradict Marx's version, but he removed from the original concept the emphasis on exceptionality which existed in Marx. In *The State and Revolution* dictatorship is seen as the normal condition of *any* class society short of full communism. All states whatsoever embody the dictatorship of their ruling classes and exist primarily, whatever their other incidental functions, to suppress the governed classes and keep them in subjection. The most democratic of existing states or any such democratic state imaginable are in reality the dictatorship of the bourgeoisie – though of course this can take varying forms, some more favourable than others to proletarian interests. Moreover, Lenin was convinced that under the stress of war and rising social discontent the ruling classes of the existing democracies were tending increasingly towards more authoritarian forms of government. On this understanding the proletarian state, being a state and with the primary purpose of keeping in subjection the overthrown bourgeoisie and repelling its foreign accomplices, must therefore also *ipso facto* be a dictatorship – to define it in those terms was not to say anything about its actual instruments of government or means of rule. It is clear that the essence of this viewpoint had been present in Lenin's mind for a long time, for at the beginning of the 1905 revolution he had envisaged a revolutionary provisional government which would represent the 'democratic dictatorship of the proletariat and peasantry': although soon becoming convinced that the very democratic soviets then emerging were a more appropriate form of the proletarian dictatorship.

The regime under both Lenin and Stalin was therefore unashamedly a dictatorship but not, in Soviet eyes, as the West understood the term. Following the expansion of Soviet power after the Second World War the regimes of the 'people's democracies' did not initially have their theoretical status precisely defined in Leninist categories. Officially the working class was leading the regimes but not exercising its dictatorship, as it allegedly did in the USSR. They were not supposed to be dictatorships of the proletariat, but certainly not bourgeois dictatorships either: were they therefore on the way to assuming the former identity? The question was left unresolved until the imposition of Stalinist systems after 1947, when the 'dictatorship of the proletariat' was declared to be in operation through a formal parliamentary system rather than a formal soviet one. The Western parties continued to assert the 'dictatorship of the proletariat' as their political objective, but the notion increasingly contradicted the programmes they advanced in their endeavours to win popular backing and electoral credibility. It had, in fact, become by the sixties no more than a theoretical talisman.

For these reasons alone it might well appear expedient as all three of these larger CPs, along with several of their minor brethren, geared themselves up in the mid-seventies to exert enhanced political influence or even hope for imminent partnership in government, to dispense with the embarrassing phraseology. The image that the word 'dictatorship' had acquired in the consciousness of the Western public cônstituted an additional and no less pressing motivation. The leaderships who proposed the change nevertheless had to overcome considerable resistance at the grass-roots of their parties (even in the PCI), among members who regarded the pragmatic manoeuvres of their parties as regrettable if unavoidable concessions to the times, hankered still after a Leninist and straightforwardly revolutionary approach, and therefore continued to cling to the traditional terminology.[7]

What it amounted to was an embrace of the established democratic systems of Western Europe (in Spain newly-established) not merely as a form of advanced bourgeois politics which had certain advantages for the working class, to be superseded in due course – which was the Leninist view – but in principle as true democracy. This was combined with an undertaking to always play the electoral game and not abandon it if opportunity offered. The democratic posture was accompanied with critique of a further aspect of the Leninist theory of the state. According to *The State and Revolution* the victorious proletariat could not simply take over the state machine (the legislative, administrative and coercive apparatus) of the defeated bourgeoisie, but must 'smash' it and replace it with an alternative apparatus of its own loyal personnel. The new thinking judged the bourgeois state to be no monolithic machine of repression and coercion but an ambiguous site of contestation upon which the workers' parties and the popular forces must try to establish positions. Finally, it was clear that the three big parties – though the PCF went less far than the other two – would, if admitted to government responsibility, not press for solving the crisis by means of a frontal assault on their national capitalisms but would indeed work to restore stability and growth by measures designed to enable capitalism to operate with greater efficiency, and call upon their following to make economic sacrifices (above all in wage demands) towards this end.[8] In the words of Adam Westoby, 'When Western European parties did embark on "Eurocommunism" they were widely considered to be undergoing not a process of autonomous radicalization, but a re-absorption in to their national polities, dissolving the distinctive forms crystallized by the efforts of the Comintern in the 1920s.'[9] The Eurocommunists themselves, not unnaturally, saw things in a different light: 'Socialism will come, it is life itself. The capitalist system, due to its internal contradictions, is condemned to death. However, it must not necessarily be defeated by violence. If we are able to implant socialism in another way, it will not be a less worthy socialism', according to Benoit Frachon, the PCF trade union leader.[10]

Of necessity, the vindication of bourgeois democracy and the acceptance of bourgeois institutions adopted by these parties had implications for their evaluation of the political and social regimes existing in the USSR and Eastern Europe. In short, it meant an increasingly critical stance, developing from criticism of specific acts – such as invading Czechoslovakia – to criticism of institutions and political systems as incompatible with the model of democracy and social relations to which the new-thinking parties were in process of committing themselves. Although none were prepared to cut their links with the Soviet bloc (for all sorts of reasons), they certainly went out out of their way to distance themselves from the character of the regimes prevailing there, for which Moscow did not fail to criticise them sharply. By moving in this direction these parties followed the logic of the programmes and principles they were adopting in relation to their own countries, but their leaders would have been less than human if they had not also anticipated that taking up this strongly independent posture would be helpful with democratically minded voters suspicious of communists' long subordination to and apologies for tyrannical regimes.

The ensemble of theoretical positions and political directions sketched above came in the late seventies to be generalised under the the name of 'Eurocommunism'. Where or by whom the term was first coined is unknown, but it had been around in informal discussion and argument for some time before it appeared in print in the title of a book by the General Secretary of the PCE, Santiago Carrillo, 'Eurocommunism' and the State. Even so, he put it in quotes. The severe criticisms of Soviet reality which this text contained caused Carrillo to be attacked by the CPSU in quite vituperative terms.[11] Thereafter the word caught on in political discourse both inside and outside communist parties. Those members who favoured the ideas which it designated were however, except in Italy, rather embarrassed by it and reluctant to apply it to themselves. Communist opponents, however, used it readily, as a term of abuse.

In its strongest interpretation Eurocommunism meant

> a situation in which the individual party was inviolate and and assured of the right to define its own brand of Socialism; to participate in whatever capitalist enterprises it chose; to collaborate with whatever foreign or domestic groups, movements, parties or governments it liked; to criticise other Communists, including the Soviet Union, its internal policies, its policies towards other Socialist countries, as well as its foreign policies generally.[12]

Stern comments that if this is what the Eurocommunists intended, then 'it is difficult to see what remains of the original Communist commitment to a shared ideology, authority structure and organisation'.[13]

The Eurocommunists, or at least their intellectual spokespeople, claimed to base the theoretical interpretations and political approach on Gramsci's writings, although in this there was an element of disingenuousness, for Gramsci had never doubted that however complex and lengthy the political 'war of position', it must culminate sooner or later in the forcible overthrow of the ruling class and its state. It is most unlikely that he would have approved of the political strategies pursued by the major Eurocommunist CPs, particularly the PCI. He might well have endorsed the search for class alliances among the middle strata of society, but scarcely the project of restoring Italian capitalism to health and vigour, above all at the expense of the workforce. In the event the Eurocommunist strategy achieved no success anywhere, or at most one so paltry as to be negligible, and which was soon erased. The minor parties which followed it discovered that it brought them no significant advances; they remained as small and isolated as ever, continuing to be distrusted by their labour movements and the bulk of their national electorates.[14] The three big Latin parties developed along different lines as they pursued the Eurocommunist enterprise – in the Spanish case, the outcome was calamitous.

Italy

Among Italian political formations the PCI was renowned for its probity and avoidance of the corruption which permeated the nation's civic life. From the middle of the decade its leaders perceived the answer to the economic crisis to be the extension of these values into industry, commerce and capitalistic enterprise generally. Previously they had indicted monopoly capital as the enemy of the working class and society at large; the shift in orientation which took place viewed it in a much more indulgent light as the sector of Italian capital which represented efficiency, honesty, the route to enhanced productivity and the model which the remainder should try to emulate. It was back-wardness, sloth and corruption that were presented as the root of the country's economic problems and the seedbed of the worrying ultra-right backlash. From all of this was born the concept of the 'historic compromise' which meant in essence that the communists accepted the continuance of capitalism for the indefinite future in exchange for a drive towards honesty and efficiency in the economy, together with a rationalised and improved system of welfare provision.

Having made a turn away from militancy following the 'hot au-tumn' so as to avoid alienating the lower middle classes and driving them into the camp of the extreme right, the PCI moved increas-ingly towards the notion of coalition with Christian Democracy and consequently blew very cool on the campaigns for legalised divorce and abortion. Such an attitude showed it to be lagging behind pop-ular sentiment, whose move away from traditional values was mani-fested in the divorce referendum of 1974.[15] In spite of its compromising behaviour the PCI also benefited, with unprecedented success in the parliamentary elections of summer 1976, where it achieved 35 per cent of the vote, though still just failing to eclipse the Christian Demo-crats. It could no longer be discounted in parliamentary calculations, though the political establishment remained determined to exclude it from governmental coalitions. Accordingly a compromise was arrived at, if scarcely a historic one. The PCI did not enter government, but its deputies became a semi-detached part of the governing bloc, abstaining in support of the administration rather than voting for it. In return it was understood that the DC government would aim to carry through the line of reforms which the PCI advocated. The experiment did not prove to be a happy one and all the benefit was reaped by the communists' new partners rather than the party. In the words of political cynics, the DC made the history and the PCI the compromise.[16]

In January 1977 its General Secretary launched a slogan of 'austerity' to 'eliminate waste, parasitism, privileges and consumeristic excesses'. 'This slogan had an unenthusiastic reception among the rank and file of the Party and among its electorate who did not appreciate its pro-gressive "socialist" aspect'[17] – as well they might not, since it placed the burden of solving the crisis on lower income groups, and 'The

Party spoke in general of the need for planning, austerity, income redistribution and a new model of development but had few detailed demands to place before other parties at the bargaining table.'[18]

In other respects, as well, the strategy foundered. Italian political and civic life during the late seventies was increasingly beset by the terroristic activities of neo-fascists and of the Red Brigades – ultra-revolutionaries who drew their ultimate inspiration from the events of the late sixties but in the absence of any mass following or political strategy, turned to individual acts of assassination and kidnapping against the state and its personnel.[19] For a time they succeeded in doing so very effectively, generating a moral panic and culminating with the kidnapping and murder of the Prime Minister, Aldo Moro. Draconian repressive measures were instituted to deal with the problem. These violated civil rights, were used against individuals not associated with the terrorists and cast suspicion over everyone politically to the left of the PCI. The party enthusiastically supported all of these measures, seeing itself, not without some justice, as the ultimate target of the Red Brigades' attentions[20] – but alienating the support of democrats alarmed by the government's response to the crisis.[21] Having been placed in a situation of responsibility without power, the party succeeded in offending many of its potential voters, distressed by its economic or political stances. At the parliamentary elections of 1979 the PCI vote receded and the episode of semi-governmental participation came to an end, with the party considerably worse placed than it had been in 1976.

Spain

The PCE experienced much worse. Its General Secretary, Santiago Carrillo, had been, as noted, the first to popularise in print the term 'Eurocommunism'. Even before the collapse of the dictatorship the direction in which he was leading the party had provoked in the aftermath of the Czechoslovak crisis a Soviet-inspired revolt by traditionalists and Soviet loyalists under the leadership of a rather sinister civil war hero, Enrique Lister.[22] The Soviet bloc had gone on to snub the PCE by sending supplies of Polish coal to Spain during a miners' strike at the end of 1976. However, there was no open rupture and formal relations were maintained, though by this time they had become fairly icy.

The frustration of high hopes about the party's likely role in the new Spain was an additional circumstance making for disunity,[23] and in the shape of the Spanish socialists, the PSOE, led by the charismatic

Felipe González, it was faced with a left-wing rival which also possessed a credible civil war record and was untainted with the Stalinist record and anti-democratic suspicions which clung to the communists – not to speak of the socialists' infinitely greater international acceptability. In the elections of 1977, under the restored, albeit monarchical, democracy, the PCE, though securing a bloc of deputies in the Cortes, performed poorly and even below expectations. Its centres of long-standing working-class support under the dictatorship, when, apart from the Basque nationalists, it had provided the most effective opposition, were eroding as its potential electorate started to abandon it for more attractive options (including constitutional nationalists). Fragmentation thereafter was rapid and Carrillo's personal style did not help. Whatever his politics might have been, his personality was authoritarian and duplicitous. He resigned in 1982 after yet more unfavourable election results, by which time the PCE was split in two, but then went on to establish another breakaway faction. The PCE ceased to count as a significant factor in Spanish politics.

France

Although the PCF, on the face of things, succeeded better than the PCE or PCI in that it both preserved its unity and actually did enter government following electoral advance, in the long term it achieved no alteration in the character of French politics, and even before communism's general debacle at the end of the eighties found itself confined as a steadily shrinking remnant in French society, bypassed by history.

From 1972 the party had maintained a working relationship with François Mitterrand's socialists on the basis of a Common Programme of fairly far-reaching and radical proposals, at the heart of which was extensive public ownership of industrial and financial institutions. The relationship represented something far less than political unity, however, and for the following five years was a rocky road with many potholes, overhung with mutual suspicion between the partners.[24] It was no great secret that Mitterrand was hoping to use the PCF as a ladder which he would subsequently kick away, and it was clear that the socialists were deriving greater benefit than the communists from the arrangement.

In 1977 parliamentary elections were approaching and the communists requested 'updating' of points in the Common Programme, aiming to take account of developments since 1972 and sharpen its radical edge. Mitterrand, who provocatively announced his party's intention of becoming the dominant force on the French left, displayed a studied lack of interest. It was thought likely at the time that the left would win these elections and presumably the Socialist leader wanted to present a less alarming image to capital, both domestic and foreign. The updating negotiations were put in hand but broke down when both the other partners flatly refused to accommodate the PCF's demands. The left-wing coalition then fell apart and in consequence the expected parliamentary victory failed to materialise – but the PS moved ahead of the communists for the first time since 1945. The real reason for the communist leaders' behaviour in disrupting the alliance was probably to try to avoid this latter outcome. They perceived their party weakening to the benefit of its rival and therefore, but too late, tried with a radical emphasis to reclaim the ground they were losing as the dominant voice of French labour. One newspaper commented that the PCF leaders chose 'the strengthening of the party amidst defeat rather than the weakening of the party amidst victory'.[25]

This was not the end of the story, however. Presidential elections fell due in 1981 and the PCF, having stepped up its support for industrial action in the intervening years and grown lukewarm in its Eurocommunist stance,[26] presented a candidate in the shape of its General Secretary, Georges Marchais. There was no hope that he could be elected, of course, and the intention was avowedly to secure a sufficiently high vote to compel a victorious Mitterrand to take account of communist strength and form a coalition administration. The electoral results in the first round proved bitterly disappointing, producing a vote of just over 15 per cent (the expectation was 17–19 per cent), symptomatic of the party's ebbing political fortunes.[27]

Nevertheless, communist support for Mitterrand in the second round gave him victory, the first left-wing President of the Fifth Republic. The new President called fresh parliamentary elections, which the left won comfortably (with a marginally improved PCF vote). An agreement was cobbled together between the two parties, which promised much less than the Common Programme had done, but was nevertheless accepted by the communists, and Mitterrand thereupon found it expedient to include four of them in his administration in minor capacities – 'errand boys', as one Socialist minister put it.

In spite of the new government's cautious perspectives compared with what the two parties had advanced in the seventies, a great deal of hope was invested in it and the conviction that fundamental economic and social change was at last in prospect. The electors who had voted for the left were soon undeceived – global economic recession and stringent financial pressure led rapidly to the failure and abandonment of all the innovative socialist measures and replaced them with a regime of financial orthodoxy. This, along with simultaneous events in Spain, was of the utmost importance in the post-war history of social democracy – but that is another story. Mitterrand, as the slide took place, had no doubt calculated that his PCF junior partners would fulfil the same role as their predecessors in the post-war administrations and that, with their anxiety to remain in the government outweighing the disillusion of seeing their hopes overturned, would help to reconcile the French labour movement to the austerity programme. The communists refused to play that game and preferred to go back into opposition, but the episode left them further weakened and discredited and now very much overshadowed on the left by the PS. For them, the strategy of left unity which they had assiduously pursued for over a decade had produced the worst of all worlds.

By 1981, although the term 'Eurocommunist' continued to be used a a definition – mainly by outsiders – for some communist parties and certain political orientations, the concepts which it embodied had, as effective strategies for transforming their respective societies, run into the sand. It had never in any case represented a cohesive programme with co-ordinated direction; it was more a climate of political feeling, though undoubtedly one widely shared by communists in the countries where it formed the dominant standpoint. It was the product of two processes going on within their ranks during the long era of economic and political stability and of consumer growth. These were, in the first place, growing realisation of the damage done by swallowing whatever the Kremlin decreed, as well as the immorality of behaving in that manner. Secondly, and connectedly, they were searching for a way out of the political ghetto and to overcome the blocks in the western political systems which kept them isolated. Whether the strategy was purely misconceived or whether it may have been valid in principle but faced with obstacles that were simply too formidable remains an open question.

Although Eurocommunism had its origins partly in a critique of the practices of the Soviet Union and its ruling party, none of the Eurocommunist parties, large or small, went so far as to sever relations with the CPSU. It is clear, if only from the published record, that the Soviet leaders did not like the development and regarded it as a derogation from 'proletarian internationalism', in terms of unwillingness to accept the CPSU as being at the very least first among equals if not something much more, and of the criticisms these parties made of the Soviet internal regime and of its foreign policies. Harsh words were exchanged from time to time, even with the PCF, the least enthusiastic of the parties in its Eurocommunist postures, and in other cases internal opposition trends were quietly encouraged from Moscow, even though these never received its official recognition. From the Eurocommunist side, however, to have gone all the way to a break would have been, apart from the practical problem of leaving a large proportion of their membership behind them, too much of a denial of their historic origins and traditions, an unsustainable rupture of their identities. Eurocommunism was a reflection of the contradictions in the West European communism of this era rather than its resolution.[28]

Light and Shadow

The events in Western Europe, while marking an interesting and significant phase in the development of international communism, brought no long-term successes. Events occurring elsewhere in the world at the same time, however, appeared to suggest a continuing momentum of communist advance and even, though very briefly, the possibility of reconciliation between the two main communist powers.

Mao himself had liquidated the Cultural Revolution when its chaotic development had reached the point at which it was in danger of posing a threat to the economic viability of the state and the continuance of his own power. The CPC, after its traumatic disorganisation and virtual destruction, was reassembled and continued as the central institution of the state. The instigators of the Cultural Revolution, however – Mao himself, his wife Jiang Jing and a close circle of collaborators – remained in charge of affairs, bypassing the veteran Prime Minister Zhou Enlai. There was no reason to believe that their ultimate aim of instituting a regime of puritanical ideological conformity and unquestioning collectivist discipline had been abandoned in the long term.

That this aroused grave apprehension among the masses was equally clear, and early in 1976 it found an opening through which it could be expressed. Zhou died, and his standing both in the Chinese party and as a heroic figure of international communism required that he be accorded a major state funeral. The partial marginalisation in which he had expired, however, led the authorities to organise a funeral on no more than a modest scale. Public response in Beijing was intense and disapproving, resulting in spontaneous massive and widespread demonstrations in his memory, which were suppressed with some violence but whose message of dissatisfaction was clear. The events

could not touch Mao himself, but they weakened the position of the
cabal around him, and when he himself died later in the year brought
about their downfall.

An intense succession struggle, which ultimately turned upon the
attitude of the military commanders, ended with the disgrace and
arrest of the 'Gang of Four' and began the ascent to predominance in
the Politburo of the pragmatic Deng Xaioping. In the altered circumstances, with Mao and his associates gone on the one hand and on the
other a greater Soviet acceptance of diversity, it might be expected
that the CPSU and the CPC would be in a position to compose their
differences and establish a new alignment of allied, if not united,
communist states and parties with a mutual strengthening all round.
Any such hopes did not last long, for the new Chinese leadership had
its own agendas, to which it regarded the Soviet power as being as
much of a threat as ever. It showed itself determined to continue
to maintain good relations with the USA on the basis of continuing
hostility to the USSR. The internal reforms towards which it moved
were certainly dramatic, leading onwards to a dismantling of the
foundations of China's centralised economy, but in international terms
these merely strengthened its pro-US alignment. Any remaining traces
of communist internationalism in Chinese postures (they were few
enough and mostly rhetorical) vanished with Mao and the Gang of
Four. From then on the state's concerns would be purely driven by
national, not to say nationalist, considerations.

National considerations were to the fore in the events of the late
seventies in south-east Asia and these illustrated in the most horrendous fashion the manner in which formally Marxist organisations
could be driven into bloodthirsty courses by a combination of social
radicalism and nationalist obsession. The Khmer Rouge regime,
evolving through a ferocious internecine leadership struggle (five of
the twelve ministers appointed in 1975 were later killed), committed
itself to creating a nationally sealed utopia of collective peasant toil
on the basis of mythical Khmer national traditions.[29] Phnom Penh
was forcibly emptied of its population in the most barbarous fashion;
all elements attached to the previous regime or thought to be tainted
with urban (i.e. anti-national) corruption mercilessly exterminated
and the residue dispatched to unremitting agricultural labour. Money,
religion, privacy and the family were forthwith abolished and draconian terror employed to keep the population in line. 'When the
[economic] programmes failed, the Khmer Rouge blamed the failure
on political enemies – a constantly changing category – and killed them
off.'[30] Vietnam was stigmatised as the national enemy and military

attacks against it commenced along parts of the border where Phnom Penh claimed territory because of Cambodians resident there.

On any analysis the Pol Pot regime displayed characteristics far closer to fascism than to communism, even in its Stalinist version. The terror regime, which made *Nineteen-Eighty-Four* appear benign by comparison, the ultra-nationalism which defined itself in uninhibitedly racist terms, the nostalgic attachment to a mythical past which was its central preoccupation coupled with its explicit rejection of modernity and attempt to dismantle it, are classic markers of fascism, though in this case carried further than any actual fascist regime ever tried.

> In fashioning their revolution the Khmer Rouge also drew on elements of the very culture – their own – which they set out to destroy. The coercive behaviour of the leadership and their casual recourse to terror, for example, fitted easily into centuries of arbitrary, authoritarian rule . . . . the Khmer Rouge security apparatus, just as in traditional Cambodia, protected the state rather than individual human rights. Buddhist ideals differed sharply from Communist ones, of course, but the two movements shared the idea that personalities could be obliterated and remade following their immersion in a collectivity such as the monkhood or the party . . . Cambodian teaching practices [emphasised] rote learning, reverence for teachers and complete obedience.[31]

Racist arrogance proved to be the regime's undoing, for the attacks on Vietnam provoked a military response at the end of 1978 which drove Pol Pot from his capital and established a government under Vietnamese protection.

One Chinese leader remarked at the time that Pol Pot and his confederates were a hangover from the Gang of Four and that Beijing would have preferred to repudiate them, but could not afford to do so, geopolitical considerations having priority. Vietnam was in the Soviet camp, and the invasion of Cambodia was viewed not as an act of liberation but an extension of Soviet influence in the Indo-Chinese peninsula. In February 1979, therefore, Chinese forces counter-invaded Vietnam from the north. The enterprise was not an unqualified success, for the battle-hardened Vietnamese resisted effectively and compelled the Chinese army to withdraw – but it was a drain on Hanoi's resources that it could ill sustain and the beginning of a campaign that would impoverish it yet further. It also represented something qualitatively new – the first occasion (apart from the Sino-Soviet skirmishes of the sixties on the Issuri River) on which avowedly socialist states had engaged in military conflict with each other.

The full implications were to become apparent only later. Elsewhere in the Third World the attractions of the Soviet model, or of the USSR and the bloc as a source of assistance, were not yet exhausted. In 1978, the Afghan communist party, well entrenched in the army, seized control of the government. The following year three revolutions overturned US clients and two of them brought the states in which they occurred within the Soviet orbit. One of these, to be sure, hardly amounted to a major piece upon the geopolitical chessboard. The tiny Caribbean island state of Grenada had been ruled since independence by an insane (though not particularly bloodthirsty) dictator, Eric Gairy. His overthrow was effected (again largely bloodlessly) by the New Jewel movement which, being strongly left-wing in its disposition and determined on extensive social and political reform (although affiliated to the Socialist International), soon incurred the displeasure of the Americans. Consequently it established links with Cuba and the bloc, thereby offending Washington even further.

The second of these revolutions was a more substantial affair and represented a further threat to the American government's hemispheric hegemony, though scarcely the military menace which the overheated US imagination assumed. The dictatorship of the Somoza family in the Central American country of Nicaragua was a particularly unsavoury business,[32] little other than a terroristic plunder of the nation's resources – even the manhole covers in the capital Managua's streets were the family's personal property. For several years guerrilla war had been conducted from the countryside by the FSLN commonly referred to as the Sandinistas, from the nationalist revolutionary martyr, General Sandino, whom they adopted as their icon. In March 1979 the regime crumbled in face of military defeat and popular insurrection and the Sandinistas established their power. Inevitability their social-reforming intentions provoked Washington's wrath and exposed the new regime to American blockade, along with armed incursions, killing and destruction by the remnants of the Somoçistas, organised from neighbouring Honduras with US assistance.

No less inevitably the usual cycle was set in motion, as was the case with Cuba and Grenada, in which the regime, whether or not it wanted to stand in the front-line of the Cold War, turned towards the rival superpower for its survival and protection. The Sandinistas, however, did not go down the same road as the Cubans of turning themselves into an orthodox Marxist–Leninist party, instituting single-party rule and collectivising the economy under centralised control. In Nicaragua, within a framework of reform and regulation, private business continued to run the economy, an uncensored opposition press remained in being and attacked the regime with extreme virulence, and hostile political parties continued to function and compete.[33] The Sandinista government gave signs of becoming the first communist-orientated regime to avoid the descent into political monopoly, authoritarianism and regimentation of its people. None of that did it any good with the US administration, indeed, it probably exacerbated its fault by setting a particularly bad example, and the unrelenting economic, political and military pressures against it never abated.

The third of these upheavals in that year was the most cataclysmic of them all and the one unquestioningly the most damaging to Washington's real interests – but also the one which was least beneficial to the Soviet Union or international communism. The Iranian regime overseen by the Shah Pahlevi was regarded at the time by democratic opinion as particularly tyrannical, which it was, although its image improved considerably by contrast with what came after. It was also the linchpin of the Western defence system in the Middle East as well as being a capital source of oil. The Shah, along with indulgence in ostentatious and sacrilegious displays of wealth among an impoverished and generally devout population, had attempted a variety of modernisation initiatives funded by oil revenues which had produced social dislocation and inflamed popular resentment. The discontent was channelled in part through outlawed political parties, among which the Iranian CP, the Tudeh (Masses), was a significant contributor,[34] but far more important was the role of the Shi'ite clergy, wholly alienated from the monarchy on account of the latter's modernisation policies and ambition to exercise control over clerical as well as civil society. The bazaar traders, economically threatened, were a further potent and linked source of opposition, but one therefore of a fundamentally anti-communist bent.

Uncontrollable protest built up and exploded into bloody revolution propelled by popular insurrection and military defection. The Shah saved his life by flight, abandoning his ministers, generals and secret police chiefs to vengeance and execution. The Western position in Iran was eradicated overnight, to be replaced with intransigent enmity and the designation of the US as the 'Great Satan'. The symbol around which the opposition forces coalesced was the Ayatollah Khomeini, newly returned from exile. No sooner had the old order been overthrown than a murderous struggle for power erupted among the rival factions of the victors, one in which Khomeini's adherents, because of the latter's respect, ideological power and capacity to articulate religious sentiments, held the aces. In the outcome the left, both secular and religious, was totally defeated and largely exterminated, the Tudeh proscribed and driven underground once more, but retaining only a shadow of the influence it had possessed before the revolution.

It was not unusual for radical Third World regimes to suppress their local communists as dangerous rivals but nevertheless sustain good relations with the Soviet bloc and lean on it for support and aid of various sorts. That was emphatically not the case in Iran. If the USA was depicted as the Great Satan, the USSR was stigmatised as the lesser devil. The Ayatollah's regime regarded itself as a revolutionary centre for the Middle East, much in the way the infant Soviet Russia had done for Europe, but this meant religious revolution, which it tried hard to disseminate, though frustrated in the end by insufficient military resources. For communism this was more than merely another severe setback, of which there had been many in the past. As Eric Hobsbawm observes, the Iranian Revolution was the first major revolution since 1789 to explicitly reject the values of the Enlightenment and the European tradition, to which Marxism was heir, and instead to found itself upon not merely different but wholly antagonistic cultural values. It was a portent of things to come.

At the close of the same year a combination of ideological and national considerations pushed the Kremlin into an adventure which in the end was to undermine its resources, its domestic legitimacy and its international credibility. Afghanistan was a classic buffer state, located between Soviet central Asia and the US diplomatic and military satellite Pakistan. Since the era of the Cold War, though domestically independent, it had been acknowledged as lying within the Soviet diplomatic orbit – a kind of Asian Finland.

By European standards the country was exceptionally backward in economic, social and cultural terms, a very loosely integrated feudal-style monarchy, deeply divided both by geography and ethnic tension. Its mountainous terrain and traditions of religious fanaticism and local feud made its population ideally adapted for guerrilla warfare. In the nineteenth century more than one invader had come to grief there as a result. Not unusually, as in comparable countries, the impetus for transformation came from inside the military, the necessarily most modernised institution within the state. In the Afghan case, however, the lead among the military reformers was secured by an indigenous (though severely divided) communist party. In the seventies the monarchy was disposed of and in April 1978 a coup against the president put the communists in power in Kabul.

To rule the capital was one thing, but no Afghan government had really wielded much authority throughout the countryside and the new regime was no exception.[35] Internal and external factors conspired to ruin it. Attempts to impose social reform such as land redistribution and improved opportunities for women heated traditionalist resentments and soon provoked widespread rebellion against the infidel government. The regime itself was weakened and its effectiveness diminished by the splits within the ruling party, so intense that there existed effectively two rival communist parties. The communist putsch also removed Afghanistan from its buffer-state status and turned it into a Cold War pawn as the Pakistani government moved to support the rebel forces and channel state-of-the art US military equipment into their hands.

By the end of 1979 it was clear that the government was unable to contain the rebellion and was on the way to being overwhelmed. Decision makers in the Kremlin were faced with the choice of letting events take their course or attempting to shape them. Geopolitics and the responsibility felt for revolutionary movements abroad conspired to lure Moscow into a fateful and fatal decision. Understandably, the Soviets were alarmed at the prospect of of US power, in the shape of its Pakistani and Afghan allies being brought right up to a sensitive border. They also had in mind the discredit likely to result from the destruction by right-wing forces of an allied and ideologically linked regime. In December the decision was taken (it appears to have been with some hesitation) to provide military support, Soviet troops occupied Kabul and moved to support the Afghan army in controlling the countryside. The brutality of the political arena into which the USSR was now drawn was demonstrated at once by the execution of the communist President Amin, who had requested the intervention – because he was held responsible for the situation which had made it necessary. The Soviet Union did not confine its role to a military one, but acted as a power broker and placed the rival Afghan communist faction in power on the assumption that it would be better able to attract popular support.[36]

The immediate consequences were political rather than military – those came later. At a stroke the West, already taking its distance from the Helsinki Accords and moving towards an attitude of greater enmity than had been manifest since the fifties, was handed an enormous propaganda advantage. Once more the USSR was stigmatised as an aggressor and punished accordingly. The 1980 Olympic Games were scheduled to be held in Moscow, a long-awaited public relations triumph, the complement to Helsinki and the seal on the international respectability the regime had been striving for. The West instead launched a boycott of the Moscow Games, and though they went ahead, they were only a shadow of the event which had been anticipated. In addition, most of the Western communist parties condemned the invasion (although the PCF, significantly, did not), thus reopening old wounds in the movement itself. The stance of the critical parties followed from their acceptance that no consideration of revolutionary gain could justify the use of military force to impose a regime against the popular will. Supporters of the intervention suggested that Western notions of the Afghan popular will might be different if the views of the country's women were taken into account. In any event Moscow paid an immediate heavy price for its action, though a much heavier instalment was still to come.

The year 1981 was supposed to have been the year when, according to Khrushchev's boast at the 22nd Congress, the USSR would overtake the USA in material consumption, not to speak of other indicators of public welfare. All that had, of course, been quietly forgotten, and the continuing dependence of the Soviet Union on US grain imports were a humiliating reminder of just how inferior in that capacity it was to a country with a much smaller agricultural sector.[37] The year 1981 was also the year of Leonid Brezhnev's seventy-fifth birthday,[38] and surveying the scene at that point, the General Secretary might well have noted with satisfaction that in spite of setbacks and deficiencies, the country he led and the movement of which he was the pre-eminient representative continued to progress in the right direction. Across the globe the previous decade had seen regimes added to the bloc or adopting postures of 'socialist orientation' which would one day bring them to full membership. 'Socialist solidarity' had been exemplified and racist South Africa rebuffed by the Cuban intervention in Africa. On the international field the rival bloc had suffered little but defeats, military and diplomatic, and had been obliged to publicly acknowledge the European status quo on Soviet terms. China, while remaining a problem, was no longer the rival revolutionary centre it had purported to be ten years earlier. Soviet military strength had been asserted and the economy, if problematic in many areas, was basically sound and growing. The Western parties, in spite of their grumbling and objections, had remained in communion and the PCF had in any case reconciled its differences with the CPSU as well as succeeding in gaining entry to government. Given the irresistible attractions of hindsight, it has to be stressed that there was absolutely nothing on the horizon in mid-1981 to suggest what would be the fate of the communist movement and regimes or the suddenness with which it would overtake them.

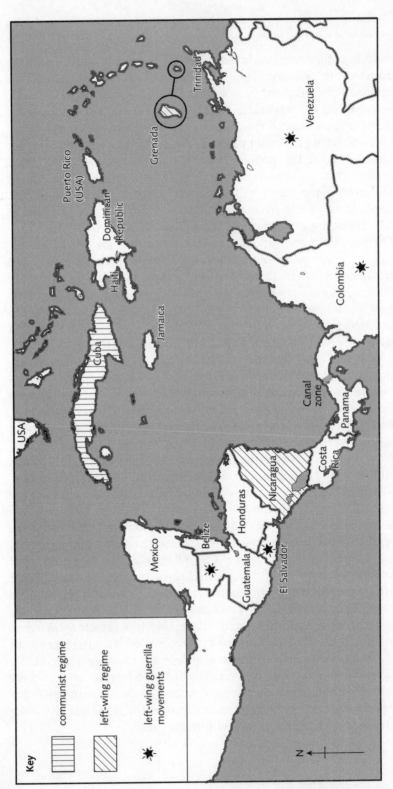

Figure 8 The Caribbean

7

The Amazed Evangelist

What happened to the communist movement between 1981 and 1991 recalls to mind the verse heading James Bridie's play:

> The sticks break, the stones crumble
> The eternal altars tilt and tumble,
> Sanctions and tales dislimm like mist,
> About the amazed evangelist.

More prosaically, Adam Westoby points out in a text published before the overturn that, 'It is clear, however, that the incidence of revolutionary crises in communist states is considerably higher than in industrialised 'capitalist' states. Most large-scale movements of industrial workers against the state now occur in the communist world.'[1] The events between 1981 and 1991 demonstrated two things. The first was the dramatic and wholly unsuspected fragility of communist states and societies, including the USSR itself; the second the organic and umbilical attachment of the non-ruling parties to the original Leninist regime. Once it was gone, few of the former could survive independently or find continued reason to justify their existences. Not many disappeared from the scene altogether, but apart from a few exceptional cases they changed their names or their character, usually both. The same applied to the ruling parties of the regimes themselves. The collapse of their power did not destroy them utterly as organisations (and some even managed to come back to government), but it twisted them into unrecognisable new shapes and it annihilated altogether the world movement which had once combined them.

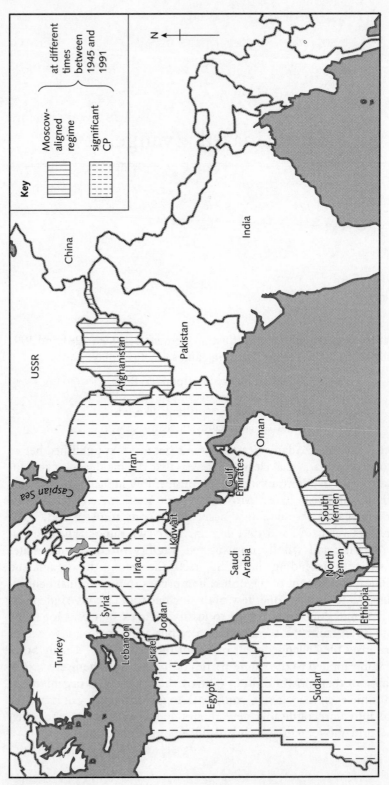

Figure 9 The Middle East and Gulf Region

The process of the bloc's collapse has been recounted frequently and subjected to intensive historical scrutiny. In the aftermath it is not too difficult to see the signs of decay whose significance was not appreciated at the time, but what continues to puzzle is the speed and comprehensiveness of the disintegration. An entire historical culture perished virtually overnight – and considering the extent of the overturn, was obliterated with a remarkable minimum of violence.[2] There are as yet no definitive answers to these questions, though some tentative suggestions will be made here. Three phases of the process can be identified: between 1982 and 1985 a growing recognition on the part of the Soviet leadership of the depth and intractability of the problems that they were facing and the implications for the communist movement; from 1985 to 1989 a serious effort to address the difficulties and further exposure of their depth; and from 1989 the accelerating disintegration culminating in the dissolution of the Soviet Union at the end of 1991. The events occurring in the Asian communist regimes during those years appeared to be moving on a different track, but in terms of the abolition of the essential tenets of Marxism–Leninism, they were headed for a similar destination. The only surviving regime upholding the classic values which had once informed the culture of the bloc is Cuba – something of a historic irony – and even that is eroding at the edges.

In the last years of the Soviet Union the Brezhnev period came to be designated as 'the era of stagnation'.[3] At the time of his death in 1982 declining growth rates could be read in all the figures, personal corruption had grown widespread and penetrated even into the leader's family circle, the structure of the party itself was threatening to fragment as powerful regional party bosses were permitted to establish virtual personal fiefs in return for their loyal support to the General Secretary.[4] In the Eastern bloc, too, economic performance was manifestly flagging, with dramatic political consequences which were seen at their most damaging in Poland.

In that country, since Gomulka's overthrow in 1970, the regime, under the apparatchik Gierek, had virtually lost all sense of direction and had stumbled from expedient to expedient trying to juggle and reconcile a variety of social and political interests – workers, peasants, the church, the military – and of course the Kremlin. So far as any consistent strategy existed it consisted of attracting foreign capital, inward investment to renew and expand the industrial base. In fact a lot of external capital was attracted but it did little to reconstruct the foundations of the economy, being mostly wasted on prestige projects which failed to fit into the productive framework. The agricultural problem remained intractable, with the sector producing well below its potential and incapable of breaking out of the cycle so long as its products were kept underpriced for social reasons.

The chickens came home to roost in the mid-to-late seventies when rises in world interest rates placed pressures upon the national budget that could only be accommodated by a programme of fierce economies that immediately jeopardised the living standards of the populace. 'This was no invisible hand of a market but the all too visible hand of a party leadership.'[5] As Oliver MacDonald points out, the regime had become dependent upon US finance for 'the most sensitive issue of domestic politics – the market supply of meat'. Per capita consumption of this commodity rose from 53 kilos per annum in 1970 to 70.3 kilos in 1975 (far above the British equivalent)[6] when the regime first tried unsuccessfully to impose austerity in 1976. The regime fell between two stools, for it was insufficiently tyrannical to prevent the eruption of organised social protest. The particular irony of this development was that it was centred in the industrial working class in the shape of the oppositional trade union Solidarity. The Polish workers quickly demonstrated what they thought of the workers' state led by the Polish United Workers' Party, for as soon as the barriers were lifted the official trade unions emptied out as their members flocked into Solidarity, which, as the government fell, assumed political as much as industrial dimensions.[7]

Agreements reached in 1980 with Solidarity as an independent bargainer failed to stabilise the situation, and in December 1981, under threat of Soviet intervention unless drastic action was undertaken, the military seized control and suppressed the opposition in order to preserve the essence of the communist system. The coup was relatively bloodless, but highly significant as the first military take-over in a socialist regime, a blatant contradiction of communist ideology from whatever angle it was viewed. Apart from being another setback in the propaganda struggle with the West, it was condemned by all the Eurocommunist parties, although these contained minorities which were prepared to argue that the Polish workers had to be instructed in the long-term interests of the working class by military force in alliance with the Kremlin.

The Polish events represented a demoralising experience for communists of an independent sensibility who still continued to hope for the possibility of communist-ruled regimes overcoming their Stalinist heritage. The PCI went so far as to declare that the inspirational legacy of the October Revolution was now exhausted. Eurocommunism itself was stalled and the hopes which had temporarily gathered around it in the 1970s proved illusory. The chronic economic recession through which the West had been passing since the oil price rises, the fallibility of social democratic Keynsianism, turned out to benefit the right and not the left in both Europe and the United States. This was particularly ironic, for the West European communist parties had long preached, during the years when the post-war boom was generally assumed to be for all time, that it was in reality a temporary phenomenon and that when it broke capital would respond by attacks upon the incomes and standards of working people. Now that these predictions were borne out, however, it was the left which was spurned by electorates and a general cultural shift back towards laissez-faire principles took place in the developed world, a process identified particularly with the names of the British and US leaders, Thatcher and Reagan. Within the Eurocommunist parties the internal opponents of the new course, who had continued to hanker for the old certainties and Soviet allegiance, resumed the offensive and some of these parties started to fragment.[8]

If the developments of the early eighties within both East and West Europe were serious enough, the world aspect was much more threatening still for the movement and its continuing centre, Moscow. The international triumphs of the 1970s were proving to have bitter fruits. The election of President Reagan in 1980 confirmed the shift, which had indeed begun under President Carter, towards what commentators have termed the Second Cold War. It embodied an attitude of uncompromising hostility from the major Western powers towards the Soviet bloc and a systematic attack on a number of fronts. The first of these consisted in a renewed round of the arms race, with a range of fresh weapons system deployments and the prospect of others, particularly the 'Star Wars' nuclear defensive umbrella. Trying to keep pace with the threat stretched even further the strained and technologically inferior[9] Soviet resources – which was exactly what was intended.

Around the world the regimes 'of socialist orientation' which had been established in the previous decade either independently or with Soviet and Cuban assistance were not permitted to consolidate themselves. Instead they were subjected to armed attack in one form or another. The normal way in which this was done was for the West to train, arm and provide bases for oppositional elements, a strategy which was pursued energetically throughout the eighties. Simply to enumerate the instances shows how extensively the policy was applied. In southern Africa the South African regime made it possible for anti-government forces in both Angola and Mozambique to devastate and ruin the respective countries, along with the destruction of large swathes of their population. In Washington's own backyard the same principle was applied to Nicaragua, while in the Caribbean the island state of Grenada was directly invaded by the USA itself and its radical and Cuba-friendly regime uprooted. The latter event, while of no great geopolitical importance, was a severe public relations rebuff for international communism and by contrast an assertion of American strength and determination.

The USA could not reverse its military defeat in Indo-China, but it could make sure that united Vietnam was internationally isolated as far as possible and subjected to punitive trade sanctions. The pressures did not stop there, for the remnants of the overthrown Pol Pot regime found refuge over the Thai border, from where they were sponsored by the Thai government, Beijing and the USA and its allies to wage destructive guerrilla war against the Cambodian society precariously restored under Vietnamese protection.[10] That too, apart from the human cost, was an immeasurable drain upon the resources of a Soviet ally. There were in addition a couple of instances where affiliated regimes imploded under the impact of their own shortcomings without (or with only very minimal) external assistance. Such was the case in South Yemen (Aden) and in Ethiopia, where Mengistu's terror, in spite of Soviet and Cuban assistance, was unable to hold together a politically, socially and ethnically divided state which finally succumbed to the armies of the internal opposition, with the Eritreans achieving their objective of national independence. Both the successor governments were still socially radical but understandably no longer Soviet aligned.

The greatest of all these disasters occurred in Afghanistan. Here Soviet forces were directly engaged and the conflict assumed for Moscow something of the character which Vietnam had done for its opponent. In spite of a growing deployment of ground and air forces the resistance, liberally supplied with US armaments through Pakistan, which also offered it safe havens, could not be overcome. The effect upon the morale of the Soviet military was considerable and extending casualty lists produced the inevitable reaction in the USSR itself, in spite of tight censorship. Communism in power had certainly been viewed by outsiders as brutal and authoritarian, but up till then also efficient where it mattered. Failure to win in Afghanistan was therefore a particularly troubling sign. Beyond that, even in instances where there was no military problem, a number of the supposed 'states of socialist orientation' in Africa (Congo and Benin may be mentioned) were in reality no more than personal or family dictatorships, whose rulers found it convenient to adopt such a posture and try to cobble together a 'Marxist–Leninist' party to consolidate their personal authority. They expected material assistance in return for their international stance but did nothing to enhance the image of international communism.

Leonid Brezhnev died in 1982. By one of the ironies which mark the course of Soviet history he achieved his objectives more comprehensively than any other Soviet leader, even Stalin, and, generally regarded as a benign figure though not much respected, left behind him an infinitely more peaceful and contented society than the dictator. But he also left behind a society whose economic cracks were showing more visibly with every year that passed[11] and with corruption eating away at its elite. He also left an economy and a government which had, owing to their international role, expanded their commitments, particularly their military ones, far beyond the level of their resources (at least in the form which they were managed) and a world movement whose morale and historic confidence had plummeted, thanks to Soviet actions since 1979, even as the ideological bonds loosened between its individual members and the socialist homeland.

The Politburo which met to determine his successor was rather in the position of a college of cardinals meeting to fill the vacancy following a particularly lengthy pontificate, aware of grave problems which had accumulated and required addressing but uncertain of the way forward and lacking in new ideas and personnel – the Soviet leadership by this point was composed almost exclusively of elderly men. In the event they played safe, choosing as General Secretary an individual who had the reputation of a reformer but who was safely integrated into the power structure, a former head of the KGB, no less. His appointment foreshadowed an intention to tackle the symptom rather than the reality of the underlying decline, for Yuri Andropov had the reputation of being an uncompromising enemy of corruption, and as soon as he assumed responsibility an anti-corruption drive was put in hand which swept into its net members of Brezhnev's own family circle.

It was emblematic of the dilemmas which gripped the Politburo, and might be seen as a sign of desperation, that the person they selected was known to be a desperately sick individual. He survived only eighteen months, dying before the anti-corruption campaign had the chance to penetrate very deeply and being replaced by the nonentity Konstantin Chernenko, whose status as a stopgap was scarcely concealed – not exactly a far-sighted thing to do for a state acknowledged to be facing critical times. Finally in 1985, the youngest member of the Politburo, a stripling of fifty-five, Mikhail Gorbachev, was elected to head the party, mostly on account of his administrative and communicative ability and energy, with the expectation that he could lead an effective reform programme. That such an apparently unlikely candidate was selected is indicative of two circumstances. Firstly, that by this time the party leadership was really so desperate that they took the chance on such a relatively untried newcomer, and secondly that the reforming ideas were emanating from Gorbachev himself – there is no reason to believe that the Politburo as a whole had evolved any reforming strategy or that they would have been capable of doing so. The expectation was that Gorbachev would prove a more effective and long-lasting version of Andropov. Throughout the communist parties internationally the development was generally welcomed – by traditionalists because they would tend to welcome whatever the CPSU decided, and by renewers because it appeared to signal the possible transformation of Soviet structures.

Gorbachev, who had a legal training, symbolised in his person the technocratic elite who were coming to the fore of the Soviet nonmenklatura in place of the old Stalinist warhorses such as Gromyko, who had nominated him at the Central Committee.[12] He was undoubtedly a dedicated communist and Marxist–Leninist, passionately committed to the essentials of the Soviet system and intent upon its perpetuation. He was aware at the same time of the system's deeply flawed reality and therefore committed all the more strenuously to remedying the defects.

Being first and foremost the leader of the Soviet Union Gorbachev, whatever he may have felt about the international movement – and the CPSU continued to maintain a very elaborate and expensive network of contacts with foreign communist parties[13] – had to direct his attentions primarily towards overcoming the intrinsic defects which were corroding society and culture. The loudly publicised antialcohol campaign (it stopped short of prohibition) was a high-profile measure chosen as much for its symbolic importance as for alcohol's adverse effects on economic performance. In the end it was probably counter-productive and did more harm than good – a portent of what was to happen to the deeper reform measures that the General Secretary moved to introduce.

The themes of *glasnost*, meaning 'openness', and *perestroika*, meaning 'reconstruction', which he made his slogans and which came to symbolise Gorbachev's reign, proved to be the undoing of the regime and the instruments of its destruction. They were combined with an approach to international issues, all of which which together signified that the USSR was truly embarking upon a new course, that implied more than a shift from earlier positions but in fact was a reversal of its previous historical trajectory.

It could be termed an increasingly national posture except that the USSR itself was a multinational state. It is clear that Gorbachev and his advisers were aware that the USSR's resources were badly over-stretched by its international role, particularly in view of the additional demands being placed upon it as a consequence of the 'Second Cold War'. They initiated a programme for liquidating it, decisions which may have contributed as much to the eventual outcome as did those relating to the internal structures of the state. The programme was pursued through all manner of initiatives and negotiations, including summit meetings, in which Gorbachev's own personality and bearing (not to speak of his wife's) were deployed as significant assets. Since the enemy, represented primarily by Reagan and Thatcher, was extremely reluctant to terminate the global contest, it was clear that the objective could be attained only on the enemy's terms – which meant in effect a surrender of Soviet positions throughout the world. Evidently the implications of this change of direction for the movement internationally were bound to be far-reaching.

The various regimes around the globe which were being supported by Soviet aid and armaments against military attack or pressures were urged to make whatever accommodation they could with their local opponents, or in the case of Cuba, with the United States itself. This applied to Angola, Mozambique, Ethiopia and Vietnam. The most dramatic of such reversals, however, occurred in the case of Afghanistan, when in 1988 the Soviet military force was withdrawn, leaving the indigenous communist regime to manage as best it could, although material military assistance continued to be supplied.[14] At the same time the Kremlin made unilateral gestures with armament reductions in central Europe and made it clear that it no longer considered this region to be a zone of contestation, using phraseology like 'Common European Home' to apply to all Europe including the USSR. It was significant that the East European regimes (leaving aside in any case the maverick Romania), though they might be pressured, could no longer be directly commanded.[15] Some, such as Poland and Hungary, were following through their own evolution a political course resembling that being pursued in the USSR, but others like the GDR, Czechoslovakia and Bulgaria were dragging their feet or actively resisting,[16] their rulers intent on perpetuating as much as they could of the neo-Stalinist structures and doubtless hoping for better times in Moscow.

The reform process there, however, once begun, acquired an unstoppable momentum which after a few years ran away with its initiators. Glasnost had two principal effects. In the first place the opening-up of the media to genuine discussion, argument and exposure of abuse resulted in the entire structure of state and society, not merely its unhealthy elements, coming under scrutiny and criticism. Stalinism was buried at last, symbolised by formal reversal of the verdicts on the purge trial defendants of the thirties. That, however, represented only the completion of the Khrushchev agenda. More significantly, Lenin's hitherto sacerdotal status began to come under question, and the argument to be voiced, at first tentatively, but then with growing confidence, was that Stalinism with all its horrors was organically related to the Leninist system and that the Bolshevik Revolution had been a historic disaster.[17] Officialdom did not surrender without a fight: throughout the eighties the broadcast media remained under centralised control and the institutional story, whether in public statues, museums, youth organisations or school history texts continued to expound the line that with the Stalinist nightmare and the era of stagnation safely behind it, a historically progressive society and state founded by Lenin was rejuvenating itself and returning to its original values. For this purpose the old practices, glasnost or no, were pressed into service. Not only did Lenin's mausoleum remain a site of veneration and pilgrimage but in the Lenin museum beside the Kremlin Trotsky, Zinoviev, Kamanev and Bukharin were totally written out of the script of his life, and only passing reference was accorded to Stalin or Lenin's early political collaborators who subsequently became his opponents.

The second major effect of glasnost was to enable political formations to come into existence outside the control of the CPSU. This was very much unintended, for none of the leaders aimed to dismantle the single-party monopoly, but it proved to be an inevitable consequence of opening up political discussion; and once contested elections were permitted it was unavoidable that the candidates should come to represent and to campaign on alternative and oppositional political platforms. When it became clear that events were moving in this direction the regime tried initially to handle the development by permitting political associations and groups so long as they refrained from describing themselves as parties, but this naturally soon revealed itself as an untenable compromise.[18] Even more portentously, the impact of the opening-up began to splinter the CPSU itself, with divergent and even opposing factions establishing themselves on the basis of attitudes to the reform programme – traditionalists, neo-Leninists, democratisers. At his first party congress after becoming General Secretary Gorbachev urged the delegates to break the tradition of unanimous approval of whatever issued from the leadership; four years later he would have probably been pleased to have had it back again.

The consequences of perestroika were no more favourable for the regime. The lumbering mechanism of central planning could function in a minimal sort of way so long as it was not tampered with, but attempts to supplement it with market mechanisms (such as permission for co-operatives to set up sales outlets and restaurants) and incentives only tended to multiply the disruption and bottlenecks in supply and distribution that they were intended to ease. Some co-operatives simply bought trade goods at controlled prices and sold them at market ones. State enterprises certainly became competitive, but not in the way envisaged. Instead they tended to take on the character of autonomous fiefs competing for centrally allocated resources and hoarding them in order to supply the needs of their dependent workforces, who relied upon their enterprise for a range of benefits and found themselves drifting into a quasi-feudal relationship with its managers. Without a genuine market the system could not cope with rising consumer demand and diverse and sophisticated preference schedules. The poor quality and unattractiveness of Soviet-produced consumer goods was notorious, as was the unreliability of consumer durables. The fervent demand for tourists' clothing and accoutrements is well known.[19]

The rouble (the same was true for East European currencies) was not exchangeable on the international money market and its formal exchange rate overvalued it grossly (it was officially worth about £1). The principal tourist-attracting cities of the USSR, principally Moscow and Leningrad (as well as Prague and Budapest), were consequently infested with illegal money traders, who operated by accosting Western visitors in public spaces and offering them deals. The perestroika programme, far from amending such deficiencies, tended to exacerbate them, and deliberate obstruction from bureaucrats whose positions were threatened by reforms made matters still worse. Perestroika's disruptive impact on production tended to cause output to decline, dislocating the economic structure, weakening the rouble even further and inflaming consumer dissatisfaction. Such developments intertwined with the effects being produced by glasnost, for they fuelled the disintegration of the political structure and the party's internal unity. It was indeed by taking advantage of discontents like these that Boris Yeltsin first turned himself into a populist figure.

The explosion in April 1986 of the Chernobyl nuclear reactor in the Ukraine symbolised the deficiencies in the Soviet economic culture and the contradictions in the reform agenda. The disaster, with numerous casualties, was due to poor design and standards of construction in the reactor, and set off by defective management. It exemplified both the shoddiness of standards in the civil economy and its dependence on this same dangerously inadequate equipment, for Chernobyl was merely one of many similar reactors, which remained indispensable to the Soviet power supply – in fact the remaining functioning parts of the Chernobyl station itself had to be brought back into operation, as the electricity it produced could not be foregone. The principles of glasnost did not stop the authorities from trying to react in the traditional manner – by concealing what had happened and imposing a news blackout. Only the nuclear cloud blowing across northern Europe exposed the reality of what had occurred and forced a confession. More was destroyed than the immediate devastation and loss of life. If any single incident was responsible for shattering confidence both internally and across the world, in the concept of centralised planning, once supposed to be the secret of communist success, it was this one.

1989 and After

All the same, as late as the beginning of 1989 the Gorbachev experiment still did not look evidently foredoomed, and the foundations of the Soviet Union still appeared reasonably secure – although there had already occurred worrying signs on the fringes of the USSR that dissatisfactions were beginning to translate themselves into national antagonisms. At that point Gorbachev himself remained a very popular figure. He was highly regarded among Western governments, not least for graceful acceptance that the USSR had in reality lost the Cold War and was seeking to withdraw from the contest on the best terms it could obtain. He was esteemed by the Western public and by most Western communists because his government's actions had significantly lessened the threat of nuclear confrontation. In visits to the GDR and Beijing he was welcomed with enormous acclaim as the symbol that communism could assume a less repressive face than the citizens of these two states were obliged to endure. At home his standing may have been on the wane, especially among the military and elements of the bureaucracy, but it was not yet fundamentally undermined.

The sequence of events which destroyed first of all the bloc regimes and shortly afterwards the USSR itself have been examined intensively and at length[20] and will not be recounted here. Our concerns are of a more general nature and relate to the overall picture. If the Soviet Union could be said to have been brought down by fragmentation at its power centres, the same was certainly not the case as far as Eastern Europe was concerned. The regimes in all of them remained comparatively united, and when their military and police capacities are considered, the opposition movements which were raising their heads looked laughably weak in contrast. In other times and other places they would have been disposed of without difficulty, as indeed was the case in China. To be sure, if the unreconciled communist rulers in the GDR or Czechoslovakia (and probably Poland) had been willing to spill blood they could have survived a little longer. The astonishing fact is that they were not, and this is in fact the clue to the nature of the transformation.

Lenin had been fond of remarking, with reference to imperialism and the Tsarist empire, that a chain snaps at its weakest link. In Poland the spring elections of 1989 commenced the dismantling of the regime, but events in Hungary precipitated the final collapse. In the course of the year the ruling party more or less lay down and died by transforming itself formally into a social democratic party (a rump broke off to maintain the communist tradition) and throwing the political system open to freely contested elections. The country proceeded to open its border to Austria, and through that exit flowed massed numbers of Czech and GDR citizens, escaping their respective regimes. A chain reaction was set in motion which brought open opposition demonstrations out on to the streets of East Berlin, Warsaw and Prague. Opposition crystallised around Civic and Democratic Forums, whose political character, unified only by commitment to political democracy, was diffuse and vague, certainly not socialist or reforming communist as the Hungarian or Czechoslovak revolutionaries had been in 1956 and 1968, but by not in the main anti-socialist either, though such elements did exist, especially in Poland.

Thus confronted, the East German and Czechoslovak regimes simply crumpled, the latter being extinguished forthwith, the former being liquidated via a token reformed communist transition. Their Polish counterpart exited in a slightly more dignified fashion, through elections which permitted a staged replacement of communist government in favour of a revived Solidarity. Why did they not fight for self-preservation? – for none of them lacked troops, and while there might be questions about the reliability of these, regimes which really believed in themselves and their historic value would presumably have taken the gamble as the Polish had done in 1981 and the Chinese did in 1989. The answer is to be found in the fact they were formed and saw themselves as part of an international movement of proletarian revolution led by the USSR. It was from this that they derived their legitimacy and their sense of identity, that which enabled the leaders to convince themselves that they truly represented, appearances to the contrary notwithstanding, the interests of their respective working classes. It appears that the GDR rulers did prepare for bloodshed and that their resolve collapsed only when Moscow made it clear that they need expect no ideological support from that quarter. It was not a material problem, for they undoubtedly had enough firepower at their disposal to impose an immediate solution. But abandoned by the fountainhead of legitimacy, their morale evaporated and they saw no further point in resisting.

It is not surprising that the Warsaw Pact regime most at odds with the Kremlin was the only one which did endeavour to forcibly resist the march of history. Ceauçescu, the Romanian dictator, fearing that the military was unreliable, mobilised the armed formations of his secret police, the Securitate, to put down the popular uprising with bullets. His fears regarding the army were well-founded, for it turned against him and crushed the Securitate. He and his wife, Elena, implicated in his crimes, were captured and shot on Christmas Day. It is reported that as they were being taken to their execution they sang the Internationale – perhaps in that extremity they recollected the ideals which had brought them into the communist movement when it was a bold and self-sacrificing step to take in the Romania of the thirties. The point is more than a trivial one, for it demonstrates that lust for power and privilege[21] alone was not sufficient motivation for the men and occasional woman who ran the communist regimes; ideological underpinning was required as well.[22]

The point is emphasised by events in the last member of the bloc, Bulgaria. No public disorder was evident here, although there had been greater toleration in recent years of intellectual dissent in the capital, Sofia, and the government was drawing unfavourable international attention to itself for the way it treated the Turkish minority in the south of the country. On the face of things, however, there was no reason why the regime, lacking much reforming inclination and firmly in the Stalinist tradition as well as the saddle, should not have perpetuated its rule indefinitely on its own resources. Yet when the international system disintegrated it too gave up, opening up the country to the West, rebaptising itself as the Socialist Party and submitting itself to freely contested and reportedly fair elections.[23]

Romania had been a semi-detached member of the bloc; two European countries which regarded themselves as communist regimes were entirely outside it, namely Yugoslavia and Albania. The significance of Yugoslavia is considered below in relation to nationalism: the instance of Albania illustrates yet again the importance of the world movement even to a party ostensibly in bitter antagonism to it. Following the liquidation of the Cultural Revolution Hoxha's regime had repudiated its alliance with China and defiantly proclaimed itself to be the only socialist country on earth. With minimal foreign trade, no external investment or foreign debt, deliberately minimising technological application in its economy, a per capita income the lowest in Europe, and without fraternal connexions to other regimes, it gave every appearance of being confined in a time-warp. Hoxha, as absolute a dictator as Stalin or Pol Pot and with no less relish for historical fabrication, though slightly less bloodthirsty, had died in 1985 and his successors were individuals of mean calibre – possibly because he had purged everyone of ability or judgement among his associates. It might perhaps be imagined that 1989–91 would have represented a golden opportunity for the Albanian regime – after all, the propaganda it had long disseminated about the anti-socialist, counter-revolutionary directions of all its former allies since 1945 now appeared to be justified in the event and it could attribute its own survival to its spartan social order and refusal to compromise with the fleshpots of capitalism. Nor, unlike Cuba or North Korea, was it threatened with a powerful and aggressive enemy close to its borders. Yet within a couple of years, without civil war or major bloodletting, Albania too had gone the way of the others; its ultra-Stalinist ruling party threw in the towel and allowed itself to be voted out of office. Isolation as a maverick beside a surviving socialist bloc in the context of a global struggle was one thing, isolation as an anachronism in an indifferent capitalist universe was something else and a source of total political demoralisation.

Nationalism Resurgent

Lenin, and Marxism–Leninism, had always been highly conscious of nationalism and national identity as social and political realities. As a weapon directed against imperialism it was esteemed positively, and once the struggle had been successful multinational socialist states were supposed to provide, within their structures of harmonious co-operation, for legitimate expressions of the national identities to which citizens were attached. Beyond that, the national question within the socialist state or bloc was supposed to be a dead issue. In reality, since the formation of a socialist state system their governments had been fitting political practices into national or even nationalist frameworks – in Yugoslavia, the USSR, China, Poland and Bulgaria, to mention only some. 'The socialisation of the nation,' according to E.H. Carr, 'has as its natural corollary the nationalisation of socialism.'[24] These government manipulations nevertheless were a different matter from explosions of disintegrative nationalist passions within the states themselves.

Even while Gorbachev appeared to be firmly in control of the Soviet Union and well before the political earthquake in Eastern Europe, worrying signs were emerging that social discontents and tensions on the peripheries of the USSR were running into nationalist courses and ethnic antagonisms. As early as December 1986 riots with an edge of national grievance at Russian hegemony and the proportion of Russians living in the country (and occupying the most favourable employments) had broken out in Alma Ata, capital of Soviet Khazakstan. Just over a year later the two Soviet republics of Armenia and Azerbaijan were literally at war with each other over a territorial issue. At the same time anti-Russian (and anti-Soviet) demonstrations were occurring in the Baltic republics in pursuit of demands for national autonomy or independence which, in the case of Lithuania, were co-opted by the local (and supposedly subordinate) communist party. Nor was the Great Russian republic itself exempt from the reappearance of Great Russian chauvinism of a particularly sinister sort. A notorious article published early in 1988 attacking the reform programme (paradoxically one effect of the reforms was that such attacks could now appear) had distinctly chauvinist and anti-semitic overtones. An organisation titled *Pamyat* (Memory), which was formed ostensibly to care for war memorials, soon developed anti-semitic and fascistic leanings, formed paramilitary squads and indulged in violent attacks on opponents and Jews. It was able to do so because it had protectors in the highest reaches of the state apparatus.

The communist regime which was most afflicted by nationalist eruption and where the state was destroyed in consequence was a non-member of the bloc, the supposedly most flexible and liberal of all communist states, Yugoslavia, particularly ironic as its regime had successfully defied Stalin on the foundation of *Yugoslav* nationalism. The federal structure of the state, however, tempted its rival leaders to use of ethnic rhetoric in power struggles within the Yugoslav League of Communists; this went back as far as the early seventies and became more pronounced around the time of Tito's death in 1980. A year later it escalated into ethnic persecution, by the authorities of the largest republic of the federation, Serbia, of the (majority) Albanian population in the Kosovo province. In 1990 the party disintegrated into its constituent national elements and with it the country. Armed conflict commenced the next year, at first in a bloodless and rather farcical manner as the northern republic of Slovenia detached itself, but thereafter turned into an uncontrollable three-way war of exceptional ferocity and brutality propelled by ethnic hatreds and territorial covetousness.[25]

The events in Yugoslavia aroused anxieties that similar processes could be in train in other parts of newly liberated eastern Europe where national sentiment and friction had been in the past scarcely less intense than in the Balkans.[26] Moreover, the people of these countries undoubtedly did have a national consciousness of themselves as citizens of historic states forced into humiliating subordination to Moscow. Major violence, however, was averted, although the new governments did indeed wrap themselves in their national flags and divert attention from their own deficiencies by inciting prejudice against national minorities, particularly the more helpless such as gypsies and the few Jews who still lived in the area. The only really serious national conflict, however, in Czechoslovakia between the dominant Czechs and perceivedly disadvantaged Slovaks, was resolved peacefully if not amicably with the sundering of the Federation.

It would be an error to regard ethnic nationalism in the disintegrating communist world as a reality that had persisted unchanged throughout the era of communist rule and which, though forcibly suppressed during those decades, had remained present all the time and only waited the opportunity to reassert itself and push aside the collapsing values of Marxism–Leninism. To see it as a form of undead politics, suspended but unchanged in essence, which rose vampire-like from the grave once the Marxist sun went down, has more substance but is still misleading. A more accurate perception would view the eruption of nationalistic and chauvinist attitudes as something largely though not entirely new – not the cause of the communist breakdown but its consequence.

It is clear from any study of the developments, particularly those in Yugoslavia, that the generation of national hatreds was not a *spontaneous* reaction of the masses but was deliberately provoked and cultivated by former communist political leaders and, in a debased caricature of Gramsci's conceptions, by former communist intellectuals reinterpreting both the historic memories and contemporary grievances of their audiences, employing the techniques of modern media dissemination as well as the traditional ones of journalism and demonstrations.[27] Ancient national identities which had been all but forgotten could be taken out and dusted off to provide an ideological framework for political and military organisation, whether in Belgrade, Zagreb, Bratislava, Tblisi or Moscow, once the credibility of the existing one had become exhausted. On the part of the political leaders and spokespeople who adopted these techniques it was a form of opportunism designed to perpetuate their authority; on the part of the populations who responded it represented a recourse to cultural driftwood in an ideological shipwreck. On what other basis could they hope to salvage, in the dawning world of global free markets, such job security and welfare provision as they had enjoyed under the old regime?

Although superficially a very different sort of episode, similar considerations should be applied to the events in Beijing in June 1989. There had always been a strong nationalist strain in the Maoist regime, as well there might, in view of the continuity of Chinese civilisation over millennia and the fact that the revolution had rescued the country from degrading subordination to the West. After the extinction of the Gang of Four and the rise of Deng Xiaoping to predominance from 1979, the government embarked upon a radical reorientation of the economy in the direction of market relations, the principal aspect of this being the abolition of the agricultural commune and the reconstitution of the peasant family as an economic unit, which provided a foundation for the encouragement of capitalist initiative in other sectors of the economy. The new directions, however, unleashed social tensions as well, and among the youthful intelligentsia questioning of governance by the geriatric autocrats who monopolised ultimate responsibility. The students' discontent and impatience was inflamed by reports of the Gorbachev developments in the USSR. After a period of wall-poster agitation, with the civil police sympathetic or wavering, the enormous demonstration assembled in Tianenmen Square which presented a challenge to the authorities to choose between major democratic concessions and major repression.

Although, from what is known of the the developments, there were apparently real discussions in the Politburo – possibly more concerned with the reliability of the army than with the principles at issue – the ultimate outcome was never in doubt and the tanks were sent in. What is interesting from our perspective is the rhetoric that the CP leadership used to justify the suppression. It was no different in tone and substance from that which might have been used by any Western power in similar circumstances. Nothing was heard of putative dangers to international communism issuing from a challenge to the leadership of the CPC, and virtually nothing beyond the merest token phrases of peril to socialism in the People's Republic itself. All the statements related to the stability of government, society and the nation, the threat of civil disorder and disruption and the horrors of national disintegration (still within living memory in China) if the protest was allowed to continue. It was as a *national* leadership not a communist one that the Politburo reasserted its authority, and it is likely to be by authoritarian national ideology following Deng's death that a future leadership will strive to hold the social structure together amid proliferating market relationships.

The Debacle and its Consequences

The CPSU and the USSR themselves did not have long to go after 1989, for by then it was clear that the communist system was too sclerotic and threadbare to sustain any reform which continued to preserve the essence of Marxism–Leninism, and the events of that year had extinguished Moscow's credibility as the centre of an international movement. It was revealed simply as a great power struggling against an avalanche of intractable domestic problems. After December 1989 the international movement was both effectively and formally dead. A minor but revealing symbol was the closing-down of *Problems of Peace and Socialism* in 1990.[28] Rather surprisingly, as political fragmentation and social disruption grew from month to month across the Soviet Union, there was little mass response on the streets apart from in the Baltic republics, now firmly committed to separatism.

Nor was there any mass response one way or the other around the unbelievably amateurish and muddled attempt in August 1991 at a coup by elements in the state and party leadership, aiming at a reassertion of the old order.[29] Such mobilisation as there was occurred on behalf of the anti-coup forces grouped around Boris Yeltsin. It was a pitiful end for the historic CPSU with its claims to be the party of the October Revolution, socialist construction and victory over Nazism. The party leadership was totally paralysed and unable to even convene a meeting of its Central Committee. Nobody lifted a finger to defend the supposed embodiment of the consciousness of the Soviet proletariat and masses when, after the coup's failure, Yeltsin proclaimed the party to be outlawed, its organisation dissolved and its assets sequestrated.[30] It was to revive, but in an unrecognisably different form. The USSR followed it into oblivion at the end of the year and its fifteen republics assumed the form of independent sovereign states. Most of them continued, in more or less democratic structures, to be ruled by their old nomenklatura – but these had all stridently and effusively ceased to be communists. Many in fact were turning themselves as fast as possible into financial dealers and entrepreneurs.

The shock waves from 1989 and 1991 rolled across the communist parties of the capitalist world. Some of these affected to remain confident in the values which had inspired the world movement and in the eventual triumph of socialism internationally. Among those who adopted this posture were the CPs of Portugal, France, Greece and the USA, but they did not escape splits and ruptures as a result which reduced their significance even beyond the low level at which it had already arrived. The CPUSA was negligible in any case, and because of its leadership's rigid attitudes lost the one outstanding figure in its ranks, Angela Davis. The PCP experienced dissidence and split. The PCF had been in sharp decline since the calamitous experiment of 1981 and its national vote had fallen below 10 per cent. Its degeneration was measured by the fact that one of its local mayors, desperately seeking grass-roots credibility, had led violent anti-immigrant demonstration. After the bloc fell it avoided splitting in any disastrous manner but its shrinkage accelerated and quarrelling intensified among its leadership. It had reached the status of a political relic with nowhere to go but downwards.

There were at the same time two CPs of this kind which experienced different fates and continued to maintain their local viability – in West Bengal and South Africa. The former was a product of particular local circumstances, and as the provincial ruling party possessed a mass base and a flexible and popular governing strategy which the international collapse could not immediately erode. The SACP paradoxically was enjoying the greatest contemporary success of them all as the apartheid regime crumbled and it assumed the position of a major force in the formation of the new South Africa. Its leaders did continue to repeat in the new situation the ancient international certainties, but they had more pressing immediate matters to concern them.

The more common reaction of the parties in Europe, large or small, was either effectively to disappear or to discard their communist identities. John Callaghan's comment (made with reference to the CPGB) that they did not 'attempt to salvage anything from the Marxist theoretical legacy or the practical heritage of the Communist tradition'[31] may be overstated, but it represents the essence of the reality. The significant member of this group, the PCI, changed its name to the

Party of the Democratic Left and turned itself into a purely national formation – that was after all the culmination of the direction in which it had been heading over several decades. It did have to endure a split in doing so: the dissidents set themselves up as Communist Refoundation, which was small but far from negligible (it held the balance of power in the Italian Parliament following the elections of 1996). It was the only traditionalist breakaway from the dissolving Western CPs which amounted to anything. Among the smaller parties the normal response was to seek collaboration or unification with organisations or parties of new left or environmentalist character. Tiny traditionalist or even professedly Stalinist splinters continued to exist in most of these countries, but they amounted to little more than societies for nostalgics and operated no international network.

After the political hurricane of 1989–91, 1.4 billion human beings continued to live under regimes which formally accounted themselves as Marxist–Leninist (the preceding figure had been 1.7 billion).[32] In reality only the population of Cuba (7 million) could authentically claim to be included in this category. The remaining survivors were either stampeding towards the market, or in the case of the North Korean regime had evolved into such bizarre form that the nearest analogy would be a crumbling pharaonic despotism. Perhaps surprisingly, in view of their records as the Kremlin's overseers in Eastern Europe, most of the successor parties to the CPs did not vanish and a few, in their new democratic costumes, even staged remarkable political comebacks. This fact emphasises that they did have genuine social bases, and that these actually were among the industrial workforce in the main, for their rule offered job security and assured welfare, albeit at a low level. They revived when it became apparent that the benefits of the new consumer capitalism were to be neither universal nor evenly distributed.

The CPSU, as the Communist Party of the Russian Federation, revived too, and formidably, at least in name, to become in fact the only party with an organisation able to reach across Russia. Its character, however, has been transformed, for its emphasis is now great power and stridently nationalist rather than social, let alone concerned with class. In this guise it was (and is) easily able to accommodate to co-operation with straightforwardly chauvinist, anti-semite and neo-fascist elements, the notorious 'red–brown alliance'. This course should not surprise any observer. The communist regime in its day, whatever shortcomings it may have had, made the USSR into a superpower feared and respected throughout the world as well as assuring a basic sufficiency and well-ordered surroundings for all its citizens

– precisely the opposite of prevailing conditions. It is these positive memories which Zyuganov has succeeded in linking to present discontents and rage against the foreigners who have imposed them to mobilise sentiment behind a pseudo-communist politics.

The rabid nationalism which in Russia now bears the label 'communist' illuminates in the clearest possible manner as an extreme case the direction in which all the ruling and former ruling parties of the quondam communist world have proceeded. Even in Cuba the main ideological resource is anti-Yankee nationalism, though it tries to mobilise international support against US pressure. Everywhere else the parties have become wholly national in their outlooks or international only in respect of fitting into the global economy. The fate of the non-ruling parties reflected in general measure what happened to their counterparts in government. Some, with hope triumphing over reality, tried to go on asserting the values in which they had been conditioned, a few disappeared utterly, most transformed themselves into something else. On thing they all had in common, however, was that if they did continue to have any political resonance it was thenceforth confined to their own country.

Evaluation

Even as early as 1939 the impulse emanating from 1917 towards international revolution under the Marxist banner appeared to have spent itself. The one established revolutionary state had closed in upon itself and descended into a paroxysm of bloodletting: the Communist International had degenerated into no more than a shrivelled caricature of its original being. The Nazi–Soviet Pact of August that year represented a proclamation that brutal raison d'état would take priority in Moscow over any considerations of internationalism, morality or even consistency.

Six years later, with unqualified victory over the Axis powers, matters were transformed in several directions. For a brief period the movement and its state were relatively popular throughout Europe and the Americas as well as having established a strong (and mostly armed) presence in parts of Asia. The other principal dimension of change was the marked expansion of the geographical area under the control of Marxist–Leninist parties. That expansion, however, represented something very different from what the founders of the Comintern had foreseen and aimed at. On the one hand it was the state power of the USSR extended westwards (though not without significant local support) and on the other a number of indigenous revolutions in the Balkans and Asia – areas characterised by their backwardness in terms of industrial and social development – the reverse of what had been anticipated in 1917. The centre of the communist movement after 1947 and more especially after 1949 was no longer a single state but a bloc – an apparent triumph and vindication of the communist historical perspective, but one containing the seeds of its own destruction as the pull of national considerations against international ones was multiplied from one state to several. Not even Stalin's iron straitjacket could prevent this becoming apparent in his own time, with the Yugoslav breakaway and the practical if unstated independence of the Chinese communist rulers.

The fragmentation of the bloc which soon followed the dictator's death was thus not a contingent process which different or more sensitive approaches might have averted: its potential was an inherent and inbuilt feature of the inter-state structure which had been created by that time. In principle, perhaps, there was no absolute reason why the states which seceded from the bloc at different times should not have gone their separate ways on an amicable basis and remained allies in face of the capitalist enemy, but all Leninist not to speak of Stalinist traditions told against such a resolution. These states were founded on ideological legitimation of a particularly comprehensive and all-inclusive sort, so that difference and disagreement were certain to be interpreted in ideological terms and perceived as deviation from the true path. This was in addition, of course, to the practical interest which the USSR had in keeping the East European states in a condition of subordination.

The emergence of a bloc of Marxist–Leninist states coincided with the commencement of a bipolar superpower conflict embracing the globe, with political, military and cultural dimensions and for forty years holding the world hostage to the threat of a nuclear armageddon. Not only were the Marxist–Leninist states participants but also the communist movement in every country, as the proclaimed aim of each communist party was to attain political power and remodel its society swiftly or slowly along Marxist–Leninist lines. Discounting qualifications and shadings to the general picture, two rival ideologies battled for the soul of humankind. For the communists of the non-ruling parties their project was first and foremost in their own eyes one of human emancipation (although it was many other things in addition), and of course if they achieved power they tried to translate that into reality even when they were aware that the populations they governed were less than anxious to be emancipated in that fashion. As

Janós Kadar was to express it in the aftermath of the 1956 repression, 'If the wish of the masses does not coincide with progress, then one must lead the masses in another direction.'[33] So a façade of popular enthusiasm was always constructed, with all-embracing mass organisations controlled by though not identified with the party; mass demonstrations of counterfeit enthusiasm; single-candidate elections.

Such practices were repulsive to public opinion in the Western democracies and so the movement in those states had to battle always against the disadvantage which their association brought them and which ensured that they would never be entrusted with serious government power. Perhaps the surprising fact is that they managed, particularly in France and Italy, to maintain their position as well as they did. As the years passed they tried in general to take their distance and emphasise their democratic credibility, without breaking the international links which remained essential to their political and cultural identities. CPs in colonial regimes, dictatorships or pseudo-constitutional states throughout the third world had less of a problem from the association: it was in those parts of the world therefore that the movement was likely to make the most dramatic advances.

The essential appeal of the movement, whether to the industrial proletariat it claimed primarily to represent or the peasants and intellectuals it wanted to incorporate, was its claim to combine economic rationality with social justice and to have developed practical mechanisms both for removing the ruling classes who stood in the way and putting in place an economic order with need in place of profit as its driving force. The economic systems established on the model of Stalinist industrialisation in the USSR were, however, substantially irrational and profoundly flawed, and destroyed by their internal contradictions far more than outside pressures, even though the latter were considerable.[34] Owing to their integration with the political structure, when they crashed they brought the latter down with them. Where the economic system was reorientated before it collapsed, in China and Vietnam, it is clear that the communist political system will perish by slow erosion rather than spectacular implosion, being transformed into some variety of authoritarian nationalist regime.

The communist movement has often been characterised as a secular religion, and there is a lot of truth in this, with its apparatus of saints, martyrs, evangelists, priesthood, and so forth – but it was a religion of a very particular sort. Its peculiarity derives not mainly from the fact that it had no supernatural elements and indeed categorically rejected them, but more from the centrality of politics to its identity. The orthodox religions can survive quite happily when the political formations to which they are attached are destroyed because the majority of their believers are not primarily concerned with political matters. Even within regimes which embody their outlook the clergy and the religious institutions are usually careful to preserve a distance from the political framework and the politicians. The communist movement, by contrast, was concerned with the political sphere first, last and all the time. When its politics and all that followed from it was not merely overthrown but utterly discredited it disappeared, as did its individual components.

In view of all its unquestionable shortcomings it might seem difficult to understand how the international communist movement succeeded in constituting such a formidable political force during the greater part of the present century, indeed to effectively *define* the character of what Eric Hobsbawm has termed the 'Short Twentieth Century'.[35] There are two principal reasons. One is that the ideas energetically promulgated by the parties of the movement were attractive to a great many people in particular places and situations; the other is the organisational traditions which were embodied in the movement. The two were not wholly unconnected. Adam Westoby notes that non-communist regimes which tried to utilise communist organisational principles were unable to do so, the transplantation was artificial and failed to survive;[36] though on the other hand individual communist defectors to other organically viable movements and institutions tended to find their communist organisational experience a great asset.

The core of the ideology lay in the assertion that the particular interests and political aims (as interpreted by the party) of one social class, the industrial proletariat, were simultaneously the general interests of society and other exploited or 'progressive' elements such as peasants or intellectuals – as well as being historically validated. Communism in its twentieth-century guise began as a movement appealing to the working classes of war-weary Europe, and though its initial capture of state power was confined to the Russian Empire, it did succeed in putting down viable roots throughout the continent. These proved capable of giving rise to vigorous growths in the succeeding crises of war and occupation in spite of the political degeneration of the movement in its original homeland, a degeneration which the communists emphatically denied, refused to recognise and indeed transformed into virtue.

The Axis defeat in 1945 turned out to be the high point of communist influence among the working classes of Europe. Thereafter, with the continent mostly divided between a coercively-imposed version of the Russian model and an alliance of militantly anti-communist states, it steadily receded – despite occasional local variations and attempts by some of the west European CPs to pioneer, with considerable modifications to the ideology, new and more attractive approaches in keeping with post-war consumer society. The west European working classes however, with the partial exception of the Italian, had however attached themselves to political formations which better represented their interests.[37]

The movement, however, discovered, just as its advance in western Europe became permanently stalled, an enormous new constituency among the peasant masses of Asia and other regions of the Third World. To these limitlessly oppressed toilers, for whom, as Westoby remarks, bare survival was good fortune and comfort an unthinkable luxury, and to the intellectuals who articulated their sentiments, communism expressed the hope for a better world, class vengeance upon their timeless exploiters and, in the image of the USSR and the 'people's democracies', a demonstration that what had never been thinkable to previous generations had now become possible at last.

Lenin, even when a young agitator and before Bolshevism had appeared upon the scene, liked to insist that the only thing the working class had to oppose to the power and resources of the rulers was its organisational capacity, and that the revolutionary party must be built upon this. Although performance frequently did not measure up to principle, one feature which distinguished the Bolsheviks from their pre-1917 revolutionary rivals was their emphasis upon organisation.[38] Once they were engaged in asserting their rule over a fragmenting state and fighting a civil war that emphasis became central. It was no accident that Stalin rose to command the party through his control as General Secretary over its organisation.

Communist ideology in peasant environments could produce a messianic zeal. Communist organisational practices supplied the structures which in east and south-east Asia turned the social energy that would otherwise have been dissipated in uncoordinated local revolts into a titanic insurrectionary force.[39] It was, culturally modified, the same form of messianic determination and organisational capacity as had placed other parties of the movement at the centre of the Resistance and Partisan activity in occupied Europe.

Communist forms of organisation, though practised everywhere in the movement, had been designed for extreme situations, initially for working-class agitation under Tsarism, then hardened and consolidated in the desperate circumstances of post-civil-war Soviet Russia. They were readily adapted to coercive forms of government and administration and were tailor-made for elites – or dictators – accountable only to their own interpretation of Marxism–Leninism and sense of history. Marxism–Leninism can be considered as the amalgam of ideological belief and organisational practice embedded in the parties of the movement. Not surprisingly, once the parties had patronage to dispense there were plenty of careerists and opportunists ready to mouth the correct phrases and go through the motions without any sincerity. That applied not only to the ruling parties with a monopolistic party-state at their disposal – though it was naturally most evident in such cases – but to the larger non-ruling ones which controlled jobs and privileges in trade unions, linked associations or their own apparatus. Nevertheless, as this text has tried to demonstrate, the genuine motivating power of the ideology can never be discounted.

An outlook and form of organisation that was well adapted to winning state power if the opportunity presented itself, could not avoid changing its character to a greater or lesser degree once it was in the position of running the state. That applied to post-revolutionary Russia; it applied to the parties emerging from the underground to take control of eastern Europe (mostly under Stalin's supervision); it applied no less to Mao's guerrillas once the CPR had been established. They were compelled to multiply their responsibilities, expand their personnel and wholly reshape the direction of their behaviour. In the Soviet Five-Year Plans they had their model. It is probable that the economic programmes of the communist regimes, with their wrenching impact upon civil society, could not have been sustained by any other means than the use of the communist parties to co-ordinate and motivate economic, social and cultural activity through the various levels of these societies. In the absence of a market the party acted as the society's nervous system, processing its informational inputs (though as Michael Waller points out the information was always distorted) and transmitting its motor impulses.

That was all the truer in that these programmes were profoundly and wastefully irrational and could not have gained acceptance and self-sustainability in the absence of the coercive mechanisms that kept them in operation.[40] Hillel Ticktin notes that they possessed neither the logic of the market nor that of authentic socialism (whatever that might be) and their irrationality was exemplified in the fact that in the early seventies the Soviet economy applied greater resources to repairing machinery rather than to manufacturing it – mostly because of intrinsic imperfection rather than routine wear and tear. The reality of these economic structures was further distorted by the large inputs of unpaid or cheap labour from women who, under the guise of formal equality, were exhorted to enter the labour market, but on terms inferior to that of their male counterparts, and at the same time to continue to take prime responsibility for domestic labour – not least the endless queueing which the irrationality of the system generated.

At the same time the movement cannot be regarded in isolation, as though it were a self-enclosed system. From the moment of its birth and more especially from the era of the Cold War it was recognised, with its global programme and rhetoric, as a mortal enemy by the established powers-that-be, above all by the centres of corporate capital and the political upholders of capital's hegemony. The Soviet Union on its own might just have been tolerable, as China was to become from the early seventies, but what could not be forgiven was the claim by the communist movement not only to a project of social transformation but to to a political loyalty transcending international boundaries. Not even Stalin himself could exorcise this spectre, although he tried, with the liquidation of the Comintern in 1943 and his subsequent efforts to reign in Tito and Mao. The hopes and expectations propelling the movement forward in the aftermath of the 1945 victory escaped his control, however. The determination by the West at all costs (both economic and otherwise) to curb the communist movement in all its manifestations (which did not exclude limited agreements from time to time) became the dominant theme of international relations and political affairs during the second half of the century, divided the world into two blocs armed to the teeth with nuclear weaponry, stretched even the resources of the United States and on at least on occasion brought the nations to the verge of thermonuclear annihilation. What frightened the West, of course, was precisely what attracted those parts of the world's population which had no reason to love it.

Ironically, that part was not in the main the one for which the movement claimed above all to speak, namely the industrial working classes. Fiat workers in Turin might weep on hearing the news of Stalin's death,[41] but that was a most untypical reaction. In general Western proletariats accommodated excellently to the welfare capitalism of the post-war years and discovered in it realisation of the ancestral hopes of their class. The working-class bases of the PCI and the PCF were shrinking assets, as the former in particular realised. It cannot be denied that where working-class insurrection, whether violent or relatively peaceful, has occurred after 1945 it has been directed overwhelmingly *against* ruling communist regimes; whether in East Berlin in 1953, Poland and Hungary in 1956, Poland subsequently in

1970, 1976 and 1981, little-reported sporadic episodes in the USSR itself, or even Shanghai during the Cultural Revolution. Equally, it cannot be denied that fear of communist advance among Western working classes in the post-war years was among the principal incentives on the part of anti-communist politicians to preserve economies of full employment and expanding welfare.

It seems reasonable to conclude that while pressures from the West almost certainly hastened the collapse of the Soviet bloc and transformation in the nature of the Chinese regime, in-built contradictions in the nature of the Marxist–Leninist regimes would sooner or later have brought about similar results in any event. It was not by accident that the movement, both states and parties, was fragmenting to a growing extent throughout the post-war years, though the full implications of this were realised only with the Soviet collapse. The immense gravitational pull of the Soviet state kept nearly all the parties apart from the CPC within its orbit, but for many of them at an increasing distance as they encountered the dead ends of Soviet-defined Marxism–Leninism. The millennial hopes of the communist movement, whether Stalinist, Eurocommunist or any modulation of Leninism, were increasingly shown to be illusory, for the only options fell between centrally planned systems of economy and social organisation which were unsustainable in the long run, or else modifications which had market restoration as its endpoint. Parties committed to the latter might or might not continue to call themselves 'communist' for historic reasons, but relationship to what went before is no more than nominal.

Now destroyed, it is inconceivable that a world communist movement could ever be re-created (though Trotskyist organisations continue to preserve that fantasy, seeing themselves as the purified version of global communism). The movement's basic presuppositions have been too emphatically demonstrated to be false, its record and ideological tenets have been too thoroughly discredited. An entire historical era has in effect sunk beneath the waves. This does not mean that it has left no legacy apart from the the socio-economic disaster which its fall has produced in the former USSR and much of eastern Europe. It stands as a foredoomed and heroic though destructive attempt to emancipate humanity from the contradictions of modernity and to pass, in Engels's words, 'from the realm of necessity to the realm of freedom'. Other social and political movements, whose shape is still indistinct, will require in the third millennium to learn from the catastrophe and resume the tasks in which the communist movement failed.

Notes

Notes to Introduction

1 In what follows the development of the movement in Latin America, apart from Cuba, is treated in a very perfunctory fashion and even more so in the Middle East or Australasia. The nationally important Japanese Communist Party is referred to only in passing. Another area which deserves fuller treatment is that of the 'front organisations' – international trade union federations, student or youth movements, peace campaigns, friendship associations, etc., which were controlled by the communists.

2 That assumption was challenged in the early days of the Bolshevik revolution by women such as Alexandra Kollontai, but the regime soon became as sexist as any, and under Stalin traditional male–female relations were made central to the Soviet concept of the family, and contraception and abortion were outlawed. In Ceauçescu's Romania young women were subjected to compulsory gynaecological examinations to ensure they were not illegally practising contraception or abortion. In the West, argument was resumed, especially in the Eurocommunist parties, with the rise of the women's movement form the seventies.

3 His broader survey, *The Evolution of Communism*, published in 1989, appeared too early to take into account the collapse of Eastern European regimes and is premised on an indefinitely continuing future for the movement.

4 Hillel Ticktin, 'Towards a Political Economy of the USSR', *Critique* No. 1, Spring 1993, pp. 23–7. Further articles in Nos 6 and 9 elaborate the thesis.

Notes to Chapter 1

1 With the exception of Mongolia, but that was scarcely different in character from a constituent republic of the Soviet Union.

2 According to the Julian calendar then used in Russia the Bolshevik Revolution occurred on 25 October and was always referred to in official terminology thereafter as the 'Great October Socialist Revolution', although as a result of switching to the Gregorian calendar used elsewhere in Europe the anniversary was celebrated on 7 November.

3 Also known as the Second International, to claim continuity with Marx's International Workingmen's Association (The First International) of 1864–74.

4 Adam Westoby, *The Evolution of Communism*, Polity, 1989, p. 164.

5 These impressions were greatly hardened by the comprehensive defeat of the newly formed German Communist Party's attempt at insurrection in January 1919.

6 Though it should be noted that at this stage the Bolsheviks were still modest enough to imagine that they would be overtaken in due course by the revolutionaries of the more advanced states. Hence it was intended to shift the headquarters to Berlin once the socialist revolution had succeeded in Germany.

7 Annie Kriegel, *The French Communists: Profile of a People*, University of Chicago Press, 1972, p. 282.

8 Comintern (i.e. Soviet) financing of foreign CPs, however, might turn out to be counter-productive, as it could encourage these parties to develop bloated bureaucracies and become reliant on the outside funds to the detriment of their own energies. Examples relating to the CPGB were cited at a conference on the Soviet archives at Manchester University on 3 February 1996.

9 Unless, like Antonio Gramsci, they had been taken out of the in-fighting by being locked up in enemy prisons.

10 Up to and including the right of secession, a right exercised by agreement only in one instance, that of Finland.

11 Moshe Lewin, *Lenin's Last Struggle*, Faber, 1969.

12 See Isaac Deutscher, *Stalin: A Political Biography*, Penguin, 1970, for an account of the unreal atmosphere of the debate, which had personal as well as political implications.

13 Which went under the title of 'permanent revolution'.

14 The personnel of that caucus changed constantly and its members at one stage might well find themselves oppositionists in the next.

15 Except through its police agents abroad assassinating enemies or defectors.

16 Well documented for the CPGB in 1928–9.

17 The capitalist rulers were held to employ either social democracy or fascism as circumstances required. According to Stalin these movements were 'not antipodes but twins'. Hence the characterisation 'social–fascist'.

18 Stalin himself was probably somewhat contemptuous of the organisation and regarded it as a irksome necessity. He had very little to do with it in person and left its running to lesser subordinates.

19 These included the by now venerable Sidney and Beatrice Webb, who visited the USSR and, though not wholly uncritical (their translated text was indeed the only one in the country where any criticism of the regime could be read), pronounced it to be a 'new civilisation'.

20 In Belgium and France, for example.

21 The French communists in consequence liked to refer to themselves as 'the party of the executed'.

22 See Donald Sassoon, 'The Rise and fall of West European Communism 1939–48', *Contemporary European History*, Vol. 1 Part 2, July 1992, pp. 139–69.

23 So far as they could be 'consulted' across the battle-lines.

24 The country in which it most singularly failed was Poland, where the Western powers had a commitment to a government-in-exile which was anti-Soviet (it had broken off relations with Moscow during the war) and whose partisans were being forcibly repressed with the assistance of the Red Army.

25 Quoted in Fernando Claudin, *The Communist Movement from Comintern to Cominform*, Penguin, 1975, p. 332.

26 Though that official stance may not have been Stalin's real preference. It has been suggested that he was perfectly content to have his potential enemies destroy themselves in mutual conflict and therefore had no real wish to see the Western collapse of 1940.

27 Again, to refer to the British example, both of the two leading figures in the CPGB, Harry Pollitt and Rajani Palme Dutt, possessed talents which would have brought them brilliant careers in the Labour Party had they been so minded.

28 See, for example, Allan Merson, *Communist Resistance in Nazi Germany*, London, Lawrence & Wishart, 1985, for an account of how the underground KPD functioned under the Third Reich.

29 Unless, as in Nazi Germany, the surviving organisation was so fragmented as to make this impossible. Merson's volume shows that nevertheless, reconstruction of a central committee remained a prime objective of the Moscow-based exile leadership.

30 That had not always been the case; the General Secretaryship of the Soviet CP was initially a second-rank responsibility.

31 However, in tiny, remote, and illegal or semi-legal parties not even the Comintern was able to apply these principles consistently and faction fights were both frequent and disruptive.

32 See, for example, the verbatim discussion in the Central Committee of the CPGB over the Comintern's insistence on it reversing its initial pro-war line in September 1939, recorded in F. King and G. Matthews, *About Turn*, London, Lawrence & Wishart, 1990.

33 Some of whom even had aristocratic backgrounds, including Zhou Enlai. This circumstance gave rise to a possibly apocryphal story that during the time of the Sino-Soviet dispute, at a reception which both were attending, he was castigated for his social origins by the Soviet leader Khrushchev, who was boasting of his own peasant antecedents. Zhou is said to have replied, 'Nevertheless, we have an important thing in common – we both betrayed our class.'

34 Though an exception should be noted in the case of Bolivia, where the tin mining, with a very militant workforce, constituted a significant sector of the local economy.

35 Witold S. Sworakowski (ed.), *World Communism: A Handbook 1918–1965*, Hoover Institution Press, 1973.

36 Except among the politically impotent Trotskyists.

37 This is not to argue that that Stalin's motives were either ethical or meritorious, merely that they were realistic in the light of his preconceptions and the existing situation of the USSR. A case can certainly be made that Moscow's war aim was to dominate the entire European continent, but the contrary evidence, in the light of Soviet capabilities and what actually happened in Italy, Greece and Yugoslavia seems overwhelmingly stronger. See Caroline Kennedy-Pipe, *Stalin's Cold War: Soviet Strategies in Europe, 1943–1956*, Manchester, Manchester University Press, 1995 for a recent assessment. The author draws attention to significant differences over international policy within the Soviet elite. There were also elements within the US administration and diplomatic service who from the other side, favoured an aggressive stance in principle. See Daniel Yergin, *Shattered Peace. The Origins of the Cold War and the National Security State*, Penguin, 1980.

38 Winston Churchill, *The Second World War. Triumph and Tragedy*, London, Cassell, 1954, p. 369.

Notes to Chapter 2

1 Until 1939 the Nazi regime proceeded in such a manner, and even after the outbreak of war showed great reluctance to impose material sacrifices on the German population.

2 The question of whether the Italian and French CPs were in a position to launch a victorious revolution in 1944–5 and were prevented only by Stalin's diplomacy, remains a strongly disputed one. The official position naturally was that they were not; critics from the left asserted the opposite. The balanced judgement of Paolo Spriano in *Stalin and the European Communists*, Verso, 1985, is that these parties would certainly have been defeated if they had tried. However, whether such a revolution was possible or not is not really the point – success or failure would have been equally disastrous for the Kremlin.

3 Noted in Adam Westoby, *The Evolution of Communism*, Polity, 1989.

4 Though the former enemy states were faced with the additional difficulty of having to transfer most of their existing industrial plant to the USSR in the shape of reparations.

5 Westoby, *Evolution of Communism*, p. 244.

6 According to Luigi Longo, one of the participants in the Cominform's founding conference, 'we had no idea that we would be presented with such a sharp political turn'. Spriano, *Stalin and the European Communists*, p. 293.

7 The Cominform organ was given the bizarre title *For a Lasting Peace, For a People's Democracy*, allegedly insisted upon by Stalin himself. It was claimed later that this was chosen so that Western broadcasters, whenever they referred to it, would be compelled to repeat the slogan.

8 The potentially disruptive effect of national sentiment upon international communist unity was hinted at in the immediate post-war period, when the PCI had to take into account passionate Italian national opposition to the Yugoslav claim to Trieste.

9 Rankovic was the chief of Tito's security apparatus and regarded as his closest collaborator. In the sixties he himself was purged.

10 The few who did were isolated or imprisoned, or in one case, killed trying to leave the country.

11 Some did refuse and maintained their Soviet loyalties. They were imprisoned under extremely inhumane conditions.

12 Though the Cominform hastened to note that the the CPSU, from its wisdom and experience, had been first to detect the Yugoslav deviation.

13 James Klugmann, *From Trotsky to Tito*, London, Lawrence & Wishart, 1951, pp. 22–6.

14 *Ibid.*, pp. 14–15.

15 No compromise was tolerated. Hitherto friendly non-communists who expressed any sympathy with Yugoslavia were attacked with the utmost vehemence, such as Konni Zilliacus by the British CP. However in Italy, the PCI now found itself in the happy position of being able to run with national feeling and attack the Yugoslav position over Trieste.

16 The Yugoslav Communist Party was reconstituted as the Yugoslav League of Communists, for example, as more appropriate to a socialist regime.

17 Mainly in that greater attention was given to legal forms.

18 Fernando Claudin, *The Communist Movement from Comintern to Cominform*, Penguin, 1975, p. 527, quoting Ferenc Fejto.

19 The court of course made no attempt to explore the contradiction. In the record of the trial published in English, *The Trial of Traicho Kostov and his Group*, Sofia, Bulgorian State Press Department, 1949, the previous written confession is inserted in place of the usual 'examination', which was abandoned. The printed documentation also included a supposed subsequent admission of the charges: a crude forgery.

20 A closed trial of military leaders took place in Poland.

21 In the Stalinist mentality the link was easily enough established, since
    in 1948 the nascent Israeli state had relied mainly on Czech arms sup-
    plies. Stalin had favoured its establishment at that point, but by 1952,
    with the strength of the US–Israel link apparent, the line had changed.
    The charges of anti-semitism were of course indignantly denied.

22 Claudin, *Communist Movement*, pp. 536ff., cites Spanish and French
    examples, noting the more restrained tone of the PCI. British examples
    include James Klugmann's, cited above, and Derek Kartun's *Tito's Plot
    Against Europe*, London, Lawrence & Wishart, 1949.

23 Not without considerable supplies of equipment and other assistance
    from the Allies. Detachments of the Malayan guerrillas marched in
    the 1945 victory parade in London and their leader, Ching Peng, was
    awarded the OBE.

24 This derived from his theory of imperialism, which postulated that
    the economic health and social stability of the capitalist metropoles was
    dependent upon colonial plunder. Though the theory was mistaken in
    detail, perception that the rise of colonial movements would have major
    impact on metropolitan politics was certainly valid.

25 They were even copied by non-communists. Up till 1927 the Chinese
    nationalist party, the Guomindang, was run (with close communist
    participation) along Bolshevik organisational lines and its leader, Chiang
    Kai-Shek, was an honorary member of the Comintern executive.

26 The fact that, as noted previously, it was mostly not led by peasants
    was nothing new – the majority of peasant revolts had leaders who had
    risen out of their class or were from other social groups.

27 One by-product of this greater flexibility, however, was a higher incid-
    ence and intensity of internal faction struggles. There was also a prob-
    lem during the period of the Popular Front and the Second World War,
    when Stalin was in alliance with these same imperialists and unwilling
    to embarrass them in their empires. This helped to check the growth of
    the Indian CP, which had to fall into line and oppose the immediate
    independence demand being advanced by the Congress party.

28 Westoby, *Evolution of Communism*, p. 88; Adam Westoby, *Communism
    since World War II* (Harvester, 1981), p. 99.

    We were told that Stalin was the 'great teacher', the 'guiding star'
    who was building socialism in the USSR and the leader of world
    socialism, and being both new to communism and relatively
    unschooled in Marxism and Leninism I accepted what I was told.
    There is a tradition in Indian politics of gurus enlightening the
    masses and this tradition suited Stalinism completely.

    K. Demoderan, 'Memoirs of an Indian Communist', *New Left Review*
    93, September–October 1975, p. 38.

29 The British Labour government, which had conceded independence in
    India, Ceylon and Burma, refused to do so in Malaya, partly because
    of communist dominance of the independence movement but more

because its supplies of rubber and tin were absolutely indispensable to the post-war British economy.

30 Mao's government was particularly offended by what it regarded as direct US occupation of its sovereign territory by protecting the Guomindag remnant on Taiwan.

31 Formally the UNO, the US having secured a UN resolution authorising intervention against North Korea.

Notes to Chapter 3

1 The formation of the post-war Stalinist regimes gave Trotskyists a lot of theoretical trouble. Since they were, on the face of it, according to Trotskyist measures socially and economically revolutionary (even if politically regressive), and yet Stalinism had been declared to be intrinsically counter-revolutionary, their emergence should have been impossible.

2 Allan Merson in *Communist Resistance in Nazi Germany*, London, Lawrence & Wishart, 1985, writes of communists released after serving concentration camp sentences in 1930s Germany who returned immediately to underground opposition.

3 According to Stalin, 'Once the political line has been agreed organisation decides everything.' Annie Kriegel comments, 'Communists believe in happiness. While their merit is to believe in it for others, their reward is to attain it for themselves.' Annie Kriegel, *The French Communists: Profile of a People*, University of Chicago Press, 1972, p. 139.

4 '[T]hese cadres led popular masses effectively and manifested a more stable spirit of discipline just because they were endowed with a *certainty of faith*.' Paolo Spriano, *Stalin and the European Communists*, Verso, 1985, p. 82.

> And the factors which produced this way of thinking of the party and of society as organisms, the health of which takes precedence over the preferences of its parts,were no doubt the same as those that led to the formation of the Stalinist system in its entirety – traditional ways of thinking about the individual and society, notions of a socialist purpose, and the pressure of circumstances.

Michael Waller, *The End of the Communist Power Monopoly*, Manchester University Press, 1993, p. 31.

5 Spriano, *Stalin and the European Communists*, p. 79.

6 Ibid., p. 85.

7 Ibid., p. 86.

8 For example, a philosophical dispute of 1908 is presented in the following terms: 'It became urgent for the Marxists to give a fitting retort to these renegades from Marxist theory, to tear the masks from their faces and thoroughly expose them, and thus safeguard the theoretical foundations of the Marxist Party.' *Short Course*, Moscow, Foreign Languages Publishing House, 1939.

9   Ibid., p. 111.
10 Ibid., p. 115.
11 They were of course not the first to do so. The thinking which pervaded the 'official' Marxism of the Second International also regarded historical development as a quasi-evolutionary process propelled by economic change and leading infallibly towards socialism and the classless society.
12 *Short Course*, p. 116.
13 Thus, in the days of the Comintern, the national leaderships of communist parties were more than once, against their better judgement, induced to abandon and completely turn around policies which had been pursued more or less with success.
14 A word of shifting meaning, but in normal communist terminology a cadre was an individual at any level of the party structure trusted to display leadership capacity combined with organisational ability.
15 The voluntarism of Marxism–Leninism never denied, indeed it insisted, that 'objective conditions' had to be appropriate before political advance or its culmination in revolution and the construction of a socialist order could be achieved. What it claimed was an ability denied to all other social forces to master the 'subjective conditions'.
16 See Marcel Liebman, *Leninism under Lenin*, London, Merlin, 1975, for an analysis.
17 Stalin, Report at the Plenum of the Central Committee, CPSU, 1937, quoted in James Klugmann, *From Trotsky to Tito*, London, Lawrence & Wishart, 1951, p. 124.
18 Klugmann, *From Trotsky to Tito*.
19 Contrary to accepted Marxist postulates on the 'withering away of the state', Engels's explicit comments on this were dismissed as abstractions and generalisations.
20 The parallel with the artistic principles of the Third Reich has been commented upon.
21 Though Stalin was capable of ordering capricious exceptions, such as in the case of Nikolai Bulgakov.
22 In the words of Roy Medvedev, 'illiterate fantasy was officially enthroned'. Roy Medvedev, *Let History Judge*, Macmillan, 1972, p. 523.
23 There are, however, latter-day echoes of the bourgeois/proletarian science distinction in the notions of 'male science' or 'western science' promulgated by postmodern theorists.
24 Which is not to deny that it nevertheless had considerable popular support at the time outside Great Russia as well.
25 Molotov is said to have done the same and to have had them turned down for publication as too arid and boring – though he was more forthcoming in conversations with Feliks Chuyev.
26 Teresa Toranska, *Oni: Stalin's Polish Puppets*, Collins Harvill, 1987.
27 One had renounced Marxism, but his mindset does not appear all that different from the other four.

28 Toranska, *Oni*, p. 23.

29 Ibid., p. 45.

30 Ibid., p. 20. The author of the Introduction, commenting on this interviewee, refers to her 'ferocious self-righteousness'.

31 Ibid., p. 233.

32 Quoted by in Dusan Hamsik, 'The Trials', Literarni List, 28 March 1968, cited in Andrew Oxley, Alex Pravda and Andrew Richie (eds), *Czechoslovakia: The Party and The People*, London, Allen Lane, 1972.

33 Roy Medvedev, *All Stalin's Men*, Blackwell, 1983, p. 151.

34 Ibid.

35 Ibid., p. 46. Molotov's wife had been imprisoned for several years in a labour camp (which did not make her any less of a fanatical Stalinist) and the brother of another Politburo member, Kaganovitch, committed suicide to escape arrest.

36 The members of the wartime Jewish Anti-Fascist Committee had already been exterminated and a general persecution commenced against Jewish culture. There are claims that once the 'Jewish doctors' came to trial 'spontaneous' public anger would result in prominent Soviet Jews requesting Stalin to deport all Jews in the country to the far east 'for their own safety'.

37 Stalin up to that point had never put one of his own Politburo members on a show trial. The ones he eliminated were done away with in secret or died in mysterious circumstances.

38 There were even disturbances in Bulgaria.

39 Strictly, since 1952, the Presidium of the Central Committee. The real equivalent of the old Politburo was the Bureau of this body.

40 See Medvedev, *All Stalin's Men*, pp. 159–60.

41 These could be preposterous as well as sinister. At his informal parties invited guests, almost exclusively male, were obliged to dance with each other while Stalin acted as disc jockey. He also enjoyed maliciously humiliating his colleagues and famously made Khrushchev perform a traditional peasant dance for which the latter's pudgy physique was hopelessly unsuited.

42 Medvedev quotes an incident in which Anastas Mikoyan (a Khrushchev supporter and 'liberaliser'), when pressed at a meeting of Moscow intellectuals for deeper criticism of the personality cult, lost his temper and shouted 'Do you want to unleash the elements?' Medvedev, *All Stalin's Men*, p. 28.

43 Trotsky once commented that compared to Stalin Louis XIV's remark that '*l'état c'est moi*' was a comparatively liberal formulation, for Stalin might truthfully claim that '*la société c'est moi*'.

44 Not even the military leaders executed after secret tribunals were cleared at that point. Their rehabilitation was only pronounced the following year.

45 John Callaghan, *Rajani Palme Dutt: A Study in British Stalinism*, London, Lawrence & Wishart, 1993, p. 267.

46 Report of the Central Committee to the Twenty-Second Congress of the CPSU, in A. Dallin, ed. *Diversity in International Communism: A Documentary Record 1961–1963*, Columbia University Press, 1963.

47 Callaghan, *Palme Dutt*.

48 Hoxha was in some respects an unusual Stalinist. Though he was a conscientious imitator of all the worst aspects of Stalinist practice and his morals were those of a bandit chief, he possessed great personal charisma and a fairly accomplished literary style.

49 'Certainly we cannot deny that this way of acting of ours has given our party a particular, original stamp in the very extensive camp of the international communist movement of today.' Togliatti, 1961, in Dallin, *Diversity*, p. 419.

50 P. Delwit and J-M. Dewaele, 'The Stalinists of Anti-Communism', *Socialist Register*, 1984, p. 327.

51 Quoted in Annie Kriegel, *The French Communists, Profile of a People*, University of Chicago Press, 1972, p. 218. She also quotes the supposed remark of Dmitri Manuliski, a Comintern functionary and himself no stranger to servility, that Thorez was 'too servile to be a great leader'.

52 Interview with Jean Pronteau and Maurice Kriegel-Valrimont, *Socialist Register*, 1976, p. 59.

53 All the communist parties, regardless of their reactions to the revelations, refused to use the term 'Stalinism' in their own discourse.

54 Political prisoners were also being released in great numbers, including members of the wartime anti-communist Home Army.

55 Rakosi was also the name of an eighteenth-century Hungarian national hero.

56 Julius Braunthal, *History of the International*, Vol. 3: *World Socialism 1943–1968*, Gollancz, 1980.

57 For Trotskyists and other left-wing opponents of orthodox communism the Hungarian insurrection was *the* post-war example of a (temporarily) successful workers' revolution.

58 Larsen, even in his Comintern days, had always been something of a maverick and but for the fact that he was a Danish MP, would almost certainly have been arrested while in the USSR. Instead his second-in-command, an uncompromising Stalinist loyalist, was purged in his place. See Steve Parsons, 'The International and the Purges – the Fate of Arne Munch-Petersen', *Socialist History* 3, Winter 1993.

59 The internal conflicts among British communists are well documented. See various histories of the CPGB and the articles in the 1976 issue of *Socialist Register*.

60 The majority established itself as the Danish Socialist People's Party and went on to play a significant role in Danish politics.

61 They could probably have saved their lives by recantations and declarations of loyalty to the Kadar regime. The delay until 1958 may have been because Nagy had been under Yugoslav protection before he was seized. In 1958 Moscow was once more on bad terms with Tito.

62 The party's previous programme, adopted in the mid-thirties, had been titled *For Soviet Britain*.
63 Pronteau and Kriegel-Valrimont, *Socialist Register*, p. 60.
64 This relationship was standard practice in every communist party, both at the centre and in its regional organisations.

Notes to Chapter 4

1 Derisively termed the 'workers' bomb' by some Western peace campaigners.
2 It was claimed, though rather unconvincingly, that Soviet threat to use nuclear firepower in defence of Egypt in 1956 had brought about the termination of the Anglo-French invasion.
3 The action of neutralist states might also be included here.
4 The technological triumph of the sputnik was cited in the editorial of *World Marxist Review* in January 1960 as proof that Soviet citizens must enjoy intellectual freedom, otherwise such scientific accomplishments would be incomprehensible.
5 In 1991 it was revealed that the British CP had been in receipt of funds from the Soviet embassy between 1957 and the early eighties.
6 The Albanian national hero, Skanderbeg, was one such rebel.
7 In 1948 its name was changed to the Party of Labour.
8 Albania was also unique in being the only state which tried formally to eradicate religion.
9 See Arshi Pipa, 'The Political Culture of Hoxha's Albania' in Tariq Ali, ed., *The Stalinist Legacy: Its Impact on 20th Century World Politics*, Penguin, 1984.
10 Though accompanied by dreadful massacres of their rural enemies: landlords, bailiffs, moneylenders – and their families.
11 His disgustingly offensive personal habits appear not to have been a foible but a deliberate statement of identification with what he regarded as peasant lifestyles.
12 This appears incredible, but actually was imposed upon the cultivators. An account of the famine is given in Jasper Becker, *Hungry Ghosts: China's Secret Famine*, London, John Murray, 1996.
13 The effects of hunger and an efficient repressive apparatus prevented revolt in the countryside, which was isolated from the cities. Such grain as was available was supplied to the urban areas as a first priority to dampen potential dissatisfaction there.
14 *Long Live Leninism!*, Beijing, Foreign Languages Press, 1960, pp. 23–4.
15 Lenin recognised, of course, that there are elements of the state which have other purposes than the immediate application of coercion – legislature, executive departments and so forth – but in Leninist theory it is the military, police and enforcement agencies which are the state's defining feature. See Lenin, *State and Revolution, Collected Works*, Vol.

10, London and Moscow, Progress Publishers and Lawrence & Wishart, 1966.

16 See also chapter 6, below. Trotsky declared that 'A working class capable of exercising its dictatorship over society will tolerate no dictator over itself.' Quoted in Isaac Deutscher, *The Prophet Armed*, Oxford, Oxford University Press, 1970, p. 521.

17 *Pravda* editorial of 14 February 1962, printed in A. Dallin, ed., *Diversity in International Communism: A Documentary Record 1961–1963*, Columbia University Press, 1963.

18 Even among the Italian communists there was a strong minority trend disturbed at Khrushchev's behaviour, even to the extent of questioning the peaceful coexistence perspective. See Grant Aymot, *The Italian Communist Party: The Crisis of the Popular Front Strategy*, Croom Helm, 1981, pp. 99–100.

19 *Pravda* editorial, 2 September 1964, translated and published in pamphlet form by Novosti Press Agency. Much of it is a polemic against Chinese claims upon Soviet territory.

20 Although the CPI(M) was popularly identified with the Chinese position this was fairly superficial and the break had taken place much more on account of domestic concerns. Consequently there was a further split from the CPI(M) by militants who took seriously Mao's theses on guerrilla warfare and tried to initiate one. This was the CPI(M-L), or Naxalites.

21 After the date of an unsuccessful attack on the Moncada barracks in Cuba in 1953, which was followed by savage repressions. The twelve were the survivors of an expeditionary force of eighty which had sailed from Mexico.

22 The violent Bolivian revolution was socially based upon the copper miners of that country, although essentially nationalist in character: it was undermined by internal fragmentation. The peaceful electoral revolution in Guatemala was suppressed by a CIA-sponsored invasion force.

23 Editorial in *Revolución*, 16 May 1959, quoted in R. Scheer and M. Zeitlin, *Cuba: An American Tragedy*, Harmondsworth, Penguin, 1964, p. 116.

24 Adam Westoby, *The Evolution of Communism*, Polity, 1989, p. 136.

25 'Message to the Tricontinental Conference', printed in John Gerassi, ed., *Venceremos! The Speeches and Writings of Che Guevara*, London, Panther, 1969. He also wrote, 'I believe in armed struggle as the only solution for people who are fighting for freedom.' Ibid., p. 568.

26 Not only in South America. Guevarist young revolutionaries staged a serious but bloodily suppressed insurrection in Ceylon in 1970.

27 On the contrary, it constituted a drain on Soviet resources. A plan to construct a base there for Soviet nuclear submarines was blocked by a warning from President Nixon.

28 The fact that China exported its culture to Vietnam did not mean that its political influence was not fiercely opposed. One of the most enduring Vietnamese traditions was of resistance to foreign invasion.

29 To strengthen unity against the occupiers, the class struggle in the villages was downplayed and rich peasants and even landlords admitted to the rural party in large numbers. According to Adam Westoby, *Evolution of Communism*, p. 84, the figure was as high as 60 per cent.

30 A less destructive, though still severe, struggle for power also took place in Laos (with relatives of the royal family on opposing sides) in which the communist Pathet Lao, closely connected with Hanoi, ultimately prevailed.

31 A point of view shared by right-wing commentators, who attributed the failure to win the war to lack of full exertion of Western power, its resolve undermined by the anti-war movement.

32 It may well be that Moscow made the suggestion only because it knew it would be rejected. The prospect of Soviet pilots in combat with American ones was not something it could have had much inclination for.

33 The most striking individual example is that of the eminent theoretician of language Noam Chomsky, whose politics were in the anarchist tradition. The difference in Western public response to the Vietnam War compared to the Korean, which only communists opposed, is striking. The change must be attributed to the weakening of Cold War presumptions in public consciousness, particularly among young people. 'Revisionist' analyses of the Cold War, together with the experience of the Cuban revolution, undoubtedly contributed a good deal to the change, while these analyses in their turn were no doubt stimulated by the questioning generated by the Vietnam War of the US international role.

34 The great Vietnam demonstration in London in 1968, said to be the biggest since the Chartists, was organised by the communists' opponents, and communists constituted only a very small percentage of its participants.

35 To cite high-profile examples again, the American Angela Davis may be mentioned.

36 The rehabilitation of Trotsky's own reputation by Isaac Deutscher's three-volume biography should also be noted in this context.

37 It was perhaps not surprising that Trotskyist organisations tended to turn into caricatures of the Stalinism they denounced. See, e.g., John Callaghan, *British Trotskyism: Theory and Practice*, Oxford, Blackwell, 1984.

38 Although one grouping had broken with this theory (which was Trotsky's own) and held that the regime was 'state capitalist' in character.

39 In 1938 a 'Fourth International' had been created under Trotsky's inspiration to unite his followers. It began life a a very small and persecuted organisation with virtually no political weight. By the fifties there were two rival 'Fourth Internationals' and since then the number has multiplied.

40 Except on the island of Ceylon, where largely accidental circumstances resulted in the major left-wing party taking on a Trotskyist rather than a communist coloration.

41 Tito, for example, was stigmatised as a Trotskyist, as in James Klugmann's *From Trotsky to Tito*, London, Lawrence & Wishart, 1951.
42 In Britain this was later to change with the rise of the Militant Tendency.
43 Stuart Schram, *The Political Thought of Mao Tse-tung*, Penguin, 1969, pp. 316–17.
44 'He proclaimed and had it proclaimed that the masses decide everything and that it is necessary to learn from them whereas in reality he built up a system that was extremely centralised politically and monolithic in tendency, based on an authoritarianism of which the boundless cult of his person was the symbol.' Livio Matian, *Party, Army and Masses in China: a Marxist Interpretation of the Cultural Revolution and its Aftermath*, London, New Left Books, 1976, quoted in Fred Halliday, 'Marxist Analysis and Post-Revolutionary China', *New Left Review* 100, November 1976–January 1977, p. 170.
45 There are parallels in this respect with the Great Purges of the thirties in the USSR.
46 In the light of what has occurred in China since Mao's death, he may be regarded as having been right in that respect.
47 From the Decision of the Central Committee of the CPC concerning the Great Proletarian Cultural Revolution (the 'Sixteen Points'), August 1966. Cited in Robert V. Daniels, *A Documentary History of Communism*, Vol. 2, *Communism and the World*, I.B. Tauris, 1987, p. 311. All the supposed bourgeois representatives who were brought under attack were members of the Communist Party or individuals in public positions. The *actual* bourgeoisie of China, the 'national capitalists', were left strictly alone.
48 The bizarre mental universe of the Red Guards is brought out in the following quote: 'After the Party Central Committee Plenum had been published (the "16 points") and the Red Guard movement launched, many groups were formed, and in the main these centred round the original two tendencies: to rebel against the Party committee, or to rebel in conformity with the lead of the Party committee.' John Collier, 'The Cultural Revolution in Canton', *New Left Review* 48, March–April 1968, p. 65.
49 Printed in *New Left Review* 54, March–April 1969, translated by Bill Jenner.
50 Lin Bao, however, did not survive to enjoy the fruits of his association with the Chairman. In 1971 he was killed in a mysterious air crash, allegedly trying to flee to the USSR after an unsuccessful plot against Mao.
51 Gregor Benton, 'Chinese Communism and Democracy', *New Left Review* 148, November–December 1984, pp. 65–6.
52 Bill Jenner, 'The New Chinese Revolution', *New Left Review* 53, January–February 1969, p. 83.
53 There were a few very insignificant groups in the West whose primary allegiance was actually to Albania rather than China.

54   In the Eastern Bloc, the Romanian regime, though maintaining amicable relations with Beijing, allowed no trace of its political notions to have any purchase in Romania.

55   See especially E.P. Thompson, *The Poverty of Theory*, London, Merlin, 1978.

56   The Maoists at this stage managed to acquire ephemeral influence in some Parisian industrial enterprises when its student militants on principle abandoned higher education to get involved with the proletariat. They took jobs in the vehicle factories (where they were ruthlessly opposed by the communist trade union organisations) and one created a cause célèbre when he was killed by security guards during a demonstration.

57   So gaining the support and assistance of Jean-Paul Sartre, who was not otherwise a Maoist. A number of these Maoist students (and their teachers, such as Michael Foucault) were later to achieve status as major intellectuals, either as postmodernist philosophers or right-wing commentators.

58   At the time of the right-wing coup of 1973 in Chile the Chinese embassy handed over Chilean Maoists who had taken refuge there.

59   Bill Lomax, 'Twenty-Five Years after 1956: the Heritage of the Hungarian Revolution', *Socialist Register*, 1982, p. 94.

Notes to Chapter 5

1   Another possible division of this group would be between those which enjoyed a legal existence and those forced to operate underground, but categorisation according to the economic level of their country is probably more significant.

2   In 1960 meat production began to decline and 1962 proved very adverse for the grain harvest. Other government agricultural initiatives also turned out to be counter-productive. Shortages all round were severe in 1963.

3   A copy of the Indian edition was ceremonially burned by unreconciled Stalinists in the CPI.

4   'Anti-Crisis Measures Are Merely A Palliative against Capitalism's Incurable Illness.' Chapter heading in O. Kuusinen, ed., *Fundamentals of Marxism–Leninism*, English edition, London, Lawrence & Wishart, 1961, p. 342.

5   Ibid., p. 362.

6   Ibid., p. 528.

7   Ibid., p. 489.

8   The economic considerations in this case were in themselves significant enough. The Congo contained incalculable mineral wealth, above all uranium, and had been, while under Belgian rule, the West's principal supplier.

9   And would have involved more if the Politburo had had its way. Foreign capital was encouraged with the offer of big concessions to invest in Soviet Russia, but was unwilling to accept the risk.

10 Lenin's pamphlet *Left-Wing Communism: An Infantile Disorder* is a classic statement of the necessity for tactical compromise to serve strategic ends. (The concept of 'infantile disorder' was not a comment on the mentality of his targets but intended to suggest that their rigidity was comparable to a childhood ailment: i.e. not very serious and soon got over.)

11 Soviet Peace Committee, *Leninist Principles of Peaceful Co-existence and the World Today*, Moscow, USSR Academy of Sciences/Soviet Peace Committee, 1973, pp. 124–5.

12 Speaking in average terms. The range of incomes within particular workforces is of course itself quite substantial.

13 No member of the former Soviet or East European nomenklatura who has become an entrepreneur since communism's collapse has claimed, to the best of my knowledge, that they were secretly longing to be capitalists at the time they were administering the communist states.

14 The states of the Western bloc, with the partial exception of France, were in a not wholly dissimilar situation *vis-à-vis* the USA. This did not discredit their regimes, partly because it had the appearance of being a voluntary alliance, but more importantly because of the material prosperity which derived from the relationship.

15 The regime's propaganda claimed that they were equivalent to those of West Germany, but nobody took this seriously.

16 The GDR (established in 1949 at the height of the anti-Tito terror) had no purge trials. This is unlikely to have been due to courage or independence on Ulbricht's part; more likely it was on account of the state's exposed position in relation to the West.

17 Outside the bloc, the Albanian regime was likewise inordinately proud of being free of any external debt.

18 The formerly large Jewish minority had mostly been deported to their deaths during the Second World War. A significant gypsy minority was still in existence, however.

19 A political joke current at the time tells of a scrawny Polish dog and a well-fed Czech one meeting at the frontier as they go in opposite directions. The Polish dog remarks, 'I like to eat from time to time!' The Czech one replies, 'I eat not too badly but I like to bark occasionally!'

20 There also existed a marked contrast with the isolated position the French communists had found themselves in when opposing the colonial war in Algeria during the late fifties and early sixties.

21 Unlike the European social democratic parties, who all moved during the fifties in the direction of closer theoretical as well as practical accommodation with the then Keynesian-influenced capitalism.

22 It was pointed out that every successful socialist revolution had been the outcome of an alliance between working class and peasantry. This

was certainly true in the Russian case, though for the others it was more of a theoretical construction.

23 Quoted in Grant Aymot, *The Italian Communist Party: The Crisis of the Popular Front Strategy*, Croom Helm, 1981, p. 38.

24 See Annie Kriegel, *The French Communists: Profile of a People*, trans. Elaine P. Halperin, University of Chicago Press, 1972.

25 According to one of the PCI leaders 90 per cent of the party's members were Catholics. Interview with Giorgio Amendola, *New Left Review* 106, November–December 1977.

26 Italy at this time possessed the one long-lasting and moderately successful neo-fascist party in Europe, the MSI, which was known to command sympathy in the highest ranks of the security services.

27 Aymot, *Italian Communist Party*, p. 4328.

28 Quoted in ibid., p. 112.

29 Amyot indicates that there were many rank-and-file members, though they had no influence on the leadership in this respect, who continued to look forward to a dramatic day of reckoning with the bourgeoisie. Some 'have not even been shaken by the things that came out of the 20th Congress' Quoted in Aymot, ibid., p. 138. Aymot comments on the traditionalists: 'They simply had a more traditional, pre-1935 idea of communism and class struggle, and were in many ways more faithful to the original working-class inspiration of the Communist movement than the supporters of the *via italiana*' Ibid., p. 165.

30 Next to France and Italy, West Germany was the principal focus for European student unrest, but there the communist party was negligible and outlawed.

31 George Marchais initially attacked the student demonstrations as incited by 'pseudorevolutionaries' and 'serving the interests of the government, the bourgeoisie and monopoly capital'. *L'Humanité*, 3 May 1968. Quoted in Annette Eisenberg Stiefbold, *The French Communist Party in Transition*, Praeger, 1977, p. 9.

32 The British press of the time assumed unanimously that it was finished and would be replaced by a Sixth Republic of whatever complexion.

33 Apart from events in France itself the international outlook seemed uniquely propitious, the USA as well as neighbouring NATO states being too distracted with their own internal problems to undertake any forcible intervention.

34 It had been negotiating for such common ground for several years and in 1965 had supported François Mitterrand in his Presidential contest against de Gaulle.

35 It was feared that this might be attempted by reinstating the old Radical politician Mendès-France.

36 '[B]y attempting at the outset to restrain this exceptional outburst, the leadership has cut off the party from a great force of Socialist renovation'. *Le Monde*, 6 June 1968, Quoted in Stiefbold, *French Communist Party*, p. 10.

37 Ibid., p. 14.

38 It was also strongly argued that the PCF's cautious approach was also influenced by the fact that Gaullist foreign policy was, among all the major Western powers, the one most favourable to the USSR. This interpretation, however, appears to be unfounded. See ibid., pp. 11–13.

39 See Tobias Abse, 'Judging the PCI', *New Left Review* 153, September–October 1985, pp. 12–14.

40 Aymot, *Italian Communist Party*, p. 185.

41 Ibid., pp. 170–93.

42 This is a very compressed rendering of what was in detail an extremely complex process.

43 Quoted in Julius Braunthal, *History of the International*, Vol. 3, *World Socialism 1943–1968*, Gollancz, 1980.

44 As becomes clear in another context from the conversations recorded in Teresa Toranska's *Oni*, Collins Harvill, 1987.

45 With the exception of the venerable war-hero President Svoboda, whose refusal to co-operate with the invaders was one of the factors compelling them to change their initial plans.

46 Alexander Dubcek, speaking to the Central Committee of the Slovak CP, December 1968, reported in *Information Bulletin of the CC of the Communist Party of Czechoslovakia, December 1968*, pp. 84–5.

47 Cited in Robert V. Daniels, *A Documentary History of Communism*, Vol. 2, *Communism and the World*, I.B. Tauris, 1985, p. 338.

48 *24th Congress of the Communist Party of the Soviet Union March 30–April 9, 1971: Documents*, Moscow, 1971.

49 Although in this respect the CPI leadership appears to have been considerably in advance of the party rank and file. A survey carried out in 1979 showed that about 40 per cent of those who were members in 1968 had approved of the invasion. (Though of course that figure is likely to be distorted by the circumstance that many who opposed it may have left the party in the interim.) See Grant Aymot, *Italian Communist Party*, p. 177.

50 Both the (non-ruling) parties who supported and those who criticised the invasion were faced with significant elements of their membership who advocated a contrary view.

51 Braunthal, *History of the International*, pp. 469–70.

52 Edward Ochab, in Toranska, *Oni*, p. 81.

53 The sentiment had extraordinarily wide ramifications. I can recall in the early eighties, while having a discussion with a Scottish communist of Polish extraction, my shock at being confronted by an anti-semitic tirade in relation to Poland. It was also possible for Moczar's followers to imply for themselves – though this could not be said directly – a communist nationalism which blamed Jews for Poland's subjection to the USSR, because of their preponderance in the higher reaches of the Party. The dementia found its furthest expression in the material issued by a bizarre Polish CP-in-exile based on Albania: 'Even less can we

tolerate the appearance in Poland of a Zionist, Trotskyite group of Jewish nationalists who use the concept of equal rights as a cover for their aspirations to establish Jewish domination over 30 million Poles.' Quoted in Geoffrey Stern, *The Rise and Decline of International Communism*, Edward Elgar, 1990, p. 237.

54 Toranska, *Oni*, p. 82.

55 Consequently they were suppressed.

Notes to Chapter 6

1 The government had its hands tied, for example, by lack of a legislative majority.

2 Enabling a Soviet commentator to declare 'the dogmas proclaimed by Mao Tse-tung represent no real danger to the capitalist system, while their schismatic essence can be utilised in the struggle against communism.' Boris Leibzon, *The Communist Movement Today*, Moscow, Novosti Press, 1975, p. 43. 'It is indeed hard to see what the Chinese could do now to take their betrayal of foreign revolutionary movements further in their attempt to win friends.' Fred Halliday, 'Marxist Analysis and Post-Revolutionary China', *New Left Review* 100, November 1976– January 1977, p. 167.

3 See D.S. Bell, ed., *Western European Communists and the Collapse of Communism*, Berg, 1993, pp. 87–9.

4 For example, a Socialist newspaper, *Republica*, printed a summary of a published article by a Soviet theoretician which it purported to be a leaked document of advice from the CPSU to the Western parties on how to seize power. When the printworkers closed down the paper in protest, this action was expounded as confirmation of the PCP's dictatorial intentions. See Annette Eisenberg Stiefbold, *The French Communist Party in Transition*, Praeger, 1977, p. 56.

5 So was that in the East Indian colony of East Timor, and so it was soon invaded in overwhelming strength by the right-wing Indonesian regime and suppressed with great slaughter.

6 Not only had the Federal Republic claimed the GDR as part of its own territory, and refused to recognise the Oder–Niesse frontier with Poland, it had under the 'Hallstein Doctrine' refused to have diplomatic relations with any state (apart from the USSR) which recognised the GDR.

7 Illustrated perhaps better by the case of a party where the consideration was purely abstract – the CPGB. Its General Secretary in 1976 provoked a furious reaction among many of his members when he declared that a future British socialist government (i.e. one composed of communists and left-wing Labour) would have to abide by an adverse verdict from the British electorate.

8 See Stiefbold, *French Communist Party*, and Grant Aymot, *The Italian Communist Party*, Croom Helm, 1981, pp. 195ff.

9 Adam Westoby, *The Evolution of Communism*, Polity, 1989, p. 147.
10 Stiefbold, *French Communist Party*, p. 11.
11 Carrillo had written, for example:

> In actual fact, one of the causes of Khrushchev's downfall may have been his inability to transform the state apparatus created under Stalin, the system of political power to which Togliatti had referred and which eventually crushed Khrushchev. That system has not been transformed; it has not been made more democratic and it has even retained many of its aspects of coercion in relations with the socialist states of the East, as was brought out with brutal clarity by the occupation of Czechoslovakia.

Cited in R.V. Daniels, ed., *A Documentary History of Communism*, Vol. 2: *Communism and the World*, I.B. Tauris, 1987, p. 376.

Ernest Mandel, in *From Stalinism to Eurocommunism*, New Left Books, 1978, p. 99, notes, '*Pravda*, meanwhile censored the speech of the delegate of the CGT (the largest trade union federation of France, dominated by the Communist Party) because he affirmed that socialism and liberty were inseparable.'

12 B. Morris, *Communism, Revolution and American Policy*, quoted in Geoffrey Stern, *The Rise and Decline of International Communism*, Edward Elgar, 1990, p. 230.
13 Ibid.
14 A partial exception should be made for the Swedish and Finnish CPs, which did have some electoral strength, albeit modest. Finnish communism, which was able to reach subordinate government office in the mid-sixties, was from 1968 divided into two rival factions, effectively separate parties, both of which were recognised by Moscow – a unique circumstance. See Pekka Haapakoski, 'Brezhnevism in Finland', *New Left Review* 86, July–August 1974.
15 Legal divorce was approved by 59 per cent of the electorate. Legalised abortion was also finally endorsed in 1981. See Tobias Abse, 'Judging the PCI', *New Left Review* 153, September–October 1985, pp. 21–5.
16 Ibid., p. 28.
17 Aymot, *Italian Communist Party*, p. 215.
18 Ibid., p. 216.
19 According to Luciana Castellina, some of the Red Brigade personnel were drawn from militant Catholics. She comments, 'After all it is understandable that once Catholics started moving left they kept the same kind of fundamentalism and sought to draw the most far-reaching conclusions.' Luciana Castellina, '*Il Manifesto* and Italian Communism: an Interview', *New Left Review* 151, May–June 1985, p. 33.
20 Ibid., p. 35.
21 Castellina, ibid., claims that 'hundreds of people were killed and tens of thousands put in jail'.

22   See Fernando Claudin, 'The Split in the Spanish Communist Party', *New Left Review* 70, November–December 1971.

23   The contrast with Portugal is striking, and may possibly be ascribed to two factors. In the first place, the PCP had real prospects of attaining power, always a unifying circumstance. Perhaps more importantly, the fact that the leadership was ultra-traditionalist avoided the strains consequent on trying to initiate new ideological courses.

24   A small third party, the Left Radicals or MRG, was also involved.

25   Quoted in M. Adereth, *The French Communist Party: A Critical History*, Manchester, Manchester University Press, 1984, p. 219.

26   It supported the Soviet military intervention in Afghanistan at the end of 1979, for instance.

27   The CPSU had again muddied the waters when in the middle of the campaign *Pravda* published an article praising the right-wing President Giscard's foreign policies.

28   Eurocommunism was not exclusively confined to Europe. The Japanese CP was as a rule also included in this category, as was the minor Australian CP.

29   See Ben Kiernan, *The Pol Pot Regime: Race, Power and Genocide in Cambodia under the Khmer Rouge, 1975–1979*, New Haven, CT and London, Yale University Press, 1996, and for a theoretical elaboration Tom Nairn's review of the volume in the *London Review of Books*, 3 October 1996.

30   David Chandler, 'Epitaph for the Khmer Rouge?', *New Left Review* 205, May–June 1994, p. 88.

31   Ibid., p. 89.

32   President Roosevelt in the thirties had said of the original Somoza: 'He's a bastard, but he's our bastard.'

33   One of these was, paradoxically, the Nicaraguan Communist Party, which remained hostile to the Sandinista regime all along, regarding it as middle-class.

34   It had a creditable record, having been one of the central supports of the abortive nationalist and anti-monarchical revolution of 1951–5, suppressed with the assistance of the CIA.

35   The lack of central power also meant the absence of a peasant class ground down by relentless taxation, who would have otherwise been an important reservoir of support for a communist regime.

36   The displaced faction was known as the 'Masses', its rival as the 'Banner'.

37   Nevertheless in the 1980s the USSR did overtake the USA in per capita steel production. As Adam Westoby, *Evolution of Communism*, notes (p. 223) this achievement went almost unremarked – it had become irrelevant.

38   Suslov is said to have assured him at the Kremlin celebrations that for Soviet citizens middle age began at seventy-five. In view of the geriatric character of the Politburo, the joke was not entirely without point.

Notes to Chapter 7

1 Adam Westoby, *The Evolution of Communism*, Polity, 1989, p. 242.
2 That fact would be little comfort to the individuals who actually did die in the overthrow or its aftermath, but in historical perspective this was, relative to its scale, the least bloody revolution of all time.
3 Giving rise to a bitter toast as the regime was crumbling, 'Here's to the good old era of stagnation!'
4 One of those, in central Asia, was alleged even to have had a private prison in which he tortured his personal enemies.
5 Michael Waller, *The End of the Communist Power Monopoly*, Manchester University Press, 1993.
6 Oliver MacDonald, 'The Polish Vortex: Solidarity and Socialism', *New Left Review* 139, May–June 1983, p. 11.
7 *Pravda* commented, very revealingly, that independent unions were a violation of Leninist principles and a bourgeois provocation. 'Trade unions can only fulfil their tasks in close collaboration with and under the direct leadership of the party'. Ibid., p. 23.
8 The CPGB was one of those.
9 Particularly in the area of computers. The West took pains to prevent the USSR gaining access to its computer technology.
10 In an act of exceptional cynicism, the West continued to recognise the Khmer Rouge as the legitimate government of Cambodia and to seat it at the United Nations, in spite of its acknowledged record.
11 In some instances both literally and symbolically at once. Grass sprouted in the cracks between the concrete slabs that formed the base of the Moscow monument to space triumphs, and nobody took responsibility for tidying them.
12 If Suslov had still been alive, however, it is unlikely that he would have been appointed.
13 Including a relatively luxurious hotel in Moscow reserved exclusively for visiting foreign communists, the best available medical attention for these visitors, and Black Sea sanatoria to which they were flown for congenial holidays. Nonetheless, one observer has noted that from the early eighties the CPSU referred less and less frequently to the international movement. Michael Waller, *Communist Power Monopoly*, p. 133.
14 The indigenous regime survived better than expected without the support of Soviet troops, holding out for several more years, though eventually overrun.
15 For example, in 1987, Dubcek's hardline successor, Husak, was induced to step down but his successor Miklos Jakes was scarcely less traditionalist.
16 The resistance went so far in the GDR as to include a ban on some Soviet periodicals.

17   An ironic sidelight on the negative re-evaluation of Leninism, the Revolution and the early Bolshevik regime was that when it at last became possible to discuss Trotsky in a meaningful way in the USSR the general verdict appeared to be that he was no more than a failed Stalin.

18   At the point of Gorbachev's maximum impact before the programme began to unravel, i.e. around 1987 or thereabouts, it is possible that the CPSU could have won an open election.

19   A colleague of mine once boasted that he had profitably traded his denim outfit, appropriately in Moscow's Park of Economic Achievement.

20   See especially the editions of Stephen White's *Gorbachev in Power*, Cambridge University Press, 1993.

21   The Ceauçescus lived in great (and tasteless) luxury. The material privileges of other communist rulers, however, were comparatively modest.

22   The same thing emerges in the *Oni* interviews (see above).

23   Which it succeeded in winning. The subsequent government, however, was undermined both by its own incompetence as well as by Western hostility manifested in economic pressure, and soon lost office.

24   In Geoffrey Stern, *The Rise and Decline of International Communism*, Edward Elgar, 1990, p. xv.

25   National distinction and identity in the parts of Yugoslavia where the war was fought were not based upon language or material culture (except that the northern republics tended to be more affluent) but only pre-communist religious identification – Orthodox, Catholic or Muslim.

26   However, newly independent Georgia suffered a less savage though still bloody version of the Yugoslav war.

27   For an account see Branka Magas, *The Destruction of Yugoslavia*, London, Verso, 1993.

28   'The last feeble co-ordinating centre for world Communism slipped unnoticed out of existence.' D.S. Bell, ed., *Western European Communists and the Collapse of Communism*, Berg, 1993, p. 178.

29   Some of the participants were even said to have been drunk at the time.

30   Gorbachev did offer an objection, but it was merely verbal and token.

31   Bell, *Western European Communists*, p. 138.

32   The figure for communist party membership on the eve of the collapse was estimated at 88.6 million, with 84.5 million in the communist states. Stern, *International Communism*, p. xii. Moscow gave the figure of 36 million in 1960.

33   Bill Lomax, *Hungary 1956*, Allison & Busby, 1976, p. 196.

34   See Waller, *Communist Power Monopoly*.

35   Eric Hobsbawm, *Age of Extremes: The Short Twentieth Century 1914–1991*, London, Michael Joseph, 1994.

36   Westoby, *Evolution of Communism*. 'The key weakness lay in the fact that political monopoly was unsupported by a comprehensive secular ideology to hold the party together, and in terms of which its bureaucracies could express practical problems of rule' (p. 131).

37 Developments in other industrialised societies such as the USA or Japan should be included in the same category – the case of South Africa is exceptional.

38 'Agitate and organise!' was a favourite communist slogan.

39 Though not invariably successful. The communist guerrilla campaigns in Malaya and the Philippines, though strong and well supported, were eventually overcome.

40 It should be kept in mind that the Bolsheviks in 1917, though convinced of the bankruptcy of capitalism, had really no idea of what a socialised economy would look like. The concept and construction of the marketless, centrally planned economy was a subsequent development.

41 Tobias Abse, 'Stalin or Pius XII: Italy in the Cold War', *Socialist History* 11, Spring 1997.

Appendix 1

Biographical Notes on
Key Personalities

Lavrenty Beria (1899–1953) Appointed to head the Soviet security services in 1938, responsible for extensive acts of repression, including deportation of 'disloyal' minor Soviet nationalities following the Second World War. Arrested and shot in the Kremlin power struggle following Stalin's death. Recently it has been suggested that he was a behind-the-scenes proponent of 'liberalising' policies.

Leonid Brezhnev (1906–82) CPSU apparatchik under Stalin. Following advancement in the party became First Secretary (later General Secretary) in succession to Khrushchev in 1964. Associated with many immediate economic and diplomatic successes, but he continued enmity toward China and presided over a long-term decline in Soviet economic potential and international influence, referred to by his successors as the 'era of stagnation'.

Santiago Carrillo (1915–) General Secretary of the Spanish Communist Party in 1960. Renowned as the major public proponent of 'Eurocommunism' in the 1970s. Following the end of the Franco regime the PCE under his leadership disintegrated and became electorally insignificant. He himself was marginalised.

Fidel Castro (1926–) Opposed the Batista dictatorship in Cuba during the 1950s and led a successful guerrilla revolution which took power in 1959. Quarrelled with the United States and became a Soviet ally. Established a Marxist–Leninist regime in Cuba but marginalised the old Cuban communists in favour of his own followers. Continues to survive the collapse of the Soviet bloc but in conditions of growing isolation.

Nicolae Ceauçescu (1918–1989) Joined underground Romanian communist party in the thirties. Advanced in party and state positions during the post-war period and succeeded Gheorgui-Dej as party leader in 1965. Sought international position independent of the USSR while maintaining rigid Stalinist practices internally. Developed megalomaniac tendencies and began to persecute national minorities in Romania. Overthrown by popular revolt in December 1989 and shot on Christmas Day.

Deng Xiaoping (1904–1997) The ultimate survivor. General Secretary of the CPC from 1952, he was a major target of the Cultural Revolution in 1966, purged and dismissed. Reinstated to the leadership in the early seventies, he was again purged at the beginning of 1976, but reinstated once more following the overthrow of the 'Gang of Four' later that year. Thereafter he gradually subordinated or marginalised his colleagues to emerge as the dominant force in the CPC. Initiated 'marketisation' programme.

Georgi Dimitrov (1882–1949) After Stalin,the most renowned communist of the 1930s owing to his performance at the Reichstag Fire trial and leadership of the Comintern. As the leader of the post-war Bulgarian regime he may initially have had national inclinations and supported Tito in seeking autonomy, but he submitted to Stalin and implemented an anti-Titoite purge.

Alexander Dubcek (1921–92) Participated in the underground resistance during the German occupation of Czechoslovakia, and after rising through the CPCz ranks under the communist regime appointed Secretary of the Slovak CP. Appointed General Secretary of the CPCz at the beginning of 1968 following Novotny's fall, he was identified with the liberalisation of the 'Prague Spring'. After the Warsaw Pact invasion he was first compelled to preside over the reversal of liberalisation then subsequently expelled from the party. Made a brief return to prominence following 1989.

Wladyslaw Gomulka (1905–82) A member of the communist leadership in post-war Poland, he was associated with the 'nationalist' wing of the party, and in the persecutions following the Cominform break with Tito purged and imprisoned. Restored to power as a national symbol following the 'Polish October' of 1956, he failed to develop a viable reforming policy, allied with anti-semites in 1968, and was overthrown by popular riots and demonstrations in 1970.

Mikhail Gorbachev (1931–) From a peasant background; qualifications in law and agriculture. Rose through the CPSU apparatus and became the youngest Politburo member in 1980. Reputation for vision and dynamism resulted in his appointment as General Secretary in 1985. Attempted reform policies in political and economic spheres to deal with long-term crises of Soviet society and to establish diplomatic and military détente with the

West. Intractable nature of problems and loss of control over reform movement resulted in his downfall in 1991.

Ernesto 'Che' Guevara (1928–67) Castro's leading colleague in the Cuban revolution. He advocated a generalised Third World guerrilla challenge to US global hegemony, summed up in the phrase 'Two, three, many Vietnams'. Left Cuba secretly to lead guerrilla undertakings in the Congo and subsequently in Bolivia, where he was captured and killed. Became a romantic revolutionary icon.

Ho Chi Minh (1890–1969) Joined the PCF in 1923. Established an underground communist organisation in French Indo-China, expanded into a left-wing nationalist movement, the Vietminh, in the course of anti-Japanese guerrilla warfare during the Second World War. Proclaimed the Democratic People's Republic of Vietnam following the Japanese surrender in 1945. Fought French attempts to re-establish imperial control and won major military confrontation at Dien Bien Phu in 1954. Following division of Vietnam by the Geneva Agreements in 1954, led North Vietnam and supported the continuing war against the US-backed southern regime and, from the sixties, large-scale US military forces.

Enver Hoxha (1908–85) The 'wily Albanian' according to his own account. French-educated, he led anti-Axis guerrilla fighting during the Second World War, and with Yugoslav assistance took control of Albania at its end. Adhered to Stalin during the Tito split, he established an ultra-Stalinist regime and purged all Yugoslav sympathisers. Allied with China following the Soviet reconciliation with Yugoslavia, but ruptured the alliance owing to changes in direction by Beijing following Mao's death. Survived all challenges and refused to compromise the Stalinist character of the Albanian regime.

Janós Kadar (1912–) Active in the Hungarian communist underground during the 1930s and wartime period, member of post-war governments. Purged and imprisoned during the anti-Titoite drive, but released by Nagy. He defected from Nagy's revolutionary government in 1956 and took over, after its suppression, under Soviet military protection. Initially engaged in severe campaign of repression, but in the mid-sixties switched to policies of cultural and economic liberalisation, developing a communist version of consumer society, until dismissed in 1988 on the eve of the regime's collapse.

Nikita Khruschev (1894–1971) CPSU apparatchik under Stalin and responsible for purges in the Ukraine. Became a member of the ruling circle and emerged as leading figure following Stalin's death, eventually combining offices of First Secretary and Soviet premier. Denounced Stalin posthumously at CPSU 20th Congress in February 1956. Negotiated agreement with nationally-minded Polish communists in October but ordered suppression of popular uprising in Hungary in November. Associated with early space successes and promises to economically surpass the West. In pursuit of 'peaceful coexistence' led the USSR in ideological and diplomatic rupture with Chinese communists. Attempted to reorientate Soviet economy towards consumer needs. Dismissed in 1964 and retired to private life.

Kim Ilsung (1912–94) anti-Japanese guerrilla leader, took power with Soviet backing in North Korea at the end of the Second World War. Survived the Korean War (1950–3) with power intact. Adopted an uncommitted position during the Sino-Soviet dispute. Established a regime of extreme regimentation and bizarre personality cult. Purged all rivals and was succeeded by his son.

Lin Bao (1910–71) Long-standing associate of Mao Zedong, appointed to high commands in People's Liberation Army and eventually commander-in-chief. Mao's principal lieutenant during the Cultural Revolution and heir-apparent, he died in mysterious circumstances in 1971, possibly following an attempt to replace Mao and certainly as a result of intrigue among the CPC ruling circles.

Liu Shao-chi (1898–?) Founder-member of the CPC in 1921 and thereafter among its leading personalities. One of the few surviving leaders with links to the urban working class. Succeeded Mao as President of the Republic in 1959 and became the principal target of the Cultural Revolution in 1966. Purged, he died in prison, probably of ill-treatment.

Georgi Malenkov (1902–79) CPSU apparatchik under Stalin, he became a member of the ruling circle during the forties and heir-apparent by the time of the latter's death. Combining the party and government leadership, he quickly resigned the former office, but continued as premier until his consumer-orientated economic policies resulted in his dismissal in 1955. Intrigued against Khrushchev, expelled from the party and retired to private life in 1957.

Mao Zedong (1893–1976) Of a peasant background, founder-member of the CPC, he was primarily responsible for the establishment of the party on a rural base after the massacre of its urban membership in 1927. Following legendary 'Long March' from southern China, established an effectively independent communist-ruled regime in Yenan. Increased support in the course of the anti-Japanese war and after the Second World War defeated the Guomindang (Kuomintang) regime in all-out civil war. Established People's Republic of China in 1949. In 1958 he initiated the disastrous economic 'Great Leap Forward', resulting in mass famine. Presided over ideological rupture with the USSR from 1960 and in 1966 instigated the 'Cultural Revolution' partly out of dissatisfaction at the increasingly bureaucratic character of the CPC and partly as a move in the inner-party struggle. Established friendly relations with the USA in the early 1970s, but by this time was probably senile. His anti-bureaucratic and collectivist ideological heritage was dismantled after his death.

Viacheslav Molotov (1890–1988) Bolshevik since 1906. Became Stalin's close associate following the Bolshevik revolution and rose to high positions in the party and state apparatus, being appointed at at various times as premier and foreign minister. Lost favour with Stalin in the early 1950s and was probably saved from purging by Stalin's death. Nevertheless opposed Khrushchev's 'Secret Speech', and intrigued against him. Consequently purged and retired to private life in 1957.

Imre Nagy (1896–1958) Worked underground in Hungary during the 1920s and became one of the state and party leaders after 1945. His premiership in 1953 was ended two years later by inner-party intrigue, but the reputation gained resulted in his emergence again as premier in the revolutionary administration formed in October 1956. Following its suppression by Soviet forces, he was tricked into leaving sanctuary in the Yugoslav embassy and arrested, being executed in 1958.

Pol Pot (1928–) Original name Saloth Sar, his family background was the Cambodian gentry. Educated in Paris, he became attached to the PCF, returning to Cambodia in 1952 and assuming leadership of the Cambodian communists in 1963. Led the Khmer Rouge to victory over the US-supported Lon Nol regime in 1975. Adopting ultra-Maoist policies, he presided over a regime of extreme anti-urbanism, rural collectivism, ultra-nationalism and institutionalised violence. Military attacks on Vietnam in the name of Cambodian (Kampuchean) nationalism provoked a Vietnamese invasion which drove the Khmer Rouge from the capital. Pol Pot, with the support of the West and safe havens in Thailand, continued to lead guerrilla attacks on the Vietnamese-installed regime.

Matyas Rakosi (1892–1971) A communist hero during the inter-war years for his underground activities and the manner he endured political imprisonment under the semi-fascist Hungarian regime, he was subsequently among the worst of the Stalinist Cold War leaders. As General Secretary of the Hungarian CP he was zealous in implementing anti-Titoite purges with many executions and later acted to thwart post-Stalin reforms. Antagonism to him was among the leading factors producing the Hungarian revolt of 1956. He fled to the USSR and afterwards lived there.

Josef Stalin (1879–1953) From an impoverished background in Georgia but with a seminary education, he was an early Bolshevik supporter. His role in the Bolshevik Revolution was minor, but his talents for organisation, intrigue and populist rhetoric enabled him to assume control of the CPSU following Lenin's death. Initiated agricultural collectivisation, the industrialisation drive of the Five-Year Plans and the massive purges of the party and the Soviet population generally in the late thirties. Having led the USSR to victory in the Second World War his already unchallengable position as the leader of international communism was doubly reinforced despite the dissolution of the Comintern in 1943. Was responsible for the establishment of the Soviet bloc in Eastern Europe in the late forties, though motivations remain disputed. Provoked the rupture with Yugoslavia in 1948 and mercilessly purged East European communists suspected of Titoist sympathies. Gave rise to the expression 'cult of personality'. Severely paranoid, he was planning another major Soviet purge upon his death.

Maurice Thorez (1900–64) From a mining background, General Secretary of the PCF from 1930 until his death. An undeviating Stalinist, he presided over a substantial decline in the party's influence from its high point of 1945.

Josip Tito (1892–1980) A Croatian metalworker and Comintern functionary during the thirties, he profited from Stalin's purges of the exiled Yugoslav CP to become leader of the party. Leading the successful Yugoslav anti-German guerrilla campaign of the Second World War, he instituted an undisguised communist regime, to Stalin's disapproval. Preserving appearances, however, upon the outbreak of the Cold War the Cominform was established in 1947 in Belgrade. Following the break with Stalin Tito presided over a distinctive form of communist development, which did not however have any imitators and remained isolated, despite semi-reconciliation with Moscow from 1955. He attempted to establish a federal system balanced by communist party centralisation, which would defuse the national animosities present in Yugoslavia. The project began to unravel almost immediately following his death.

Palmiro Togliatti (1893–1964) Leader of the exiled PCI and Comintern functionary during the thirties. Returning to Italy after 1945, he presided over the expansion of the PCI into a mass organisation and the strongest European communist party outside the Soviet bloc. Following Stalin's death he increasingly emphasised the national particularity of each communist party and the need to work out independent programmes and strategies, an outlook summed up as 'polycentrism'. Under his leadership the PCI also maintained a more open and flexible internal regime than most communist parties. He is frequently viewed as a precursor of 'Eurocommunism'.

Walther Ulbricht (1893–1973) A leading figure in the pre-1933 German communist party, then survivor of the thirties purges among foreign communists in the USSR, his loyalty to Stalin was total and unquestioned. As head of the reconstituted KPD in the Occupation Zone after 1945, he carried out Soviet policy and compelled the Social Democrats into unification. Becoming Premier when the Zone was turned into the German Democratic Republic in 1949, his policies of pressurising the workforce to meet Soviet reparations payments provoked the 1953 Berlin rising. Thereafter, under an extremely repressive (though relatively bloodless) regime, the state developed economically, assisted by the erection of the Berlin Wall in 1961 to block the exit of scarce labour. Among the most active of the Eastern Bloc leaders pressing for the Warsaw Pact invasion of Czechoslovakia in 1968.

Appendix 2

Chronology of Major Developments

1945

May – War in Europe ends.
July – USSR declares war on Japan.
August – Japanese surrender.
'Popular Front' governments established in most formerly occupied European countries.

1946

Tension grows between former allies.
Churchill's 'Iron Curtain' speech at Fulton, Missouri.

1947

March – 'Truman Doctrine' announced.
June – European Recovery Programme (Marshall Plan) announced.
Popular Front governments break up; communist monopoly in Eastern Europe, communist exclusion in West.
October – Communist Information Bureau (Cominform) established.

1948

February – Czechoslovak communists seize power with Soviet backing.
June – Berlin Blockade begins.

June – Yugoslav–Soviet rift. Yugoslavia expelled from Cominform. Chinese communists gain advantage in civil war.

1949

January – Comecon formed.
September – Hungarian purge trial.
October – Communist victory in China.
November – Bulgarian purge trial.
Repression of suspected communist 'deviationists' in other East European states.

1950

June – Korean War begins.

1952

Czechoslovak purge trial.

1953

March – Death of Stalin – power struggle among associates. Georgi Malenkov prime minister.
June – East Berlin revolt.
Beria purged.
June – Korean armistice.
September – Nikita Khrushchev appointed CPSU First Secretary.

1954

May – Vietminh defeat French armies at Dien Bien Phu.
July – Geneva Agreements for temporary partition of Vietnam.

1955

February – Malenkov dismissed as Soviet premier.
May – Occupation forces withdrawn from Austria.
Soviet leaders visit Yugoslavia and apologise for Stalin's behaviour.
Warsaw Pact signed.

1956

February – Khrushchev's 'Secret Speech' denouncing Stalin at CPSU 20th Congress.

April – Cominform dissolved.

October – Crisis in Poland, resolved by installation of reforming communist government (but loyal to CPSU) under Wladislaw Gomulka.

October–November – Crisis in Hungary. Reforming communist government under Imre Nagy announces abolition of single-party system and withdrawal from Warsaw Pact. Overthrown by Soviet armed intervention. Janós Kadar installed to head Hungarian government.

1957

'Hundred Flowers' episode in China, followed by reimposition of restrictions.

June – 'Anti-party group' of veteran Stalinists excluded from CPSU leadership.

October – Sputnik artificial satellite launched.

November – Conference of communist parties in Moscow.

1958

March – Khrushchev appointed head of government as well as CPSU First Secretary.

May – 'Great Leap Forward' launched in China.

October – Coup in Iraq politically favourable to Iraqi CP.

1959

January – Fidel Castro's forces take Havana. Steady worsening of relations with USA.

1960

Developing relations between USSR and Castro regime.

First clear signs of Sino-Soviet rift.

September – Albanian CP attacks Khrushchev.

End of 'Great Leap Forward'.

November – Moscow meeting of eighty-one communist parties.

1961

April – Cubans defeat US-backed exile invasion at Bay of Pigs. Draw closer to USSR.

Yuri Gagarin makes first manned orbit of earth.

October – 22nd Congress of CPSU. Khrushchev promises society of abundance in twenty years.

1962

October – Sino-Indian war in Himalayas. Soviet diplomacy leans towards India.
October – Cuban Missile Crisis. Third World War narrowly averted. Cuban regime dependent on Soviet aid. Begins to form new communist party.

1963

February – Anti-communist coup in Iraq. Iraqi CP decimated.
Sino-Soviet breach becomes explicit.
Growing commitment of US forces to South Vietnam.

1964

October – Khrushchev dismissed. Replaced by Leonid Brezhnev as CPSU General Secretary and Alexi Kosygin as Soviet premier.

1965

February – USA begins to bomb North Vietnam.
October – Military coup in Indonesia. PKI destroyed, 500 000 communists massacred.

1966

May – 'Cultural Revolution' begins in China.
November – Hungarian New Economic Mechanism proclaimed.

1967

Cultural Revolution continues, with military intervention.
Anti-semitic agitation in Poland.
Public unrest in Czechoslovakia.

1968

January – Dubcek takes over as CPCz leader.
February – Tet offensive in Vietnam.
May – Student uprising in Paris. PCF calls general strike but restrains militancy. De Gaulle recovers control.
Development of 'Prague Spring'.
Student and industrial unrest throughout Western Europe.
August – Warsaw pact forces invade Czechoslovakia. Prague Spring reforms reversed.

1969

March – Sino-Soviet frontier fighting.
April – 9th Congress of CPC reorganises party and proclaims success of Cultural Revolution. Main report given by Lin Bao, Mao's heir-apparent.
May – Communists enter Sudanese military government.
June – International conference of communist parties in Moscow.
Continuing student and industrial unrest. 'Hot Autumn' in Italy.

1970

May – Pro-US coup in Cambodia followed by US invasion and intensive bombing.
September – Popular Unity coalition in Chile elects Salvador Allende as President.
December – Food riots in Polish cities.

1971

January – Gomulka resigns. Replaced by Edward Gierek.
July – Sudanese CP destroyed following association with unsuccessful coup attempt.
September – Lin Bao killed in mysterious circumstances, denounced as traitor. Development of Chinese–US relations.

1972

February – President Nixon visits Beijing. Adoption by China of pro-US postures in opposition to the USSR.
June – French Communist and Socialist parties agree on Common Programme.

1973

January – Paris Accords for withdrawal of US forces from Vietnam.
September – US-sponsored coup in Chile overthrows Allende and suppresses left.

1974

April – Portuguese regime overthrown by left-wing military coup. Emergence of Portuguese CP as major political force.
September – Revolution in Ethiopia produces regime of the Derg, allied to Soviet bloc.

1975

April – Khmer Rouge under Pol Pot capture Pnom Penh; institute terror regime.
April – North Vietnamese and NLF forces capture Saigon.
September – Helsinki Accords accept Soviet hegemony in Eastern Europe.
November – End of Franco regime. Spanish communists emerge from illegality.

1976

February – Cuban military assistance preserves MPLA regime in Angola.
April – Communists lose dominant position in Portuguese revolutionary government.
June – International conference of communist parties in East Berlin.
July – Communists removed from Portuguese government.
September – Mao dies. 'Gang of Four' arrested.

1977

July – Deng Xiaoping reinstated to CPC Central Committee; becomes dominant personality.
Deterioration of Vietnamese–Cambodian relations.
September – PCF renounces 'Common Programme'.

1978

March – French general elections result in defeat for divided left.
April – Afghan communists seize power with military support.
July – Sino-Albanian rift.
December – Vietnamese forces invade Cambodia (Kampuchea).

1979

January – Khmer Rouge defeated by Vietnamese; pro-Vietnamese regime established in Pnom Penh.
January – Iranian revolution.
February – Chinese forces invade North Vietnam.
March – Left-wing revolution in Grenada.
July – Sandinistas overthrow Somoza regime in Nicaragua.
December – Soviet military intervention in Afghanistan to support communist regime.

1980

July – Strikes and factory occupations in Poland protesting at food price increases. Rise of 'Solidarity' trade union.

August – Gdansk Accords.
September – Gierek dismissed and replaced by Stanislaw Kania.

1981

January – Ronald Reagan takes over as US President; adopts confrontationist stance towards Soviet bloc.
May–June – Informal PCF–PS alliance in French elections. Communist ministers in government.
September – Kania replaced as Polish CP leader by General Wojciech Jaruselski.
December – Martial law declared in Poland. Solidarity leaders arrested.

1982

November – Brezhnev dies, succeeded by Yuri Andropov.

1983

October – USA invades Grenada.

1984

February – Andropov dies, succeeded by Konstantin Chernenko.
July – PCF ministers leave French government.

1985

March – Chernenko dies, succeeded by Mikhail Gorbachev.

1986

February–March – 27th CPSU Congress. Gorbachev announces reform programme.
April – Chernobyl nuclear disaster.

1988

February – National unrest in Baltic states.
February – Armed hostilities between Soviet republics Armenia and Azerbaijan.
May – Independent political party established in USSR.
December – Dialogue between Polish government and outlawed Solidarity.

1989

February – Soviet troops complete withdrawal from Afghanistan.
Pro-democracy demonstrations in China.
June – Demonstrations crushed by military force in Tianenmen Square.
August – Non-communist government in Poland.
October–December – Communist regimes collapse throughout Eastern
Europe.

1990

January – Disintegration of Yugoslavia commences.
Free elections in eastern European states.

1991

July – Warsaw Pact dissolved.
July – Yugoslav civil war begins.
August – Failure of coup attempt by CPSU traditionalists. Yeltsin domin-
ates Russian politics, Gorbachev sidelined.
December – USSR dissolved.

Select Bibliography

The number of texts in English alone which exist on the regimes, parties and organisations of the world communist movement (and even on its postwar phase) is incalculably large and sufficient to occupy more than a lifetime's continuous reading for any single individual. What is presented here is no more than a minimal selection of what the author regards as the most crucial and useful texts available in book form. Others are cited in the text of this volume. Journal articles thus cited are not separately included in this bibliography, nor are pamphlets. The numerous pamphlets used were mostly published by the Foreign Languages Publishing House, Moscow or Novosti Press. For excellent and full, though by now outdated, English-language bibliographies readers are referred to those in Adam Westoby's *Communism since World War II* and *The Evolution of Communism*.

Journals

Apart from journals concerned with particular regions or states ruled by communist regimes, there are several which deal either exclusively or frequently with the affairs of the movement at large. The movement's own international journal was *Problems of Peace and Socialism*, the English-language version being entitled *World Marxist Review*, edited in Prague, established in the fifties and publishing articles by writers from all the parties which maintained relations with the CPSU. It tended to be more revealing for what it omitted than for what it published. Following the break with the USSR the Chinese regime published, along with numerous English-language pamphlets, the political periodical *Peking Review*.

Problems of Communism (now *Problems of Post-Communism*), which commenced in the fifties, is published by the United States Information Agency but is fairly dispassionate in its analysis. *Survey*, commencing in 1956 with a cultural emphasis and with a number of varying titles, was published by the CIA-funded Congress of Cultural Freedom and later taken over by the London School of Economics. Its emphasis is strongly anti-communist. *The Journal of Communist Studies* (now *The Journal of Communist Studies and Transition Politics*) is an academic publication which commenced in 1985. *Socialist Register* and *New Left Review*, though their scope is far broader than the communist movement, have published much analysis of regimes and parties. As the titles indicate, they are left-wing in their orienatation, but from a critical perspective.

Documentary Collections

Dallin, Alexander (ed.), *Diversity in International Communism: A Documentary Record 1961–1963* (New York and London: Columbia University Press, 1963).

Daniels, Robert V. (ed.), *A Documentary History of Communism*, Vol. 1, *Communism in Russia*, Vol. 2, *Communism and the World* (London: I.B. Tauris, 1987).

Books

Ali, Tariq, *The Stalinist Legacy: Its Impact on 20th Century World Politics* (Harmondsworth: Penguin, 1984).

Aymot, Grant, *The Italian Communist Party: The Crisis of the Popular Front Strategy* (London: Croom Helm, 1981).

Bell, D.S. (ed.), *Western European Communists and the Collapse of Communism* (Oxford: Berg, 1993).

Birchall, Ian, *Workers against the Monolith: The Communist Parties since 1943* (London: Pluto, 1974).

Braunthal, Julius, *History of the International*, Vol. 3, *World Socialism 1943–1968* (London: Gollancz, 1980).

Claudin, Fernando, *The Communist Movement from Comintern to Cominform* (Harmondsworth: Penguin, 1975).

Djilas, Milovan, *Conversations with Stalin* (Harmondsworth: Penguin, 1969).

Fejto, Ferenc, *History of the People's Democracies: Eastern Europe since Stalin* (Harmondsworth: Penguin, 1974).

Khrushchev, Nikita S., *Khrushchev Remembers* (London: Sphere, 1971).

Kriegel, Annie, *The French Communists: Profile of a People* (Chicago and London: University of Chicago Press, 1972).

Lomax, Bill, *Hungary 1956* (London: Allison & Busby, 1976).

McInnes, Neil, *The Communist Parties of Western Europe* (London: Oxford University Press, 1975).

Mandel, Ernest, *From Stalinism to Eurocommunism* (London: NLB, 1978).

Medvedev, Roy, *Let History Judge* (London: Macmillan, 1972).

Medvedev, Roy, *Khrushchev* (Oxford: Blackwell, 1982).

Medvedev, Roy, *All Stalin's Men* (Oxford: Blackwell, 1983).

Medvedev, Zhores, *Andropov* (Oxford: Blackwell, 1983).

Merridale, Catherine and Ward, Chris, *Perestroika: The Historical Perspective* (London: Arnold, 1991).

Pike, Douglas, *History of Vietnamese Communism 1925–1976* (Stanford, CA: Hoover Institution Press, 1978).

Rozman, Gilbert, *A Mirror for Socialism: Soviet Criticisms of China* (London: I.B. Tauris, 1985).

Sassoon, Donald, *The Strategy of the Italian Communist Party from the Resistance to the Historic Compromise* (London: Pinter, 1981).

Schram, Stuart, *The Political Thought of Mao Tse-tung* (Harmondsworth: Penguin, 1969).

Schram, Stuart, *Mao Tse-tung* (Harmondsworth: Penguin, 1969).

Spriano, Paolo, *Stalin and the European Communists* (London: Verso, 1985).

Stern, Geoffrey, *The Rise and Decline of International Communism* (Aldershot: Edward Elgar, 1990).

Stiefbold, Annette Eisenberg, *The French Communist Party in Transition* (New York: Praeger, 1977)

Sworakowski, Witold S., *World Communism: A Handbook 1918–1965* (Stanford, CA: Hoover Institution Press, 1973).

Toranska, Teresa, *Oni: Stalin's Polish Puppets* (London: Collins Harvill, 1987).

Waller, Michael, *The End of the Communist Power Monopoly* (Manchester: Manchester University Press, 1993).

Westoby, Adam, *Communism since World War II* (Brighton: Harvester, 1981).

Westoby, Adam, *The Evolution of Communism* (Oxford: Polity, 1989).

White, Stephen, *Gorbachev and After* (Cambridge: Cambridge University Press 1993). [4th edition, formerly *Gorbachev in Power*]

Yergin, Daniel, *Shattered Peace. The Origins of the Cold War and the National Security State* (Harmondsworth: Penguin, 1980).

Index